THE BIBLE IN CHRISTIAN NORTH AFRICA

Mr. Albert E. Schneider, Jr.
867 Poplar Rd.
Hellertown, PA 18055

THE BIBLE IN
CHRISTIAN NORTH AFRICA

———————— ◈ ————————

The Donatist World

M AUREEN A. T ILLEY

FORTRESS PRESS   MINNEAPOLIS

THE BIBLE IN CHRISTIAN NORTH AFRICA
The Donatist World

All scriptural translations are by the author from the Vetus Latina unless otherwise marked.

Cover design by David Meyer.
Cover photograph by Maureen A. Tilley. Copyright © 1996.

Library of Congress Cataloging-in-Publication Data

Tilley, Maureen A.
    The Bible in Christian North Africa : the Donatist world / Maureen A. Tilley.
        p.   cm.
    Includes bibliographical references and index.
    ISBN 0-8006-2880-2 (alk. paper)
    1. Donatists.   I. Title.
    BT1370.T55   1997
    273'.4—DC21   97-19198
                                                                        CIP

Manufactured in the U.S.A.   AF 1-2880
01   00   99   98   97   1   2   3   4   5   6   7   8   9   10

Contents

Acknowledgments

Christians treasure the concept of the communion of saints, the union of those who have struggled and those who are still struggling to live a life of fidelity. The living rely on the example and prayers of those dead and those still on pilgrimage. Likewise there is a communion of scholars. In church history it includes Ruinart, who provided texts scholars still mine as witnesses to manuscripts no longer extant, and Tillemont, who asked penetrating questions that contemporary writers have not even begun to exhaust. Modern authors have a "brilliant cloud of witnesses" who provide models of perseverance.

I am particularly grateful to those in the communion of scholars whose work has been helpful to me in writing this book. Elizabeth A. Clark was the "mother" for the writing of a dissertation on Donatism that formed the groundwork for this study. She also encouraged my persistence through the years. Robert C. Gregg taught me many strategies for questioning ancient texts. These inspired the techniques for evaluating the works of Optatus and Augustine. Reginald H. Fuller taught me that when faced with a lack of absolute certainty, timidity and silence are not academic virtues.

I acknowledge the Andrew W. Mellon Foundation for support for a year of research and writing and The Florida State University for a sabbatical during which I wrote the penultimate draft of parts of this book. Marshall Johnson and Michael West of Fortress Press provided encouragement and guidance during the long editorial process.

Finally, I thank those intimately involved with the entire process. Daughters Elena and Christine have exercised the patience with parental moods and schedules that only children in academic families know. My husband Terry has been the faithful companion and advisor for every step.

Thanks to all.

Abbreviations

AB	Analecta Bollandiana
BA	Bibliothèque Augustinienne
CCL	Corpus Christianorum Series Latina
CSEL	Corpus Scriptorum Ecclesiasticorum Latinorum
DMS	*Donatist Martyr Stories: The Church in Conflict in Roman North Africa.* Translated with notes and introduction by Maureen A. Tilley. Translated Texts for Historians 24. Liverpool: University of Liverpool, 1996.
LCL	Loeb Classical Library
MPL	Patrologiae cursus completus. Series Latina. Edited by Jacques Paul Migne. 121 vols. Paris, 1844–94.
MPLS	Supplementum to the Patrologia Latina. Edited by Adalbert Hamman. 5 volumes to date. Paris: Editions Garnier Frères, 1958–.
REA	*Revue des Études Augustiniennes*
SC	Sources Chrétiennes
T&U	Texte und Untersuchungen

A Methodological Preface

IN AN AGE of hermeneutical suspicion, Leopold von Ranke's construal of history as recording each event *wie es eigentlich gewesen,* "exactly as it happened," is no longer tenable. But how can one paint any better portrait than the previous historians? How can one reconstruct the world in which they lived? This book attempts to go beyond a rejection of von Ranke and beyond a hermeneutic of suspicion. It uses a hermeneutic of "suspicious retrieval." The case in point is the history of the Donatist movement in Roman North Africa.

Investigating Donatism once seemed a simple task. The historical record appeared sparse, but clear. The scholarly consensus on the movement developed early and remained constant: these fourth-century North African heretics were all violent lower class revolutionaries obsessed with martyrdom; they all considered themselves the only true and pure Church; they avoided any intimate contact with the polluted Catholics who had cut their deal with the satanic state; and, the Donatists suddenly disappeared from the North African scene around 420. (Throughout this work, common era dates are referred to by numerals only. Dates before the common era are marked as B.C.E.)

But the standard account is partial at best. It is based on a record written by the winners—the church deemed orthodox by later Christian authorities. The winners decided which records to

1

preserve and what spin to put on the story. Their cache of documents and their construction of the selected evidence was canonized as the only record. It was taken in the Rankean sense as history, that is, exactly what happened. But the documents and interpretations of history's "losers" were missing. There was no counterbalancing story to jostle the Catholic story toward some *via media,* some *via veritatis.*

When I first began to investigate Donatism, no matter what source I read, I kept encountering the identical assertions. That the comments were so uniformly censorious made me very curious. Finding the same assertions in text after text was not in itself especially remarkable. What I did find extremely suspicious was the monotonous use of the same words, the identical phrases (even from French to German, to English, to Spanish, etc.), "millennialist," "Church of the pure," and so on. When I discovered that all the footnotes referred to the same very limited number of ancient sources, Optatus of Milevis and Augustine of Hippo,[1] I was tempted to think that perhaps there were not a significant number of other witnesses which survived and that I would be forced to rely on the Catholic record—the only record, tendentious though it was, to extract some sense of the Donatist platform.

However, Donatist sources do exist. Although better historians admitted the existence of materials of a Donatist provenance, most clung to the works of Optatus and Augustine as their primary and utterly reliable sources. They still generally ignored as useless materials written by the Donatists themselves. Admittedly, extracting history from hagiography and sermons is problematical, as the labors of hagiographers such as Hippolyte Delehaye and the Bollandists have shown.[2] But even the documents more amenable to the historian's craft were neglected. For example, nearly all scholars ignored the official stenographic record of the Conference of Carthage in 411, a government-sponsored meeting to resolve Catholic-Donatist issues.[3] The minutes recorded the debates between Donatists and Catholics verbatim, including rude, close to crude, interruptions by bishops and the understandable complaint by the stenographers that they had spent all day taking notes in the summer heat, and that they were tired and wanted to go home. Instead of mining this resource, church historians based their analysis of the conference solely on Augustine's tendentious summary of the events, the *Breviculus collationis.*

I quickly became convinced that there might just be more to the story, and that the additions might explain why the Donatists and their church attracted so many people, both rich and poor, both violent and pacifist, and why this movement provoked such a strong response by Augustine and what came to be called Catholic Christianity. Perhaps the Donatist documents might provide the way to a via media.

In contrast to the last major study of the movement by W. H. C. Frend,[4] the present volume privileges the specifically religious character of the Donatist controversy, which was the construction both sides gave it at the time.[5] Unlike the authors of previous accounts of the Donatists, I shall be looking first to the Donatists' own texts and testimonies to construct a history of the movement, and only then to the opinions of the "orthodox" victors, Optatus and Augustine.

The Donatist sources span a period of more than a century from the legalization of Christianity to the Vandal invasion. There are stories of martyrs, sermons and pamphlets, and the records of the gatherings of bishops. Yet none of these Donatist stories is a narrative history of the movement. The methodological problem is to write a new history from non-narrative sources. How can one tell the story of a community when the remaining documents appear to be isolated fragments?

Educated in an era of hermeneutical suspicion, I cannot assume that the Catholic sources record the progress of the controversy whole and unbiased. Nor do I presume that the Donatists simply narrate the persecutions and deaths of their saints and record their beliefs in a dispassionate manner. The literature of *both* sides is tendentious and impassioned. Hence, one cannot take either of them entirely at face value. To retrieve the story, one must be suspicious.

The methods used in this study draw on a variety of disciplines and approaches to analyze the available materials in order to nuance and on occasion correct the story as it has been told. If one takes for granted that Donatists wrote to defend themselves and to attack the Catholics, the first methodological problem concerns the sifting of evidence. Beyond the obvious—that the extant Catholic evidence was likewise written to disparage the Donatists—what can one say about the evidence from the Catholic side? I would not want to reject it out of hand. If it had absolutely no contemporary credibility, it would hardly have survived. But its use as propaganda renders it problematic. To dispel some of the difficulties associated with using the materials of Optatus and Augustine, I have subjected their evidence to the following five tests.[6]

1. Multiple attestation. Does the material in Optatus or Augustine reproduce what is already known from Donatist material? Can it be corroborated by another source? In many cases, corroboration of Optatus by Augustine or vice versa is inadmissible because Augustine is often directly dependent on Optatus. Augustine, however, has access to traditions not recorded in Optatus, although not necessarily unknown to him. Confirmation of statements in Optatus or Augustine ideally would come from a Donatist source.

2. Congruency. Is the material congruent with the results of other investigations of Donatist materials? Passages that utilize a method similar to those found in Donatist texts will be more highly regarded than those that diverge far from established Donatist practice. Optatus provides the only evidence for Donatist use of Cant. 7:2, "Your navel is a finely wrought bowl which never lacks its drink."[7] Although there is no other source to corroborate the Donatist application of this passage to the Church, the interpretation conforms to the Donatist tradition of applying the attributes of the body of the beloved to the Church. Therefore, on the basis of the congruency of the statement with genuine Donatist evidence, Optatus' testimony could be accepted as probably reliable.

3. Extrapolation. Does testimony appear to be an extrapolation from what the Catholic author knows about Donatists rather than firsthand information? Here one needs to differentiate polemical statements whose force is the declarative "You say . . ." from the assertive "You would (or should) say . . . ." If it appears to be an extrapolation, does it seem to be a reasonable one on the basis of comparison with similar Donatist materials? Again, Optatus provides the only testimony to Donatist use of Wis. 3:16, combined with 4:3, to condemn the offspring of illicit (spiritual) union.[8] This follows the pattern set in genuine Donatist works of applying texts against adultery against the Catholics as offspring of bishops who, in Donatist eyes, are outside of Church law.[9]

4. *Dissimilarity.* Is a report of Donatist material a case of *obiter dicta* that does not significantly assist the Catholic author in making a polemical point, or does it even contradict the point? Such a statement would have more value than those directly serving polemical purposes. A significant example here is Optatus' argument regarding the Donatist exegesis of Matt. 26:51.[10] He argued against a contemporary pacifist interpretation of Jesus' disarmament of Peter at Gethsemene, which he claimed Donatists supported. In so doing, he undermined his own case for the Donatists as warmongers[11] and reveals what must have been a genuine Donatist interpretation.

5. *Strength.* How strenuous is the objection to an alleged Donatist statement? A relatively large quantity of time and ingenuity expended in refuting a supposed interpretation lends credence to that interpretation as genuinely Donatist.[12] One example is Optatus' long harangue on the Donatist bishop Parmenian's discussion of the navel of the Church.[13] Another is Augustine's extended argument against the Donatist use of Cant. 1:6 on *meridie* as "the south," not as "noon."[14]

The results of these tests allowed me to enlarge the body of material that may be attributed reliably to Donatist teachings. In general, Augustine's reports seem to be more accurate than those of Optatus, and the least reliable material from Optatus comes from the portion of his text usually attributed to a later editor.[15]

Once a more adequate body of materials about the Donatists has been retrieved, what is one to do with it? In construing this material, I draw principally on the insights of sociologists of religion and the techniques of New Testament scholars.

Sociologists of religion have explored ways in which people make sense of their surroundings and tell their stories, using what they know about the world from their social and political position to construct a world in which they can live.[16] In times of stress, those who live in a particular constructed world must work especially hard to preserve it or to transform the old construction to maintain cosmic and social order. As Peter Berger notes, "The less firm the plausibility structure becomes, the more acute will be the need for world maintenance."[17]

Even before sociologists of religion formulated their concepts of world-construction and world-maintenance, New Testament scholars had begun to explore the ways in which biblical texts acted as instruments for the ordering of experience. In their work on form and redaction criticism, they have showed how the Christian communities of the first century shaped the received materials about Jesus to meet the crises of faith they faced in the generations after his death. By comparing and contrasting gospels, one could find what was unique in the experiences of each of those communities. If the scholars' methods were valid, one could then turn the process around and work back from the literary works we know as gospels to the historical circumstances of Jesus' own community.[18]

In the last two decades, scholars such as John Gager, Wayne Meeks, and Howard Clark Kee have begun to use a combination of methods from sociology of religion and biblical studies to render their own pictures of the earliest forms of Christianity.[19] If one may cross the great canonical divide, might not these same techniques be useful for the historian of Christianity beyond the first century?

The same mechanisms promoting world-construction and world-maintenance are visible in the postbiblical history of Christianity. It is possible to see them at work especially in the use to which the Bible is put, especially as the uses of Scripture change over the years. Changes in the use of the Bible should alert the reader to changes in the needs of the community's strategies for world-construction and maintenance. When authors use the Bible to make sense of their world, the adequacy of the world-construal is breaking down or has been under direct attack. When they use the Bible to vindicate or attack particular people, it is not the construction of the world that is at issue but the personalities or leadership policies of the persons involved. Finally, when policies, not personalities, are the issue, the source of tension in the community is not worldview or the content of the leadership cadre but the implementation of policy.[20]

Ascribing such power to reshape the world of the reader/listener to biblical texts was not foreign to the world of late antiquity. From Plato to the Renaissance, rhetoricians and students of language recognized the power of language to transform the reader for good or ill. More recently, Averil Cameron has shown her readers language's world-reforming power as Christian rhetoric remade the ancient world.[21] This volume narrows the focus from Cameron's broad picture of the battle between pagan and Christian rhetoric to a specific instance of intra-Christian conflict.

In much of Donatist literature, the prime authority warranting the construction of the social order was the ultimate religious authority, the voice of God. The Bible approved ideals and conduct that conformed to the world-construction of the author, or it disapproved what did not. Never did it merely convey to the reader or listener information about the past, about the times of the patriarchs, prophets, and apostles. In the Church of the Donatists, the Bible became the storehouse for texts that made sense of their own world, that approved or disapproved both the characters who inhabited that world and the conduct enacted there. The Bible itself testified that "every scribe who has been trained for the kingdom of heaven is like the master of a household who brings out of his treasure what is new and what is old" (Matt. 13:52). Construing the past, the sacred past, as model for, or type of, the embattled Donatist community represented a trump card for the maintenance and transformation of the Donatist worldview. Hence, investigating Donatist hermeneutics is a necessity if we are to understand the Donatists' view of the world.

The current study remains heavily indebted, as are all studies of Donatism, to the work of Jean-Paul Monceaux and of W. H. C. Frend, but it is more conscious of sociology of religion than Monceaux could have been and it takes Donatist texts and the records of the Conference of Carthage more seriously than Frend. To the voices of Donatists it applies the insights of sociologists of religion and a hermeneutic of suspicious retrieval. Specifically, I look at the ways in which Donatists used the Bible in service of world-maintenance, in creating and transforming their world, in approving and disapproving the characters who inhabited it and the actions they took. This study will approach the Donatist controversy with a combination of a hermeneutic of suspicious retrieval and a theory of world-construction. By charting the changes in the first century of Donatist history, I will show that far from being a monolithic, apocalyptic community of pure Christians seeking martyrdom, Donatism responded to changes in its situation by constructing and restructuring the world of its own experience. In this way it was able to survive the transition from persecuted minority "sect" to the "church" of the majority.

Introduction

O martyr, you have the Law of the Lord written not in ink but by the Spirit of the Living God, not on tablets of stone but on the tablets of your heart.[1]

IN 304, ROMAN SOLDIERS arrested a group of Christians worshiping in a private home in the North African village of Abitina. Since this small town had no proper judicial authority in residence, the soldiers transported those charged with illegal assembly to the city of Carthage. There they were incarcerated and awaited their trial.

Their prison was cold, dark, and dank. Faithful friends came to bring them food, water, and the other necessities Roman jails did not provide their prisoners. But their supporters were never able to deliver these supplies. The bishop of Carthage, Mensurius, and his deacon, Caecilian, sent their own guards to embargo—forcibly, if necessary—the provisions brought by the friends and families of the confessors. Physical force was indeed necessary. In the ensuing brawl, children were forced to watch as the bishop's guards beat their fathers and mothers. Dishes were smashed. Food brought for the prisoners was scattered on the ground and eaten by the dogs.

History does not record the fate of the prisoners. One presumes that they, like many others, died in prison or were executed. Even their supporters did not focus on their deaths. Those outside the prison fixed their attention on a much more important issue: for the first time in the history of Christianity, officials of the Christian Church conspired with the Roman state in the persecution of the faithful.

Seven years later, in 311, the same deacon, Caecilian, was elected bishop of Carthage. At his election, opponents alleged that he was unworthy of the office because he had been ordained by a *traditor* (one of his consecrators had defected from Christianity when he gave up the Bible to the Roman persecutors, who burned it). The Abitinians and many other North Africans refused to accept this man and found their own candidate, Majorinus, whose successor Donatus lent his name to their movement, Donatism.

Standard treatments of the ecclesiastical history of North Africa date the beginning of the Donatist schism to the election of the rival bishop Majorinus.[2] However, the disputed election was merely a symptom of a cleavage that began years before. The issue was not only the betrayal of the Bible by Caecilian's consecrator but also Caecilian's own acquiescence in the destruction of the men and women who embodied the words of the Bible in their lives, the Abitinian martyrs.

An analysis of the Abitinian incident and its influence on Donatist hermeneutics demonstrates that what the Donatists held dear in times of persecution was not so much the Bible itself, but the people whose lives embodied the Bible. The paradigm case was the Abitinian martyrs. Donatist respect for the martyrs predominated over their respect for the physical text of the Bible because the martyrs were the true interpreters of the written word they had memorized. They explained the words of the Bible by enacting its stories. The martyrs were the living exegetes and exegeses of the text. Thus martyrs outranked even bishops.

But if martyrdom was the lifeblood of Donatist Christianity, how did the Donatists survive for centuries after the legalization of Christianity? How did they provide for group cohesion during periods when they were not persecuted? A comparison of exegetical trends before and after 304 demonstrates that the Abitinian incident not only gave rise to two churches, Donatist and

Catholic, but it also shows how the incident molded Donatist self-identity and provided the impetus for a hermeneutical shift that ensured the survival of the Donatist "church of the martyrs" long after there were no more martyrs.

Most church historians have written of the Donatists from the viewpoint of the victors in the struggle for orthodoxy. They depict these deviant Christians primarily as a foil for the great North African theologian Augustine of Hippo.[3] In such a context, they are the quintessential heretics of late antiquity: intransigents, millennialists, dreamers who looked for a return to a simpler time when martyrdom was a readily accessible and sure ticket to heaven. Such historians capture Donatism in one moment of its centuries-long history. But the history of Donatism covers a much longer time, from the beginning of the fourth century to the eclipse of Christianity at the advent of Islam. What kept the movement alive through more than three centuries of relatively peaceful coexistence with Catholic Christians?

The sociopolitical aspects of the movement have intrigued religious historians of the twentieth century. Chief among these were Ernesto Buonaiuti, Jean-Paul Brisson, and W. H. C. Frend.[4] These scholars rightly saw the insufficiency of the purely literary approach of Paul Monceaux, the grandfather of the study of North African Christianity.[5] They also avoided the problems associated with a purely confessional approach. Praising Augustine of Hippo was not their main concern.

However, their strategy failed to provide a specifically religious context for the Donatist-Catholic schism. The problem is not that they highlighted one or another type of data, whether it was racial, linguistic, social, or economic. Rather, they neglected the one factor most important to the participants: religion.[6] In ignoring the specifically religious nature of Donatism, literary and sociopolitical historians failed to integrate available materials into a coherent whole. They could not account for the perdurance of Donatism in Romanized areas or of Catholicism in the Donatist hinterlands of Numidia. The financial resources available to the Donatists surely do not fit their image of Donatism as the popular uprising of poor indigenous peoples against Romans and

Romanized Catholics. Nor could historians justify the single-mindedly theological tenor of the arguments between Donatists and Catholics, disputes that centered on the nature of the Church and the sacraments.

Only a few scholars since Frend have tried to scrutinize the theological aspects of the movement in their own right, that is, as something other than the background for the development of Augustinian theology.[7] But even here, Christian Scriptures hold no part in the equation. In spite of his own probing work in the area, Robert B. Eno echoed the prevailing attitude toward the Donatist use of the Bible when he classes Donatist hermeneutics among the esoterica of Christian history. He simply finds their use of Scripture unimportant:

> Scriptural texts were a minor consideration. The cornerstone of their tradition was to be sought in Cyprian, his time and also in the era of the beginnings of Donatism. All their subsequent history was to be measured by the heroic era.[8]

He attempts to sever the link between the Donatists' theology and their use of the Bible, asserting that Donatists looked only to Cyprian, bishop of Carthage (d. 258), as authority, but Eno considers only a particular and narrow band in their history (the early fourth century) for the model of their behavior. But the evidence proves this a mistake.

First, there is the unwarranted denigration of Donatist interest in the Bible. The surviving Donatist literature tells a different story. When one surveys Donatist works and Donatist thought embedded in opponents' critiques, one finds that scriptural texts were more than "a minor consideration." Some works have hardly a connective between their scriptural quotations and nearly every argument is studded with references to the Bible. With a community so oriented toward the Bible, a study of exegesis provides an entry into the world of theology. In the case of the Donatists, examining their exegesis and thereby discovering their hermeneutics will provide insights into their theology otherwise unavailable. The results of such an investigation will sharpen the picture of Donatism now left out of focus by sociopolitical histories and by apologetically motivated writing that reads Donatism as simply heresy by viewing the movement through Augustine's eyes rather than directly.

As for Eno's assertions that Donatism looked only to Cyprian and the heroic age of the martyrs, the chapters that follow will show the contrary. Previous studies have produced the impression that Donatism was monolithic and one-dimensional.[9] This is because these studies rely on the works of Donatist opponents who have an unalloyed interest in portraying them as unable to cope with historical change. However, a diachronic study of Donatist uses of Scripture shows that their hermeneutics changed markedly over the period of the group's existence, supporting their evolution into a viable church.

The question then arises: Why has there been little study of the Donatists and even less of their Bible-based theology? Study of this group labors under the same burdens as that of any group labelled "heretic" or "schismatic" in antiquity. The first is difficulty in documentation. Finding the texts produced by members of the movement may be complicated. Often the orthodox victors have destroyed their writings, inscriptions, iconography, and architecture. Since their writings were considered less valuable than those of other authors, the works themselves were reproduced less often and frequently were lost in the course of time. More complex problems arise with secondary sources. Most of them were based on the writings of the theological victors. These works express the interests and concerns of the dominant group. They emphasize differences between orthodoxy and its opponents and minimize similarities. Such chronicles and theological studies may dramatize what is distinctive about a marginalized group rather than portray what was central to its beliefs and way of life.

All of these problems afflict the study of Donatism. Very few Donatist works remain. Many of the fragments of those that do survive are embodied in larger polemical works and have not been mined to any great degree for their insights into Donatist life. Nearly every work on Donatism, including those of Frend, takes for granted the truth of the accusations by their primary literary opponents, Optatus of Milevis and Augustine of Hippo.[10]

Although some Donatist epigraphy and architectural monuments do survive, there are problems with the attribution of Donatist or Catholic provenance and dating.[11] So historians whose primary training is literary tend to ignore them.

There is one additional problem in the study of the Donatists. Scholars do not always know the text (and sometimes texts) of the Bible that the Donatists used. When exegetical questions are the heart of the matter, inattention to the correct text can result in incredible misunderstandings, as even Augustine admitted.[12]

Each of these problems will be discussed in its proper context in the following chapters. For the present, three comments on methodology suffice. First, this work proceeds on the assumption that the Donatist controversy was what its participants claimed it to be: a dispute over the proper way to be a Christian *in a changing world*. The Catholic-Donatist schism was based on disagreements over admissible and inadmissible religious practices. Social history illuminates but cannot independently explain all facets of this disagreement.

Second, this work does not start where other writers have begun. It does not take for granted the veracity of all the comments of Optatus and Augustine, but gives priority to the often neglected Donatist works. Only in the latter stages of analysis does it use the works of Donatist opponents to complement the material derived from Donatist sources. Even then, a hermeneutic of suspicion is the guiding principle, lest Optatan or Augustinian opinions about the Donatists be confused with what Donatists thought about themselves.

Third, the retrieval of Donatist hermeneutics is a complex task. Only one Donatist work that deals explicitly with hermeneutics survives. It is the *Liber Regularum* of Tyconius. But its testimony is hardly definitive. Its author was a maverick among Donatists and represents only one period in the history of Donatism. Therefore, to understand Donatist hermeneutics, one must not only consider the text of Tyconius but also extract method from Donatist exegetical practice in other works.

Where it has been practical, I have subjected the Donatist texts to two kinds of interrogation. I have asked questions regarding the content of the biblical verses and their rhetorical use. Questions of content are rather straightforward. They are directed toward the referents of the texts and the themes these verses support. This sort of questioning serves to isolate the issues that Donatists considered important. These will change over the course of the history of Donatism.

The second kind of investigation answers questions about the functions of the texts; that is, How do these texts serve the needs of the community? The three functions of these citations include, first, making sense of the situation in which the audience finds itself. Scriptural quotations construct and maintain a religious world. Second, words from the Bible help members of the audience judge the character of their contemporaries. The verses guide a biblically constituted community in defining who is in and who is outside the Church. Third, they provide the justification of religious practices, commands, and condemnations.

The hermeneutics of the Donatists are then inferred from changes in subject matter and in the use of the texts.

This study is divided into six chapters. The first, "Donatist Predecessors," sketches the North African tradition before the Donatists. The works of Tertullian, Cyprian, and the authors of the early North African martyr stories provide a standard against which one can measure changes occurring in later centuries among Donatists. Then, "Stories of the Martyrs" and "Donatists in Controversy" explore hagiography and controversial literature from the middle of the fourth century. "New Times, New Ecclesiologies: Parmenian and Tyconius" looks at how Donatists survived as a majority church. "Harassment and Persecution Again" takes the story up to the times of Augustine and the Vandals. The final chapter, "A New Image of Donatism," draws together the results of the investigations from the preceding five in support of two conclusions: first, that Donatists continued the primitive Christian tradition of North Africa more faithfully than their Catholic counterparts by interpreting the Bible both typologically and literally, with the latter method dependent on the former in nearly every case; and second, that Mensurius and Caecilian's interdiction of supplies for the Abitinian martyrs was the decisive event for the shape of Donatist hermeneutics. The hermeneutical changes that it occasioned differentiate Donatist use of the Bible and its conception of the Church from both its predecessors and its Catholic opponents.

The results of that incident are the four hallmarks of Donatist exegesis as it spans the centuries:

> *first,* a turn from the future as a source of hope to the past as a model for coping;
>
> *second,* a change in typological models from biblical figures who promoted a martyr's death to those who provided support in the struggle against assimilation;
>
> *third,* the adoption of the *collecta* or assembly of Israel as the model for the Church faithful to the observance of the Law of God; and
>
> *fourth,* the adoption of commands of separation as the essence of the Law of God and the sine qua non of survival for the Church.

In thus reinterpreting the Bible, Donatists provided for the endurance of their church at a time when their old methods of interpretation (glorification of martyrdom) would not have brought them through changing sociopolitical circumstances (a society in which they were not martyred). This group of Christians presented the meaning of the Bible in such a way as to promote the survival of a community that grew apart from other groups of Christians. In a land where many other Christians accepted the political and moral status quo, this separatist church found new ways to resist assimilation to the larger worldly society.

The result of this exploration of Donatist hermeneutics is threefold. First, it provides more accurate notions of the theology and practice of the Donatist movement as one of the many varieties of Christianity in late antiquity. Second, bringing into focus one portion of the Christian Church makes possible a clearer assessment of other segments traditionally accorded more importance but belabored by misunderstanding. It allows one to see why contemporary Catholics misconstrued Donatist theology as they did. It provides an avenue of approach to such questions as why Augustine's reports on Tyconius do not accord with the text of Tyconius and how Donatism itself shaped the theology of Augustine.[13] It clarifies a neglected (not esoteric) area in the history of Christianity and thus sharpens the picture of the whole. Finally, by studying Donatist resilience through the prism of hermeneutics, it provides a method for the scrutiny of the survival and growth of modern "fundamentalist" movements.

CHAPTER 1

Donatist Predecessors

THE DONATIST MOVEMENT was a particular form of Christianity that grew up in North Africa in the fourth century. Although the area is often called *Roman* North Africa, its Christianity was not entirely identical with that of the city across the Mediterranean. African Christianity was shaped by an environment marked by the remnants of Punic culture, including its religion, making it different from other forms of Christianity. To understand the life and history of Donatism, this chapter takes a look at Christianity in North Africa before the schism between Donatists and Catholics formally began in 311. After outlining a brief history of Christianity in North Africa up to the fourth century, this chapter will focus on the ways the African Christians used the Bible in their literature. The chapter will consider the two premiere theologians, Tertullian and Cyprian, and then pre-Donatist martyr stories. In addition, it will look at one council of North African bishops at Cirta in 303/305 as an example of North African religious policy. The results of this investigation provide a basis for comparison with the Donatist movement as investigated in the other chapters of the book. With a solid knowledge of pre-Donatist Christianity in its North African setting, it will be easier for the reader to perceive how Donatism responded to changes in the ambient culture in such a way as to ensure the survival of the movement.

CHRISTIANITY IN NORTH AFRICA

North Africa had entered the Roman orbit long before Christianity arrived. Africa Proconsularis was brought into the Roman empire at the close of the Third Punic War in 146 B.C.E. Numidia was annexed in 46 B.C.E. at the close of the Jugurthine War. By 35 B.C.E., Mauretania in the west had also come under Roman control. Although nominally Roman by the advent of Christianity, these areas of North Africa enjoyed their own senses of local pride, based on their independent pre-Roman histories. They also had their own dress and languages, and their own religious traditions, especially outside the areas of direct Roman supervision.[1] Even in Carthage, the most important city and Roman since 146, vestiges of their Levantine religion survived far into the Roman period. It was characterized by the hegemony of the divinities Ba'al and Tanit, syncretized but barely to Saturn and Juno-Caelestis. W. H. C. Frend and Marcel Le Glay enumerate survivals of the old religion in Christianity: unswerving devotion to a single central deity, the veneration of holy persons, pilgrimages, fatalism, fasting, sleeping at shrines to obtain healing, and trust in dreams as the voice of the divine.[2]

No one knows how and when Christianity came to North Africa. Some have suggested Jewish Christians resident in North Africa or missionaries from Asia Minor as the progenitors of the tradition.[3] In either case, North African liturgy and ascetic practices differ from those of the Roman communities to their north. The oldest literary evidence for Christianity in this area of the world indicates that by the year 180 there was at least one community near Carthage.[4] We know very little about its Latin-speaking Christians except that they considered themselves in some way separate from the rest of their world, that they cultivated the leadership of women as well as men, and that for these people martyrdom was a most glorious end.[5]

By the turn of the second century, the dominant liturgical language, at least at Carthage, was still Greek.[6] The first theologian, Tertullian, was himself bilingual. There were flourishing communities of faith in Carthage and its neighborhood by this time. During the next hundred years, Christianity spread to most parts of the African littoral and far into the hinterland, probably as far as the *limes*.[7]

By the mid-third century, the dominant liturgical language was Latin, and by the time of Constantine many people of all classes claimed Christianity as their religion.

According to the surviving literature, Christians in North Africa were concerned with many of the same issues as other Christians: differentiating themselves from Jews, keeping their members from sliding into heretical beliefs or non-Christian practices such as playing board games and dice, and dealing with Christianity's ascetic impulses.[8] The prime issue, though, was martyrdom and its effects on their ecclesial communities.[9]

Christians in North Africa were subject to the same sort of occasional and local persecutions as Christians overseas. Notable in the North African context are persecutions under Severus (*ca.* 202–3), Decius (250–51), and Valerian (256–58), and under Diocletian and Maximian (303–5). Each of these periods will be treated in the context of the discussion of Christian literature that follows.

The remainder of this chapter will survey the ways in which Tertullian, Cyprian, and the authors of the martyr stories spoke of and employed biblical materials. The final part will deal with the Council of Cirta in 303/305.

Tertullian

The first North African theologian was Quintus Septimus Florens Tertullianus (*ca.* 160–*ca.* 212). A Carthaginian and an adult convert, he was well educated in both oratory and Christian doctrine. Both rhetorical and religious training inform his approach to the Bible and set standards to which later North African Christians adhered in their use of Scripture. Although the early part of his life was spent during a time of relative peace, the last decades of his life were marked by Severus' persecution of Christians. Reflections of the harassment and Christian quandaries about proper conduct during persecution appear in his essays, *De fuga*, *Ad martyras*, and *Apologeticum*.

Although Tertullian never wrote any programmatic essays on the interpretation of Scripture, as Tyconius would nearly two centuries later, in one way or another he acted as an exegete throughout his works. Often he argued scriptural points explicitly; at other times he used biblical quotations to buttress his moral arguments or allowed words from the Bible to provide phrases for his own sentences. His hermeneutics can be gleaned from the various works in which he addressed scriptural problems or used quotations and allusions for polemical, moral, or apologetic purposes.

Tertullian as Heir of Tradition and Innovator

Tertullian inherited a rich treasury of interpretive rules to apply to the Bible as written document. His sources included Roman law and rhetoric. Cicero's *De Inventione*, one of the more famous Latin manuals of rhetoric, had a great influence on him, as did the *Rhetorica ad Herrenium* and Quintilian's *Institutio Oratoria*.[10] The methods of earlier Christians, namely Justin Martyr (d. *ca.* 165) and Irenaeus (*ca.* 115–*ca.* 202), also inspired him.[11] This section shows Tertullian as both heir to tradition and innovator in his influence on Donatist interpretation.

In Tertullian's time, one of the most common areas for the interpretation of written documents was the explication of wills, *testamenta*, expressed in the formal laws of the period, and the traditions of rhetorical training familiar to all well-educated students in classical antiquity. By their nature, wills were addressed to their readers in the present, just as North Africans believed the Bible was. The earliest Christian authors saw the Hebrew Scriptures as speaking directly to them. Their theory of inspiration involved both the action of the Spirit of God and the mediation of human beings (Matt. 22:43; Acts 4:25).

In law courts, the principle most frequently invoked was one of a simple, literal reading.[12] Attending to the exact wording may make a difference. Irenaeus cautioned Christians such as Tertullian that when there was a doubt, one might be forced to resort to the Hebrew text.[13] Thus Tertullian was also careful to note the wording in passages from the Bible. Often his argument hung on the precise words of a passage; for example, in his argument against the work of Marcion, he shows how there is no dichotomy between the Father God of Jesus and the Creator God who made the world by unpacking the meaning of the word *Emmanuel,* "God-with-us."[14]

Cicero's prime rule was the use of the ordinary sense of words. This was Tertullian's most basic rule also.[15] That simple, literal reading depended on knowing the definitions of the words involved. Rhetorical manuals such as the *Rhetorica ad Herrenium* and the *Institutio Oratoria* of Quintilian provided an additional *caveat* to Tertullian and later the Donatists: consider the definition of the terms used in the documents.[16] Many of these same principles reappear in Donatist interpretation, especially at the Conference of Carthage in 411, when the rhetoricians on both Donatist and Catholic sides displayed their eloquence, but Donatists in particular adhered to the older tradition on such issues as *persona* (the identity of disputing parties and their fitness to go to law) and the definition of terms.

When in doubt about the meaning of a disputed word or phrase, Cicero resorted to intratextual evidence, then the evidence of works by the same author. Tertullian followed this practice and made it one of the cornerstones of his practice of interpretation.[17] And when two equally good documents appeared to be contradictory, authors applied their best reasoning powers to show that they were compatible with each other or with some *tertium quid*.[18] This matches the practice of the Apostolic Fathers, who read obscure texts in the context of other, clearer texts.[19]

Besides paying attention to the words of the text and their analogues in other works, one could try to imagine the implications of a particular interpretation. Both Cicero and Tertullian tested the veracity of particular interpretations by playing out the results of adopting such interpretations.[20]

When faced with conflicting interpretations of written testimony, that is, totally different constructions of the text, different tactics were needed. Here Tertullian could fall back on the same rule as Roman jurists and earlier Christians such as Irenaeus: when there is doubt about the meaning of a particular writing, and reason has failed to provide a clear answer, the ultimate authority must be found outside the words themselves. The jurists sought the higher authority in the character of the person speaking or writing.[21] The issue is faced in the New Testament itself. The author of 2 Peter discussed what stance the community ought to take over the differing interpretations of the writings of Paul (2 Pet. 1:20; 3:1–8, 16; cf. 2 Tim. 4:4). The suggested resolution to these problems was often the same appeal to authority: know your instructor, know from whom you receive your teachings (1 Cor. 15:1–3; 2 Tim. 3:3–14, 4:3).

The Apostolic Fathers continued the earliest traditions of considering the characters of the interpreters and those from whom teachers received their doctrine.[22] At least one could check the lifestyle of the witness for its general upright character. This was exactly what Roman law and rhetoric had taught and Christianity had appropriated.[23] This concern with *person*, which moderns castigate as the *ad hominem* argument—or even fallacy—was a cornerstone of Roman and, later, Donatist interpretation.

The appeal to human authority could be problematic when authorities themselves disagreed. Beyond the Bible and one's teachers, Irenaeus taught that the tie-breaking method in interpretation was the apostolic tradition and the *regula fidei*, the baptismal creed; Tertullian would add to these a variety of sources, for example, natural law, custom, reason, the lives of believers, and the continuing inspiration of the Spirit.[24] The latter three, reason, living witness, and the abiding presence of the Spirit, were also important for the Donatists.

Beyond appropriating Roman and Christian methods of textual interpretation, Tertullian made his own contributions. The first of these is his theory of inspiration. He attributed Scripture both to God and to the human author.[25] God spoke through the

Scripture, and the Spirit provided understanding to those who inquired.[26]

But if more than one inquired and there were more than one interpretation, what was one to do? Tertullian countered with two answers. First, since all parts of the Bible had the same divine author and could not be contradictory, one verse or part of the Bible ought to illumine another. This led Tertullian to proscribe atomistic exegesis. Verses had to be taken in their context. That context could be construed as narrowly as the succeeding verse or as broadly as the Pauline corpus or the entire Bible.[27] Even single widely spaced verses could be mutually illuminating.[28]

The unity of Scripture was a theme for Irenaeus, who also taught that the Scriptures, both Old Testament and New Testament, formed a single whole, all of which was to be interpreted Christologically.[29] The unity of Scripture would be of paramount importance to Tertullian, too, in his writings against the Marcionites.[30] Both Irenaeus and Tertullian saw Christ, the Word of God, manifesting himself in all of the utterances of God in the Old Testament.[31] Donatists will adopt this whole-Bible approach because their prime self-image will be an Old Testament one, that of the assembly of Israel surrounded by infidels, and the commands for separation that they will especially like are from the New Testament.

His second tactic appropriated and refined that of Justin: he excluded the (mis)interpreter from the office of interpretation. Justin in his *Dialogue with Trypho* had asserted that the Bible was not intelligible to all, only to those to whom God has given wisdom; presumably, in this context, Christians.[32] He tried to provide material by which his readers could preclude Jewish interpretations of their common Scriptures. In a formal sense, Justin denied the propriety of Jewish interpretations, alleging that they had lost their right to interpret Scriptures by their failure to observe the Old Law. Moreover, the Old Law had been superseded by the New.[33] Tertullian will adopt this tactic in dealing with those outside Christianity, that is, the Jews. His reason differs only slightly from his mentor's. Whereas Justin thought the Old Law was superseded by the New,[34] Tertullian saw the Old Law as a temporary manifestation of the Eternal Law. In Tertullian's eyes, the Jews proved themselves unworthy custodians of the Law by their failure to understand both the temporary nature of the Mosaic Law and the divine requirement for the nonliteral interpretation of the rites of the Law.[35]

Tertullian also used his conclusions about Jews and applied them *mutatis mutandis* to the Valentinians. He barred them from using Scripture because it was not their book any more than it was that of the Jews. Only orthodox Christians—those whose creed and lives demonstrated their adherence to Truth—could interpret the Bible.[36] Donatists will use this tactic as they profess that the minds of their opponents are under diabolical control and, therefore, are not fit to interpret the Scriptures that they once gave away to be burned.

Not only context but also style figured in the interpretation of texts. Tertullian had no general rule on whether Scripture was to be taken in a specific sense, for example, literally, morally, allegorically, or typologically.[37] He advised his readers to notice the exact wording of a sentence and to avoid taking literally some figure of speech.[38] Generally, however, Tertullian started first with the literal meaning, abandoning it only when a literal construal would produce nonsense.

Even when a verse had a literal meaning, taking it literally might not exhaust all its meanings. In addition to the literal meaning of the texts, nearly all of the verses of the Bible had some moral value. A reader had to differentiate a rebuke meant to effect fear from a condemnation meant to effect suffering and death.[39] Tertullian's works provide examples of several kinds of moral admonition. Sometimes the Bible was the voice of God speaking directly and literally; at other times the Bible contained both divine and human injunctions.[40] When it was speaking literally, the words of the biblical injunction often fit the situation in biblical times as well as in Tertullian's day. The words of Paul's tirade against false doctrines (Gal. 5:20) were, in Tertullian's mind, as appropriate to his contemporaries as to Paul's. Among those injunctions one finds some with a general character and others of a particular audience. Both Cicero and Tertullian shared several other exegetical principles. In interpreting texts of a moral sense, Tertullian shared principles with Cicero: one needed to consider whether the document contained a command or simply a recommendation.[41] Both interpreters of the written text would advise a reader to inquire whether a ruling needed to be enforced immediately or if it admitted a delay.[42] In this respect, Donatists would be stricter than their Catholic opponents, taking Scripture as command more often than as counsel and regarding the Word of God with urgency in contrast to their laxist opponents.

When the literal meaning was exhausted and direct moral commands had been interpreted, Tertullian encouraged his readers to note whether parables or typology were being used. Parables were not to be allegorized, to be stretched and warped to fit subjects not intended by the original author.[43] In fact, Tertullian's usual propensity was to avoid allegory, as it was a mainstay in the arsenal of his opponents, the Marcionites. This he inherits from Irenaeus, who battled Valentinians who relied extensively on an allegorizing exegesis of the Bible. Against them, Irenaeus preferred any method but allegory.[44]

This left typology as the final method of interpretation. Typology was exceptionally important for Tertullian,[45] and, as subsequent chapters of this work will show, it forms the heart of North African hermeneutics. Typology allowed Tertullian to maintain the primacy of a literal meaning of the text against the allegorists while still allowing the Bible to speak to his own community. Although insisting on the historical reality of the type, Tertullian did not encase the figure solely in its own era. In a sense, time was dissolved.[46] The same verses that spoke of the past might provide a figure of what was occurring presently or a prediction of what was to come in the future. A future event might even be predicted by the announcement of an event that had already occurred. One example he gave was that of the story of the angels who were expelled from heaven in Gen. 6:2 (LXX). They were the type of the astrologers who would be evicted from Rome.[47] Another is the Pauline warning against the messengers of deceit masquerading as the messengers of light in 2 Cor. 11:14. No doubt it had some first-century referent, but it also helped Tertullian to point out the troublemakers of his day. The Holy Spirit foresaw both uses of the words of Scripture, those in biblical times and in Tertullian's own.[48]

Typology was often Christological; it told how to recognize the Messiah and what to expect concerning his advent and life. Typology was also moral; figures from the past provided the types of what had happened or could occur in the life of individual Christians or, more usually, the whole community.[49]

Against both Jews and Marcionites, Tertullian fought not only the misuse of allegory but also the misapplication of typology. In Tertullian's thought, only an actual historical event could act as a type for another event. For example, the dry bones of Ezek. 37:1–14 never actually rose in the vision or in history; therefore, they could not be the type for a future restoration of the historical Israel. The verses are restricted in meaning to being a prophecy of the resurrection of the dead. The resurrection was for him a historical, although future, event. Since the resurrection of the dead was a future event, it could not be the basis of allegorization for another future event, the restoration of Israel. Tertullian had tied typology firmly to past historical events.

Summary

Tertullian wrote no single treatise on hermeneutics, yet a survey of his works reveals his principles in operation. His contributions to the North African tradition of biblical exegesis are significant. He appropriated the methods of both his Roman and Christian literary predecessors for dealing with disputed testimony. From the Roman forensic tradition, he adopted a tendency toward literalism and noticing the rhetorical context of a quotation. From both traditions in interpretation, he took up the possibility of an appeal to an authority higher than the text itself, that is, the conduct of those to whom the texts belonged. Tertullian utilized the contributions of Christians of the past in his stance on the unity of Scripture and the identity of those allowed to interpret it. In addition, he provided his own contributions to North African hermeneutics. He refined the use of nonliteral methods by firmly tying typology to historical events in the past. These contributions, especially Tertullian's own additions, will resurface in Donatist exegesis.

Cyprian

The second of the Donatist predecessors, Caecilius Cyprianus of Carthage (*ca.* 200–258), presents another style of exegesis. Donatists found in him their patron saint and hero. Not only was he a local martyr but he also faced many of the same problems they did: how to deal with persecution; how to define the boundaries of the Church; how to judge the validity of sacraments. Consequently, the range of Bible verses he quoted and his interpretive practices proved very influential in the Donatist community. As prelude to a consideration of Donatist writing as survival tactic, we should examine how Cyprian's life and writings converge.

Pastoral Issues of Cyprian's Episcopate
Cyprian lived about a generation after Tertullian's death. His education and journey to faith were similar.[50] He was the energetic bishop of his diocese (248/249–58) during two periods of persecution, those under Decius (250–51) and Valerian (256–58).[51] Throughout his episcopate, Cyprian placed a high priority on the unity of the Church, which was endangered in times of harassment.

During the Decian persecution, many Christians in Carthage had apostatized. Cyprian had been in exile and had deferred the reconciliation of penitents, who were called *lapsi*, until his return. During his months away from the city, various practices regarding reconciliation had arisen. Some penitents were readmitted to the church by presbyters on their own authority. Others were admitted to full communion on the basis of letters of recommendation from confessors awaiting execution in prison. Some presbyters even interpreted these letters, the *libelli pacis*, as guarantees of forgiveness. When the persecution ended, Cyprian was faced with the task of readmitting to communion penitents still unreconciled and of making theological and practical sense of divergent practices of readmission to full communion. In addition, he was forced to think through the role of martyrs with respect to the ongoing life of the Church. This is an issue that would resurface during the time when the Christian emperors persecuted Donatists. The importance of the martyrs would be the issue over which Donatists and Catholics would split.

After the Decian persecution, there were rigorists in North Africa and at Rome who opposed what they considered the too-lenient terms under which penitents were readmitted to communion. They were known as Novatianists, from the name of their chief at Rome. Novatianists were excommunicated at both Carthage and Rome. Cyprian took a mediating position between Carthaginian presbyters influenced by confessors and the intransigent Novatianists, and required penance and rebaptism before readmission to the Church, but denied the validity of Novatianist baptism, because they had been excommunicated. This is the position Donatists would later hold: the validity of rebaptism and the invalidity of the baptism of those outside the true Church.

Since unity meant not so much doctrinal orthodoxy as an orthopraxis, the controversies over the readmission of the *lapsi* and over rebaptism were crucial ones for Cyprian. No less crucial to his ecclesiology was an issue entwined with both of these questions: that of the relationships of bishops with other bishops and with their presbyters and deacons. Cyprian's attitude toward other members of the ecclesiastical hierarchy was generally one of cordial fraternity. Each bishop took care of the affairs of his own diocese, guiding the day-to-day life of his churches only as necessary. For Cyprian, diversity of practice might be anticipated and acceptable, but not when divine law was concerned. Then any bishop and perhaps even the bishops in council had to take action.[52] Cyprian thought such action was demanded in both the questions of the validity of schismatic baptism and the propriety of issuing the *libelli pacis*. He even advised Spanish Christians in 254 that it was right for them to separate themselves from their bishops who had apostatized: "The people should not flatter themselves . . . reject the unworthy."[53] Although the issue of episcopal authority was not so central to Donatist ecclesiology as the role of martyrs and the issue of rebaptism, Cyprian's use of the Bible to warrant separation would be a strong influence on the Donatists.

When persecution began again under Valerian in 256, it was no longer directed only at the higher clergy, but at Christians as a whole (with an eye toward the confiscation of property). Cyprian's advisees were now counseled not to cease their daily praise of God, even in the mines to which they had been sentenced, and to remember that the Holy Spirit was with them.[54] Although Cyprian may have been referring to continual fidelity to the Christian faith, Donatists, as we shall see, will make it their claim that they never gave up the regular celebration of the Eucharist, even during persecution. In addition, they will claim the Holy Spirit was with their church and theirs alone. Cyprian also advised his correspondents that all Christians must be prepared for martyrdom, for the eschaton was just around the corner.[55]

Cyprian's choice of texts influenced the working canon of the Donatists, who considered him an authority in their controversies, especially those that were analogous to his: the purity and unity of the Church, rebaptism, and the role of the martyrs.

Within the specific books of the Bible that Cyprian used, he had his own favorite verses. Although he employed much material from the Gospels, he was selective in their use. Cyprian gave lip service to both the words and deeds of Jesus, but he made little use of the stories of Jesus' miracles or any of the narratives of the gospels save the passion and the story of the Magi's dream. As we shall see, these are the very stories Donatists would find congenial to their own situation.

Although the Bible was a unity for Cyprian, as it was for Tertullian, there was a hierarchy within that unity. The Gospels were the privileged texts in the New Testament, taking precedence over and confirming the Epistles, but it was the Old Testament that confirmed and provided the typology for the New.[56] Even this hierarchy will resurface among the Donatists.

Cyprian and Tertullian

Cyprian was steeped in Tertullian's works. According to Jerome, he read "the Master" daily.[57] They were in basic agreement about the relationship between the Bible and its role in revelation. The

Bible was for Cyprian, as it had been for Tertullian, the voice of God or God's Spirit filling the human writer.[58] As Irenaeus and Tertullian found a large role for Christ, the Eternal Word, in the theophanies of the Old Testament, so Cyprian saw Christ revealing God throughout the entire Bible, especially in the words of God to the nation of Israel.[59]

However, as indebted to Tertullian as Cyprian was, he demonstrated considerable independence in his exegetical practice. There are three major differences between the two in this area. The first difference, one that will be very important for the Donatists, concerns Cyprian's view of biblical inspiration. When Tertullian accounted for all the ways by which one might interpret the Bible, he included, among others, the continued inspiration of the Holy Spirit. That inspiration gave guidelines of a practical sort that permitted an exegete to adjudicate differing interpretations of a single passage from Scripture. Cyprian's theory of the guidance of the Holy Spirit was slightly different. It was not only a help in adjudication but also was revelation; it provided directly to the reader a communication from God, a direct interpretation of a text. It was this personal revelation that informed Cyprian's dreams and those of others he held in similarly high regard.[60] Contemporary martyr stories and later Donatist authors will claim the authority to interpret Scripture just as well.

The second difference between Tertullian and Cyprian is dependent on the first. Cyprian used verses of the Bible in argumentation very differently from Tertullian. Tertullian marshalled scriptural quotations like several separate pieces of evidence, along with custom and the revelation afforded by nature, as parts of a rational argument. In contrast, Cyprian saw sentences from the Bible not as evidence, but as direct commands from God. The respective polemical situations of the two men account for their differences in strategy. Most of Tertullian's controversies involved disagreements with those outside his ecclesial community over the referents of scriptural verses. Cyprian's debates, on the other hand, were intraecclesial and involved disputes not over the referents of the verses but over the implications of the texts for life in the Church.[61] Because Donatists were in a similar situation, they would rely on Cyprian's method more than Tertullian's.

Cyprian's work manifests his independence from Tertullian in a third way, in his treatment of the unity of the Bible. Tertullian had two approaches to this subject. They were conditioned by the polemics in which he was engaged. With the Marcionites, his task had been to present the Old and New Testaments as the products of the same God and hence coherent. Late in his life he encountered difficulties with Catholics whom he considered laxists. Against them he justified his ascetic practices by asserting the superiority of the rigorous commands of the New Testament by painting the Old Testament as gentle and propaedeutic. Cyprian's situation was much different. Unlike Tertullian's aims for much of what he wrote, Cyprian directed his letters and treatises to people with whom he still shared communion. Cyprian's correspondents had no trouble with the idea that the Bible was one unified book. Thus Cyprian was able to apply verses from any part of the Bible to the problems of his community. In this respect, Cyprian provided a pattern for Donatists in their dispute with Catholics. Since both shared a respect for the Bible and a presumption of its unity, Donatists were able to use Old Testament citations to apply not only to New Testament stories but also to events of the fourth and fifth centuries.

Cyprian's Exegetical Presumptions
Cyprian's practice reveals some very basic presumptions. The first of these is that the Bible was written for the sake of the troubled Christians of his congregation. Rarely did their problems involve doctrinal issues.[62] They were faced with practical questions such as those outlined above, and Cyprian's approach was, exegetically speaking, a very practical one. He found in the words of the Bible guidance for the Carthaginian church: yes, martyrdom was what God and the times required; no, baptism by excommunicates did not convey the power of the Holy Spirit. Since the Donatists' problems with the Catholics would be largely disciplinary rather than doctrinal, Cyprian's method will suit them well.

Growing from Cyprian's first presumption was the second:

the unity of the Bible. Like his predecessors in the Church, he believed verses in the Bible were mutually illuminating. One illustration of this comes from a letter he wrote to his fellow bishop Magnus.[63] It is an important example as the verses he used in this case will be key ones for the Donatists.

In writing to Magnus on the question of rebaptism, Cyprian employed three verses consecutively. From each of these three verses, he chose one word that he equated with the other two words.

> *One* is my dove, my perfect one, the only child of her mother, the chosen one of her parent (Cant. 6:9).

> An enclosed garden is my sister *bride*, a sealed fountain, a cistern of living water (Cant. 6:12).

> Christ loved the *Church* and handed himself over on her behalf, that he might make her holy, purifying her with a bath of water (Eph. 5:25–26).

The juxtaposition and equation of *one*, *bride*, and *Church* licensed Cyprian's conclusion:

> If there is one Church which is loved by Christ and it alone is cleansed in his bath, how can anyone who is not in the Church either be loved by Christ or be washed and cleansed in his bath?[64]

The scriptural passages quoted above take pride of place complemented throughout by Eph. 4:5, "One Lord, one faith, one Baptism."[65] There was one field of operation for the Spirit, the Spirit that was conveyed by the water in the baptismal ceremony. That field was Cyprian's ecclesial community.[66] These passages and the logic they engendered warranted Cyprian's exclusion of Novatianist priests from ministry and the rejection of the baptism these heretics administered. So, too, the Donatists would adopt this world set up by Cyprian and use these texts to negate claims of Catholics on a true and effective Baptism.

By restricting the operation of the Spirit to his own Church, Cyprian was free to use other quotations from the Bible to liken those outside to unfruitful branches, gangrenous limbs, priests blemished by sin, broken cisterns, or even dead bodies that pollute those who touch them.[67] His advice to his own congregation was couched in biblical terms: "Separate yourselves and avoid pollution." Again, the commands the Bible offered Cyprian and his church will become the commands the Donatist church had to obey.

Cyprian's Methodology

For Cyprian, determining the meaning of a text generally involved three steps.[68] First, he began with his chosen biblical citation. Like Tertullian, he refused an atomistic reading of texts. His practice involved noting all of a verse.[69] Second, he found it important to notice who the original audience was and why the verses were written.[70] But the third element both built upon and nearly negated the first two. Once one knew the entire text and its historical context, he applied it directly to his community.[71] In this sense, Cyprian's exegesis lacked a sense of the temporal progression from one part of the Bible to another and from biblical times to his own. Any verse could speak equally well to the present as it had to the past, and interpretation of the verse no longer depended on the literary or rhetorical contexts in the biblical book from which it came.[72]

When it came to the application of scriptural texts to the particular situations of his congregation, Cyprian rarely began with a direct command from the Bible. This would have been too easy to controvert. One would have needed merely to say that the verse quoted did not apply to the particular instance for which it was cited. To make sure that his interpretation and application would be accepted, he proceeded in two stages. First, Cyprian used biblical texts to describe the situation and to assess it. Then and only then did he issue directives. This order is important; it is the key to his hermeneutics and will reappear in Donatist interpretation.

His treatise *De unitate ecclesiae* provides a good example of his method. First, he sets up his audience for the moves he will make by establishing the link between biblical times and his own. According to Cyprian, the prophets, apostles, Jesus, and the Holy Spirit all warned explicitly of the contemporary situation.[73] Then he constructs a world in the biblical image by using verses from the Bible to describe and evaluate the Carthaginian situation. Biblical verses regarding Peter, the dove in the Canticle of Canticles, Baptism, Noah's ark, Rahab, and many other figures provide direct analogues for events in his own church.[74] No believer could contradict his description without contradicting the Bible itself. Second, he passes judgment on the situation and tells his congregation what they ought to do. In this case, he takes the words of 2 Thess. 3:6 as a Pauline endorsement of his command to his people to separate from the Novatianists:

> And we order you in the name of the Lord Jesus Christ to separate from all the brothers who behave in an irregular manner, not according to the tradition which they accepted from us.[75]

At other times he will use verses from the Bible to put into the mouths of his opponents the words by which they should express sorrow for sin and repentance. He will write scripts for others to play, as in *De lapsis*, in which the prayer of Ananias, Azarias, and Misael (alias Shadrach, Meshach, and Abednego) becomes the prayer of the lapsed for mercy. He even writes in the lines of the merciful God who would answer them.[76]

Thus, although Scripture spoke to the Carthaginian situation, it rarely did so by naked, direct command. More frequently, Cyprian used the verses to describe the Carthaginian situation. The uncontroverted texts he chose made it hard to resist *his* ensuing controversial commands, especially when those commands were reinforced by echoes from the Word of God.

Cyprian's Interpretation of the Bible: Literal and Typological
Cyprian's use of the Bible to direct his congregation falls into two types of interpretation, the literal and typological. Cyprian used both of these kinds of interpretation separately and, often, together. It is their joint use that will be most wholeheartedly adopted by the Donatists.

Cyprian's literal use of scriptural verses involved the use of specific words taken from a situation in the Bible, uttered without change, to address the contemporary situation. Perhaps the best example is Cyprian's *Ad Fortunatum*. In it he provided a systematic handbook of biblical verses for people facing persecution. Individual verses were assembled and arranged by topic, for example, attacks on idols and idolaters, promises of future beatitude, and so on. This treatise provided not only what martyrs might say to their captors but also what verses they might use to increase their fervor and reinforce their determination to resist.[77] Cyprian did not always ignore the original context of the passages, but here he manifested his belief that what appeared in the Bible appeared there explicitly for the benefit of third-century readers who would read the verses literally and personally.

This sort of employment of scriptural texts might lead Cyprian's readers to infer that the authors of the biblical texts knew the events of all time, in a sense making time irrelevant. This is the point at which the typological interpretation may be found. In fact, the whole Old Testament sometimes appears to be a "minute prefiguration" of the New Testament.[78] Christ, Baptism, Eucharist, Christian priesthood, and Church are all found there.[79] Figures in the Old Testament are not only types for the New Testament but also models for Cyprian's congregation.[80]

As Cyprian employs this principle, however, it is male figures who become types of human beings and their despicable or heroic actions. Old Testament priests become the type of Christ or of the presbyters of Carthage. Obedience to God (or Cyprian), or their opposition to kings, links all of them.[81] The opposition between David and Saul or between the prophets and their royal persecutors became typical of the opposition between the just and their persecutors in the New Testament or in the Decian persecutions.[82] So also the oppositions between brothers in the book of Genesis become the type of opposition between North Africans.[83] Female figures regularly become types for institutions: the Church and the Synagogue. The male children of the favored element in the pair become types of Christ.[84]

Cyprian's understanding of how the clergy ought to act was based on a reading of the contemporary situation through the typological lens of Scripture. The types he found in the Bible provided him with two ways for evaluating deacons, presbyters, and their bishops: unquestioning obedience and ritual purity.

Moses, Aaron, Samuel, and the priest Azariah were the models for episcopal authority. Those who opposed them provided the types for the rebellious and schismatic deacons and presbyters and the unworthy bishops of Cyprian's day.[85] Cyprian attempted to shore up his own authority by identifying the deacons, presbyters, and bishops who opposed him and his allies with those who opposed proper authority in the Bible, and by asserting that all that was happening was forewarned by the Lord, the Holy Spirit, and the apostle Paul.

This identification of the clergy of Cyprian's day with the priests of Israel made possible for Cyprian a second kind of typological application. Warnings about the ceremonial purity for priests in the Bible could be applied to the clergy of Cyprian's time to enforce discipline among his own clergy and to arbitrate disputes referred to him from outside his diocese. He used citations from and allusions to Exodus, Numbers, Leviticus, Deuteronomy, 1 Samuel, and Hosea, but only rarely New Testament passages, to rationalize disciplinary measures against deacons, presbyters, and other bishops who communicated with schismatics, held too lively festal banquets, or celebrated the Eucharist in a state of sin.[86]

This fascination with purity extended to a consideration of sin as contagion. It was communicable by both touch and proximity. Such a conception promoted the application to his congregation of biblical commands regarding separation from the sinner. He applied these disciplinary mandates not only to the clergy, who had to remain clean to offer proper sacrifice, but also to laity who were part of the worshiping, sacrificing community.[87] This idea of sin as contagion will play a prominent role in the controversy between Catholics and Donatists. Donatists, too, will interpret verses on contagion, applying the biblical texts to Catholics and justifying separation from them on the grounds that the Bible commanded it.

Strangely, for a bishop guiding a community in persecution, Cyprian had little to say about church-state conflict, perhaps because he saw persecution less as a contest between Church and state than as a God-given test of the members of the Christian community.[88]

However, in contrast to Tertullian, Cyprian is not so concerned with the rhetorical context of quotations. Cyprian's use of typological interpretation systematized biblical typology by the sex and institutional status of the type and antitype. Although these are significant contributions to the North African tradition, Cyprian's most important legacy to the Donatists is his combination of the literal and typological interpretations, which we shall examine next.

Interplay between the literal and typological interpretations is extremely common in Cyprian. The two are often difficult to separate. However, a careful reading of Cyprian's works demonstrates his cardinal principle of exegesis: the typological interpretation licenses the application of the literal to the life of Christian community. Two examples illustrate the complexity of the literal and typological relationship, as well as the logical priority of the latter. The first example utilizes Cyprian's favorite verses, Matt. 10:17–20. In them, Jesus tells his disciples:

> Beware of people; for they will hand you over to the assemblies and they will flog you in their synagogues. And you shall stand before kings and officials giving testimony to them and to the nations for my sake. And when they hand you over, do not think about how or what you shall say. What you are to say will be given to you at that time. For it is not you who speak, but the Spirit of your Father who is speaking in you.[89]

According to Cyprian's typology, the disciples in their promised persecutions were types of the martyrs. So the martyrs too could expect the help of the Spirit. The locus of the words of the Spirit in Cyprian's time was the Bible, as interpreted by the Church, so Cyprian saw in their training by the Church the verbal ammunition for the martyrs in their trials.

In the second example, Cyprian combined literal and typological interpretations of the Bible in his attempt to settle the problems surrounding the confessors' issuing of the *libelli pacis*.

Cyprian's previous literal and typological reading of Matt. 10:17–20 had put the martyrs in a very special position, in direct and close communication with God.[90] This position allowed them, in the eyes of many, to be mediators of divine forgiveness, issuing the *libelli*. Cyprian opposed this role of the martyr, despite the fact that his literalist interpretation of Scripture could have licensed it.[91] However, in *De Lapsis* he marshalled both the literalist and typological interpretations of biblical verses to refute the practice of relying on the *libelli*. He made a literalist reading of Jer. 7:15 his rallying cry: "Maledictus homo qui spem habet in hominem."[92] He then presented the justification for the application of that verse from the prophet to his own time. He did this by employing his talent at scriptwriting based on the Bible. In his attack on the issuing of the *libelli*, the saints of the Book of Revelation cry out: "How long, O holy and true God, will you pass judgment over our blood on those who live on the earth?" (Rev. 6:10).[93] The fact that the saints (with their panoramic vision of the earth) are still crying to the Lord for judgment regarding their martyrdom indicates that up to Cyprian's time such judgment had not yet taken place. If the judgment that is reserved to God has not yet been given, the confessors on earth, who are antitypes of those already in heaven, cannot be in any position to utter a judgment of either condemnation or pardon.[94]

The typological element in the attack on the conduct of the confessors presupposed that they were to act like their types: the martyrs of Scripture, those who become the saints of the Apocalypse. Using the Bible, Cyprian documented the idea of martyrdom: predicted by the prophets, presented by Jesus, performed by the apostles, it was made manifest in the death of the confessors.[95] Beyond the direct predictions of the prophets, the Bible provided figures such as Abel, the three youths of the Book of Daniel, and the Maccabee brothers, who functioned as types of both Christ and the confessors of Cyprian's day.[96] The use of types with reference to martyrs was not simply a help to the discernment of martyrdom as a state approved by God. Martyr figures from the Bible also functioned as models against which contemporary martyrs were to be measured, as a control on the behavior of the confessors.

Since it was the Gospel that provided the opportunity and the means for martyrdom, martyrs had to conform to the Gospel in order to be true martyrs.[97] So, on Cyprian's view, they could not proclaim forgiveness of sins. They issued *libelli* in their own names when the Gospel proclaimed forgiveness of sins only "in nomine patris et filii et spiritus sancti."[98] Therefore, Cyprian accused presbyters who encouraged the issuance of the *libelli* of remaining deliberately ignorant of the Scriptures, as God had foretold.[99]

Those who persisted in encouraging the confessors to issue the certificates were also tarred with the brush of typology. Cyprian likened those presbyters at Carthage to the elders in the story of Susanna in Dan. 3:15.[100] As the elders sought to corrupt the pure Susanna, the presbyters of Cyprian's day tried to break down the discipline of the Church.

The solutions Cyprian gave for the problems that resulted from persecutions were controlled by two exegetical principles, both a combination of literal and typological. First, the words spoken by confessors, especially in their trials, were provided by God. Second, the martyrs of the past—those in the Bible—provided controlling types for the recognition and judgment of martyrs in Cyprian's own day, as the priests of the Bible provided the types by which the priests of Cyprian's own day were to be judged.

Summary

For the consideration of Donatist hermeneutics, Cyprian has been important for two reasons: his exegesis was founded on the unity of the Bible, and his application was most often based on a combination of literal and typological interpretations.

First, Cyprian saw a unity in the Bible, with all parts applicable to the Christian community. Combined with an atemporal literalism, this allowed all parts of the Bible to speak to the contemporary community, especially the commands of the Old Testament. In this respect, the Donatists will be the heirs of Cyprian. However, they will also be innovators. Although Cyprian thought of his battles as within the Church and used the language of the restoration of unity, the Donatists will adapt his method of quoting Scripture to battles they envision as between themselves and those they characterize as outsiders—not schismatics, but idolaters.

Second, Cyprian's work is important for the emphasis he, like Tertullian, placed on typology. Unlike allegory, which requires an extended correlation between items in two settings before it can be invoked, typology convinces by its initial correlation of two figures. Once that correlation is accepted, subsequent correlations do not support it but flow from it. Once one accepts one's own place in a typological scheme, the rest of one's world will be seen through the typological lens. Whereas most of Tertullian's typologies were Christological, Cyprian's, because of his different opponents, were ecclesiological. The Donatists will take the typologies set forth by Cyprian and place themselves in the same correlations as Cyprian placed the just and the righteous.

MARTYR STORIES

The Donatist community was proud of being one with the Church of the third century, which had produced so many martyrs. In fact, in their debates with their opponents they held that their own persecution was a mark of their being the true Church.[101] One key link between the earlier Church and the Donatists was that they both produced numerous martyr stories in which scriptural warrants and presumptions impelled readers to accept the views of the authors. This section will consider the roots of Donatist hermeneutics in the exegetical practices exemplified in nine pre-Donatist *acta* and *passiones*. In these stories, Christians used the Bible to evaluate their situation with respect to persecution, to judge themselves and the people who persecuted them, to provide for themselves the proper attitude toward the world, and to find the words with which they were to address their friends and foes. The uses to which they put the Scriptures reveal their apocalyptic framework for understanding the Bible and their propensity toward typological interpretation of character. Although the apocalypticism will be severely tempered in Donatist literature as the years pass, typological interpretation will flourish.

Early Martyrs

The most influential of the North African martyr stories come from the provincial capital, Carthage. They are the *Passio Perpetuae et Felicitatis*, the *Acta Proconsularia*, the *Vita Cypriani*, and the *Passio Montani et Lucii*. Within this group we shall see how the Bible is used first to establish a world, then to populate it, and, finally, to offer instructions for the lives of Christians.

The earliest of these stories, the *Passio Perpetuae*, records in diary form the imprisonment of a noble Christian woman, her pregnant slave, and several of their companions. The *passio* details their sufferings during their imprisonment, their interrogations regarding their adherence to their religion, and their mutual encouragements, along with visions and dreams. Very shortly after their executions, the account was edited to include the narration of the deaths of the protagonists.[102]

The story dates from about 203; Perpetua is a contemporary of Tertullian. It comes from the time of the first organized empire-wide persecution of Christians. W. H. C. Frend captures the impact of the times:

> The Severan persecution was the first co-ordinated world-wide move against the Christians. While it affected only the relatively small class of Christian converts and was confined to the major centres, it provided a precedent for later official actions. Perhaps because of the relatively high social standing of some of its victims, it produced a profound impression on the Christians themselves.[103]

No longer were persecutions only the result of mob violence, personal vendetta, or Christian bravado. Persecution could fall on anyone, women of the upper classes like Perpetua or even household slaves like Felicitas. Any Christian naivete regarding the state and its attitude toward each and every Christian must have been shattered. Under those circumstances, Christians had to search for a new paradigm for life in this world. Tertullian provided one consisting of the battle of Christians against Satan at the end of the world.[104]

The *Passio Perpetuae* reflects this new situation in its use of Scripture. It reinforces Tertullian's construction of the world. Eschatology is one of the themes that pervades the *Passio Perpetuae*. The editor of story presented Perpetua and her friends as living in the decisive days before the Final Judgment. Biblical language that described the saints of the Final Days was transferred to the martyrs. The present was the day of tribulation when prophecies came to pass and all God's children prophesied.[105] Then they would trample on evil, represented as a hideous dragon, and play in a heavenly garden, constantly singing the praises of God.[106]

Any personal endorsement of Perpetua and her companions is always in service of the main function of the story, that is, providing a construction of the world that would help Christians make sense of systematic persecution. Like Perpetua, they were the elect of God and would not be truly harmed by persecution. If she were prescient in view of her closeness to God, what she saw benefited the whole community, assuring them that they too would triumph in martyrdom.[107] Any words of exhortation were in service to the goal of uniting the entire Christian community as one against a single foe, the Devil, aided by his minions the Romans.[108]

No other pre-Donatist martyr story will spend so much of its biblical capital in establishing a construction of the world in which Christians were persecuted. Because of the broad influence of this account, Christians needed no such effort until the Donatist period, when a brand-new construction will decipher the riddle of Christians persecuting Christians.

When the second great wave of persecutions came at mid-century, biblical verses would be used to populate an already established world of martyrdom.

Cyprian, whose memory and writings were very influential among the Donatists, is the subject of the first two martyr stories from the mid-third century. His martyrdom is recorded both in the *Acta Proconsularia*, the account of his trials by Roman authorities as a Christian leader, and in his *Vita* by Pontius, a biography that treats the years of his episcopate, his sufferings at the hands of Roman authorities, and, finally, his beheading. They were composed shortly after Cyprian's death in 258 and were both based on court records. The *Acta* provided a model of martyrdom, whereas the *Vita* is the defense of Cyprian's conduct during his tenure as bishop of Carthage, especially with respect to his self-imposed exile during persecution.[109]

In these two pieces, the authors are not concerned with constructing a world. Unlike the story of Perpetua, they contain no eschatological motifs. With the Decian persecution hardly over, Christians were not caught by surprise, as Tertullian's generation had been. Hence, they did not need to make sense of what was happening as much as Perpetua's contemporaries did.

All sorts of biblical verses endorse Cyprian as a role model and fulfill the function of populating an already established world. Ninety-five percent of the quotations and allusions—in fact, the purpose of the entire *Vita*—was an endorsement of the holiness of Cyprian. The citations were used to defend him from his detractors, who criticized him for going into exile during persecution rather than becoming a voluntary martyr. This was the dispute that the *Vita* was meant to settle. Between the *Vita* and the *Acta Proconsularia*, we have the description of Cyprian as the perfect martyr. He is the elect of God.[110] The ministrations of angels in the story of Daniel provided the models for Cyprian's dependence on God for all his needs.[111] Cyprian's biographer found positive models for his subject in the suffering of Job, the good works of Tobias, and the reliance of Elijah on God. The incredulity of Zachary in Luke 1:5–25 provided a countertype of belated belief to Cyprian's unhesitating faith.[112] Finally, the passion of Christ was the model for the sufferings of Cyprian; like his savior, he was tempted to flee, arrested in a garden, led to the praetorium, and surrounded by the crowds.[113] In his modeling of appropriate behavior for later Christians, he provides the words that ring across the decades of Roman persecution: "I am a Christian . . . I know no other gods but the one true God who made heaven and earth and all that is in them."[114]

From farther west, in Numidia, which was to become the stronghold of the Donatist church, comes the *Passio Sanctorum Mariani et Iacobi*. These martyrs and their friends died near Cirta in 259. This *passio* records the story of two good friends, James, a deacon who had already suffered as a confessor under Decius, and Marian, a lector, and a few of their friends. They were members of a church torn by internal problems over the authority of confessors.

As in the *Passio Perpetuae*, one finds here some eschatological language: there were to be epidemics, earthquakes, plagues, trumpet calls, and pallid riders on glowing horses. Death would be conquered.[115] The saints would sparkle like the stars, with shining skin and radiant robes.[116] But these verses do not function to establish a world. Instead, the very fact that the martyrs have these visions and can prophecy constitutes, in this story, an endorsement of these people as martyrs. Cyprian himself welcomed Marian to heaven in a premonitory dream.[117] Marian's mother even resembles the mothers of prototypical martyrs, Jesus and the Maccabees.[118]

However, the endorsement is not the end for which these statements were made. The editor writes:

> When they were on the point of waging their sublime struggle against the distresses of a cruel world and against the pagan onslaughts, it was their wish that their battle, which they had joined under the influence of the Spirit of heaven, should be communicated to their fellow citizens through me. And they did this not because they wanted the glory of their martyr's crown to be arrogantly broadcast, but rather that the ordinary men [sic] who constituted God's people might be given strength in the test of faith by the sufferings of those who had gone before.[119]

The test of faith is not only suffering torture and death in persecution but enduring under the daily uncertainty of whether they will be martyrs or not. The revelations of the stalwart band of men on their way to death assure those who remain, whether one suffers for a long or short time, that the reward will be the same and, no matter what, one need not be anxious for martyrdom, as God will provide martyrdom as gift.[120]

Again from Carthage during the persecution under Valerian is the *Passio Sanctorum Montani et Lucii*. The first half is a letter from several clergy, including Montanus and Lucius, written while they were awaiting martyrdom. The second part is an account of how they were beheaded, narrated by one of their friends who was imprisoned but not executed with them. Here one finds a community that was willing to admit that it was rent by internal quarrels. It was these divisions that were the diabolical foe over which the confessors had to triumph. In this *passio*, Roman persecutors were not the enemy, the agents of the Devil. The real foe, the insidious instrument of the Evil One, was the internal squabbling that beset the community.[121] So while Perpetua exhorted her friends to unity against a common foe outside the church, Montanus was forced to deal with the enemy within the community.

This difference between the way the authors dealt with unity and charity in the two stories should be no surprise, considering the literary environments in which the works were composed. The *Passio Perpetuae* comes from Tertullian's time. His works paint persecution as an instrument of the Satan.[122] On the other hand, the *Passio Montani et Lucii* comes from the period of Cyprian's episcopate, when the problem of internal divisions over how to deal with the *lapsi* was very important. The issues at that time were who should be readmitted to the church after apostatizing and under what conditions. Whether the *Passio Montani* came from the pen of Pontius, Cyprian's biographer, or not, it reflects the problems of mid-third-century Carthage, the locus of Cyprian, and not the Carthage of Perpetua and Felicitas a half century earlier.[123]

Like the *Passio Perpetuae*, it is full of visions.[124] But these are not apocalyptic revelations; instead, they are messages of comfort. Through them the persecuted Christians understand that God is really taking care of them. Even the blessed martyr Cyprian tells them not to fear the pain of execution.[125] Lucius, Montanus, and their associates were likened to the three youths in the fiery furnace in the Book of Daniel when they underwent their martyrdom.[126] Their skin shone and their robes sparkled; they were like shining stars.[127] Lucius' friends, like the Good Thief of Jesus' passion, asked that the martyr remember them in the hour of his glory.[128] The Maccabee matriarch and the hemorrhaging woman of Luke 8:24–33 provided patterns of faith for the mother of his friend Flavian.[129]

As in the stories of Cyprian and of Marian and James, Bible-based endorsement of the martyrs allowed them to speak words of encouragement to the community. The messages of the *Passio Montani et Lucii* were promises of a return to their heavenly home and a treasure that would not fail, encouragement to persevere, and emphasis on the value of unity couched in the words of Jesus ("'This is my commandment,' he says, 'that you love one another'").[130] These point to the pastoral problems of the community whence the story came: endurance to the end and solidarity in time of stress.

In the *Passio Montani et Lucii*, the use of the quotations and allusions reflects only secondarily a concern with the role of persecution. The identity of approved martyrs is important but only instrumentally. The majority of the biblical texts, especially those positioned strategically from a literary point of view, focus the attention of the audience on the value of endurance to the end. Here the community's problem is how to maintain perseverance. The biblical material provided that support.

Martyrs under Diocletian

The final four stories come from the time of the persecutions under Diocletian. The first is the *Acta Maximiliani*, based on events in Tebessa in 298. It tells of a soldier who became, in modern parlance, a conscientious objector. He was executed for his refusal to conform to contemporary non-Christian society. The world of persecution and the endorsement of the martyr are presumed in the format of trial and in Maximilian's opening statement: "I cannot fight. . . . I am a Christian."[131] What little recommendation Maximilian does garner is his own self-endorsement. He uses biblical language to claim that he cannot take on military insignia because he bears the mark of Christ; he is sealed like the saints of Revelation.[132] But this statement could be applied *mutatis mutandis* to any Christian. This allusion and every bit of the remaining scriptural material are supportive of the credal message that Maximilian offers as his defense and as his teaching for those who will read the *Acta* as a model for their own behavior.[133]

Mauretania, even farther to the west, produced two more military stories. The first is the *Acta Marcelli*, an account of a soldier who renounced his military commission by refusing a bonus and by taking off his uniform in public. The incident probably took place in 298. Like the *Acta Proconsularia* and the *Acta Maximiliani*, the *Acta Marcelli* contains no quotations or allusions that establish the setting. However, the story presents a very curious form of endorsement. Ordinarily, a martyr's endorsement takes the form of the narrator applying a scriptural verse or allusion to the person or action of a principal character. In this case, the martyr obliquely endorses himself by performing an action previously rendered only by the prototypical martyrs, the Maccabees. Marcellus' final words to his judge Agricolanus were the sarcastic "May God do well by you."[134] Not only did he employ the words of the Bible, but his use of the quotation cast him in the mold of his holy predecessors, the Maccabees, who were close enough to God to use the heavenly words to curse their own enemies as divine enemies.[135]

The remaining biblical testimony is arranged as a litany of credal affirmations, a lesson for any aspiring martyr.[136] This conduct, with its concomitant use of biblical verses, will sanction Donatist boldness at the trials not only of adult men but also those of young women. Marcellus provided a type of bold action in the face of state harassment.

The *Acta Crispinae* provides the same sort of message as the *Acta Marcelli*. It tells of Crispina, a young woman of Tebessa in Numidia who was executed in 303/304 for failure to offer sacrifice to the Roman gods. The format of the story is a narration of the trial, with little extraneous narration and few interpolations.

There are no scriptural verses giving the reader a setting within the life of the Christian community, nor are there any quotations or allusions endorsing Crispina as an individual or as a model martyr. Christians have gotten so used to the situation and the heroism of the martyrs that these are taken for granted. The young woman's trial contains a veritable litany of biblical verses that profess her monotheism and enrage her judge. All of the quotations, and nearly all of them are direct quotations rather than allusions, form a handbook of credal affirmations directed against idolaters.[137] Crispina's story showed its audience how they too should answer their persecutors—with divinely sanctioned impudence: "Let your gods speak and then I shall believe."[138]

There is an air of unreality about this story. It seems less a report of a life-or-death trial than a recitation from a catechism. Stories of martyrdom are no longer grisly torture but a battle of wits in which the ultimate security of the martyr is a foregone conclusion.

The last narrative is the *Passio S. Typasii Veterani*, the story of a Mauretanian veteran who refused to answer a recall to military life. It is dated to about 304.[139] The *Passio Typasii* begins quite formally, with a chronological statement that situates this passion in its political environment. There are no biblical verses to set up Typasius' world. The *passio* provides two messages for the reader, neither of which are surprising for martyr stories: denigrate death and glorify God.[140] However, in their context, their force is ambivalent. It is almost as if it is not Typasius-the-martyr who is being glorified but Typasius-the-hermit, or the eremitic life in general. He did not reject a recall to the military because it would involve idolatry, as did Maximilian and Marcellus. He refused to fight for the Roman emperor because he was finished with that kind of combat and had graduated to a spiritual version of warfare.[141] Although he was not allowed to continue in the uniform of the ascetic and was beheaded, he did continue to serve under the standards of Christ, for the miracles that occurred at his grave were patterned on those performed during the ministry of Jesus: paralytics were cured and demons were expelled.[142] The reader is in the presence not of a martyr but of a man who mediates the power of the holy. Martyrdom is no longer even interesting.[143]

In these final four stories, little biblical material is spent on establishing a world or on approving the persons of the martyrs. Instead, the content of these latest stories provided their audiences with messages about their own lives, whether martyrdom was red with blood or white with self-denial.

Summary

The use of the Bible in martyr stories from Perpetua to Typasius has demonstrated three major functions that biblical material played in the narratives. The verses and allusions helped Christians make sense of the situation of persecution. They helped believers to recognize real heros and true villains in the martyrs and their persecutors. Finally, they showed the faithful what to do in their own lives through the encouraging remarks and the commands issued in the stories.

In general, the strongest use of the world-constructing verses occurred in the earliest persecution, when the whole phenomenon of repression would have offered the strongest challenge to Christians. The verses supporting particular figures, especially Cyprian, appear during the second period of persecution in the mid-third century. These stories come from communities that understood the nature of persecution but needed to be sure of which leaders to follow. The final stories about martyrdom come from the persecutions under Diocletian at the turn of the fourth century. By that time, Christians understood the nature and ramifications of persecution. In none of these stories was ecclesial leadership an issue. Therefore, the biblical material was used to bring the lessons of the martyrs home to the lives of Christians, whether martyrs, soldiers, or catechists. The use of biblical material then fluctuated, depending on the needs of Christian communities. In every case, the Bible was used to keep Christian communities faithful and united.

In the chapters that follow, we shall see how similar concerns shape the use of biblical material within the Donatist movement from its inception to the mid-fifth century.

THE COUNCIL OF CIRTA

Before launching into a discussion of the next few decades of the fourth century, it will be useful to see how church leaders viewed the issues that will figure heavily in the schism in North Africa. A prime example of the parting of ways already developing before the Donatist-Catholic schism is the debate at the Council of Cirta, which is dated between 303 and 305, more likely the latter date.[144]

At this Council, a dozen bishops assembled to identify those qualified to consecrate a successor to Bishop Paulus of Cirta, who had recently died. The bishops were examined one by one. They had the opportunity to refute any charges lodged against their conduct. The criterion proposed for suitability was whether a bishop had been faithful in persecution and had not handed over the sacred books to be burned by the Roman authorities. At least one of the bishops pointed out the incongruity of a church that required martyrdom rather than have its sacred books be burned, and yet let those who burned the books ordain a new bishop.

Bishop Purpurius of Limata was accused of the murder of two of his nephews. His guilt or innocence was not a question: he freely admitted what he had done. The issue was whether this crime, like those of the *traditor*-bishops, was germane to his qualifications as an elector. No crime, even this one of murder within the family, seemed to cause as much consternation as handing over the Scriptures.

Any hesitancy to allow ordination by the bishops who were sinners of any kind was overcome in the face of the possibility of schism. The presiding bishop fell back on the discipline used under Cyprian, who had considered it unseemly for bishops to submit to canonical penance. Bishops were responsible before the face of God. God would judge them and that was more than enough. So at least at this meeting, schism was more of a danger to the Church than murder or even handing over the Scriptures.

Thus one sees the issues of the Donatist-Catholic split prefigured long before the traditional dating for the Donatist schism in 311. The issues exposed at the Council illustrate that the major sins worth speaking of in some circles in the proto-Donatist Church were the same as those among the early Donatists: betraying the Bible and the memory of the martyrs. The Council also reveals that, in the proto-Catholic Church, schism was the ultimate sin. At this gathering, proto-Catholics carried the day and proto-Donatist qualms about *traditio* and the martyrs were sacrificed to the cause of unity. For both groups, maintaining group cohesiveness in the face of a common foe, Roman persecution, was the strongest concern. Group cohesion, under changed circumstances, will remain the primary concern in Donatism too and, under those new circumstances, will call for schism.

CHAPTER 2

Stories of the Martyrs

O NCE CONSTANTINE RECOGNIZED Christianity as a legal sect in 313, the state could no longer engage in the sort of persecutions that had generated the *acta* and *passiones* of the previous chapter. But the production of such literature did not die. Instead, the legitimation of Christianity gave rise to a new form of martyr stories, the *passiones* of faithful Christians executed by the state at the behest of or with the collusion of other Christians.

This chapter analyzes the significance of key thematic shifts in the utilization of the Bible in North African literature. It traces those changes from the stories of the pre-Constantinian period, through *passiones* used during the Constantinian persecution of Donatists (317–21), to those written in the post-Constantinian period of repression (346–48). As the pattern of persecution changed, so did the use of the Bible. The shifts in the use of the Bible signal profound changes in self-perception within the Donatist communities of North Africa. Historians of Donatism, both ancient and modern, do not even hint at these transformations. Of course, it was in the interest of Catholic propagandists to conceal them, to characterize Donatists as intransigent apocalyptic traditionalists. So we must turn to the literature of the community itself to discover who the Donatists were and how they changed during the first fifty years of the movement.

Four biblically based themes change markedly over the first

five decades of Donatism, from the pre-Constantinian persecutions to the middle of the fourth century. It is not as if old themes simply dropped out and new ones emerged; rather, themes that were important in the early period faded or were transformed and minor themes rose to prominence.

First among these is the martyrs' confession of Christian faith before Roman officials. This became less and less necessary since the rulers of the empire were at least nominally Christian or were familiar with and tolerant of Christian beliefs. Thus Donatists who were persecuted could assume that their oppressors knew the main tenets of Christianity.

Second, eschatological motifs employed the Bible to support the martyrs' perseverance before 312. But now that Donatists no longer expected a speedy end to persecution, these motifs faded, as Donatists learned how to deal with long-term persecution.

The third and most striking change was the dwindling of affirmations of love and unity within the community and the emergence of language licensing division between those who are members of the true Church and those who are not, between supporters and persecutors of the Donatist martyrs. If the present time was no longer construed as the dawn of the eschaton and some Christians were now perceived as enemies, there had to be concomitant changes in self-identity. No longer could the harmony and unity of the Christian community be a source of strength in facing an oppressive and non-Christian state. No longer would all Christians be supporters of those who saw themselves as the true Church. Division was the order of the day. Lines drawn between persecuted and persecuting Christian communities served to define the boundaries that gave the persecuted a distinctive group identity. The solidarity of those who saw themselves as the true Church against the allies of the Antichrist could become a new source of strength.

Fourth, this shift in the definition of the Church required the development of a new biblical type or model to define the Donatist community. In the waning days of persecution, Donatism could no longer see the Church as a group of individuals bearing suffering until their lives were gloriously crowned by martyrdom.

Instead of being threatened with death, Donatists were subject to harassment by neighbors and bribes and fines by the civil authority. The temptation was not to apostasy in the face of death but assimilation in the face of daily social and financial pressure.

The typological model they chose was the *collecta*, the assembly of Israel. That earlier *collecta* had been the faithful Jews liberated from bondage in Egypt. So also the Donatists were liberated from persecution by a pagan government. But the *collecta* was also the biblical people of God on the long pilgrimage through the desert of temptation and into the holy land. There they were subject to the oppressive government of the emperors Nebuchadnezzar and Antiochus Epiphanes, who supported assimilation. Like the early *collecta*, the Donatists faced the temptation to assimilate, to follow in the footsteps of the Catholics who supported the oppressive government of the Roman Empire. This revolution in typology helped Donatists to endure alternating periods of outright persecution and periods of peace during which the policies of the Roman government encouraged Donatists to join Catholic congregations. The change also helped Donatists make judgments on the character of the people with whom they continued to have contact, whether those people were inside or outside the community.

The use of the Bible in martyr stories shaped the identity of Christians in North Africa. Striking thematic shifts in four key themes within martyr stories signal profound changes in Donatist self-identity. Examining the historical and legal settings, sketching the stories, and analyzing how they used the Bible during the Constantinian persecution and afterward will show how Donatist identity evolved in the fourth century.

HISTORICAL SETTING

This new kind of martyr story, in which Christians were persecuted by a Christian state, developed in response to changes in the religious and political environment. Understanding the transition from the world of the pre-Donatist martyrs to that of the

Donatists requires knowledge of the function of religion within the Roman state. In the empire both before and after Constantine, the role of religion was to ensure the equanimity and the favorable disposition of the gods or God toward the state. If the gods looked beneficently upon the state, the emperor and the Roman people would be spared any danger and the commonwealth would experience prosperity.[1]

It was the responsibility of the emperor as head of state and, indirectly, of all civil servants to ensure that proper worship was conducted and that functionaries of approved religious cults were not hindered in the performance of their duties. Christians accepted and expected such treatment from the state, as is evinced by their appeals to the state for judgment in religious controversies.[2] In the case of Christian North Africa, the relationship of the emperor to the Christian Church was demonstrated by Constantine's provision of funds for restoring buildings and property seized during persecutions, his promulgation of a law freeing priests from duties to serve in municipal governments, and his subsidy of the day-to-day activities of churches.[3]

For those groups of Christians not on the lists of approved congregations, the situation was very different. Because of the legal link between officially recognized Christianity and the state, congregations not recognized as affiliated with recognized Christian communities received no money and no official protection. When groups of Christians battled one another, the emperor Constantine considered it his duty, both religious and political— as if those duties could be separated—to intervene in the quarrel, to pass judgment, and to use civil and military authority to ensure peace on earth and harmony with the heavens.[4] Typically, of course, the government favored previously approved congregations and their leaders and opposed the claims of unrecognized groups such as the Donatists.

Whether the Roman authorities considered Donatists schismatics or heretics in a formal sense is irrelevant to de jure punishments or to de facto treatments. In either case, imperial troops disrupted their assemblies, executed members of their congregations, and offered financial incentives to their leaders to persuade them to submit to the authority of officially recognized bishops.[5]

During the periods of especially severe repression, specifically from 317 to 321 and from 346 to 348, the stories of the martyrs of Donatism were popular. This chapter divides the martyr stories into the two periods of persecution with an intervening period of peace. After summaries of the stories of the periods of persecution, it examines the particular uses of the Bible that characterize those stories in order to chart the shifts in Donatist self-perceptions and theology. The way in which the Donatists enlist scriptural support for their views reveals their attitude toward the Bible, but, more importantly, it reveals how they saw themselves and their world. Most importantly, it will disclose how their self-identity changes over the first fifty years of persecution.

Donatist Martyrs, 317–321

The Stories

During this first period of persecution, the state confiscated Donatist churches and sent some bishops into exile. The persecution was intense. At one point, a whole congregation was slaughtered inside a Carthaginian basilica.[6] However, the persecution was concentrated in coastal areas where Donatists were probably not an overwhelming majority. On the whole, the military actions against the Donatists were unsuccessful. They merely succeeded in creating heroic martyrs instead of subservient new Catholics.[7]

The martyr stories popular during this first period or written at this time are the *Passio Ss. Dativi, Saturnini presbyteri et aliorum* (also known as the *Acts of the Abitinian Martyrs*), the *Passio Ss. Maximae, Donatillae et Secundae*, and the *Sermo de passione Ss. Donati et Advocati*. Although the first two stories deal with events occurring before 317, they were circulated during the period of the first persecution of the Donatists.

The first of the stories, *Acts of the Abitinian Martyrs*, details events occurring in February 304.[8] The narrative about these confessors involves their arrest in Abitina, a village near Carthage, their removal to and imprisonment in Carthage, their individual interrogations, and the remarkable event that took place outside the entrance to their jail.

In this incident, the Carthaginian bishop Mensurius and his deacon Caecilian placed their own guards at the gates of the prison to prevent supporters of the Abitinians from entering with food and other supplies for the imprisoned Donatists. The author of the *Acts* represented the bishop and deacon as simply hostile to the martyrs, and never mentioned the existence of a contemporary law promulgated by Licinius in his capacity as Augustus in the Western Roman Empire that prohibited feeding those sentenced to starvation.[9] The penalty for such interference was a similar death by starvation. It was possible that the bishop and deacon, in respecting that law by preventing prison visitations, were trying to preserve the rest of the Christian community from arrest. However, the writer of the preamble and epilogue to this story saw nothing redeeming about the bishop and his deacon interfering with support for the martyrs. The epilogue records a letter from the imprisoned martyrs excommunicating those who associated with the evil bishop and his deacon.

The theme of division between true martyrs (and their supporters) and other, at most nominal, Christians is very strong in the *Acts of the Abitinian Martyrs*. The story contains no narration of the executions of the martyrs. The text merely states that they died in different places at different times.[10]

The *Acts* were written close in time to the events they narrated. Their compilation, including an added preface and epilogue, dates between 304 and 311, or the period before the deacon Caecilian's election as bishop in late 311 or early 312.[11] Although the *Acts* do indeed antedate the traditional moment for the beginning of the Donatist schism, the election of the lector Majorinus as bishop in opposition to Caecilian, there are three reasons to call it a Donatist story: the environment in which it was produced, the way it was transmitted, and the manner in which it was used.

The milieu in which the *Acts* were written is a church community that had drawn lines in the sand as early as 305 on two intertwined issues, the *traditio* or the betrayal of the Bible and the importance of martyrdom.

Already at the Council of Cirta in 305, when state persecution was on the wane, one finds what may be termed "proto-Donatist" and "proto-Catholic" attitudes toward persecution, martyrdom, and church unity.[12] The record of this council demonstrates that the environment in which the *Acts* were written was not substantially different from that of the Donatist period and existed long before the *Acts* were written in *ca.* 311.

Besides being a good representative of proto-Donatist sentiment, the second reason the *Acts* are grouped with Donatist stories involves the history of the text itself. The *Acts* survive in two recensions, a version supportive of Donatist tendencies and a heavily edited version useful as Catholic propaganda.[13] The fact that there was a story that had to be edited to deny support to Donatism makes the story Donatist. This chapter uses the earlier version, that is, the Donatist account.

The *Acts of the Abitinian Martyrs* should be considered a Donatist story for a third and final reason: it was suitable for and actually did provide propaganda for the Donatist cause. It contained the statement of excommunication that became the rallying cry of the Donatists: "Si quis traditoribus communicaverit, nobiscum partem in regnis caelestibus non habebit."[14] Whether written or merely appropriated by Donatists, the *Acts* qualify as a Donatist document for the purposes of this chapter.

The second of the martyr stories considered in this chapter also predates 311. The *Passio Ss. Maximae, Donatillae et Secundae* records events that occurred in 304 after the Roman emperor Galerius ordered all Christians, not only clergy, to offer sacrifice to the genius of the emperor.[15] According to this *passio*, when the edict was promulgated in North Africa, many people apostatized. Two brave young women, Maxima and Donatilla, refused and were betrayed by their own neighbors (perhaps owing to the neighbors' own guilt). The proconsul Anulinus seemed hesitant to condemn the young women on account of their tender age. But despite many delays, changes in venue, repeated interrogations, and various tortures, the young women still refused to give up their faith. Instead, they boldly challenged the proconsul; they turned the tables by accusing *him*—of being in league with the

Devil. On the road to their final interrogation, they passed through the town of Thuburbo and under the balcony of twelve-year-old Secunda. Being a properly trained Christian maiden, she had rejected several proposals of marriage (much to the consternation of her family) and chosen Christ as her spiritual spouse. Being a properly trained North African Christian, she held martyrdom in high regard. To hasten her mystical marriage, she volunteered to join her sisters in faith and jumped down off the balcony into the street through which they were passing. After brave testimony and mutual consolation and encouragement, all three were delivered to the amphitheater to be executed by being mauled by a bear. The animal, sensing their holiness, refused to participate in the desecration of their bodies. So, finally, by the order of the same Anulinus who was the judge in the *Acts of the Abitinian Martyrs*, the three young women were beheaded on July 30, 304.

Unlike the *Acts of the Abitinian Martyrs*, this story has no fascinating early text history, but, like the *Acts*, its sentiments and use are Donatist, and, like the Abitinians, Maxima, Donatilla, and Secunda were venerated by the Donatists.[16] Therefore, this *passio* is included among the Donatist martyr stories.

The next account, the *Sermo de passione Ss. Donati et Advocati*, details events from 317 to 321, the first period of Donatist repression under the direction of Roman military officers, the *dux* Leontius and the *comes* Ursatius.[17] It tells how they attempted to enforce Constantine's will regarding the subjection of Donatists to Catholic leadership and how they recognized as legitimate ecclesiastical authorities Catholics who had been apostates during pre-Constantinian persecutions. The sermon provides the grisly details of a mass execution of Donatists. Under the pretext of organizing a religious service, Roman troops herded the Donatists into the Basilica Maiorum at Carthage, locked the doors, and then slaughtered men, women, and children. The sermon reaches its first emotional crescendo as it describes family members coming to the cathedral to identify the hacked-off limbs and mutilated torsos of their relatives.

As if this savagery were not enough, the Romans enticed the bishop of Avioccala into the city, wined and dined him, and then

dispatched him too. The account is set forth in the context of a
sermon designed at its climax to inflame catechumens with a
desire to follow their fellow citizens and the revered bishop into
martyrdom.

This *Sermo de passione Ss. Donati et Advocati* is attributed to
Donatus, the eponymous founder of the movement, and is
thought to have been delivered not long after the events narrated.[18] Like the *Acts of the Abitinian Martyrs*, it survives in ver-
sions labelled "Donatist" and "Catholic." The Donatist version
again is the earlier of the two and is the one used here.[19]

Analysis

Examining these narratives from the Constantinian persecution
with their reliance on biblical materials to carry the stories forward allows the reader to see how very different these stories are
from the pre-Constantinian martyr stories. Themes once strong
were replaced by their opposites and new themes arose. All of the
biblically based themes provide brush strokes for a portrait of the
Donatist community that we could not view in any other medium.

Biblical support for the theme of confession, a strong element
in stories in the previous chapter, is found only in the Donatist
martyr stories written before the legalization of Christianity, the
Acts of the Abitinian Martyrs and the *Passio Ss. Maximae, Donatillae et Secundae*. Most of the confessional statements in both of
these stories are concerned with obeying the eternal and unchan-
ging law of God, which is written in the hearts of the martyrs.[20] As
such, these texts functioned equally well in the period before 312,
when they manifested Christianity generally, and after 312, when
their referent was the belief of the Donatist community. However,
the biblical verses used in the first period of Donatist persecution
are not always the same as those used in the pre-Donatist stories.
Instead, they are characteristically intransigent affirmations of the
martyrs' closeness to God. This foreshadows a trend that will typ-
ify the later stories.

The few remaining confessional statements affirm the unity of
God and the redemptive role of Christ, assertions that would not
have distinguished partisans after 313 and, in fact, do not appear

in the later Donatist stories.[21] In this respect, the first two *passiones* begin a bridge between the pre-Donatist stories and the first of the Donatist accounts properly speaking. They contain a only a few credal statements that could have been used before Constantine. The final story from the first period of Donatism, the *Sermo de passione Ss. Donati et Advocati*, completes the bridge by containing no credal affirmations.

In summary, the use of the Bible as a source for confessional formulae is less prominent in the earliest Donatist stories than it was in the pre-Constantinian period. It occurs only in the two *passiones* written before 313, the *Acts of the Abitinian Martyrs* and the *Passio Ss. Maximae, Donatillae et Secundae*. In these acts what was confessed was not so much what differentiated Christians from non-Christians, such as the unity of God or Christological assertions or even the Christian way of life. These commonly held Christian affirmations had been the overwhelming bulk of the confessional statements in the *acta* and *passiones* of the pre-Donatist communities, but the historical situation of Christians warring against other Christians vitiated the value of these types of affirmations. The unity of God, the role of Christ, and the moral way of life were what Donatists and Catholics held in common. Consequently, in their affirmations of faith, Donatist martyr stories relied on the Bible to prove what they did *not* have in common with their Catholic opponents. Donatist authors depended on the Scriptures to buttress their own contention that the essence of being a Christian was tenacious adherence to whatever laws God has promulgated. Donatists thus relied on the Bible to define the Christian way of life as adherence to tradition. In this way, Scripture as a whole provided guidance on the way one ought to act. It offered the standard by which all intra-Christian affirmations of faith were to be judged. Scripture as a *book* was the tradition, and it was to tradition generally, not to specific rules or texts within that Bible, that a faithful Christian had to adhere.

This attitude represents a period of transition from the pre-Donatist period, when credal affirmations had to be gleaned from the Bible for ammunition in debates with non-Christians. As this early Donatist period unfolded, Christian credal citations were no longer necessary in the same way, because the opponents of the Donatists were Christians. However, the Donatists had not yet achieved the consensus necessary for a literal application of the Bible to their own situation. Instead they referred less to particular texts than to Scripture as a whole.[22]

It should be no surprise that the Donatists appealed to care for Scripture as the hallmark of the true Christian community, for the one thing that they felt differentiated them from Catholics was their refusal to cooperate with a government that, less than a decade before, had burned the physical texts of the Bible.[23] Only later, during the second wave of persecution, would Donatists be secure enough in their interpretation of specific texts to begin citing specific texts in doctrinal debates with Catholics.

Eschatological language, which had figured so heavily in the pre-Donatist martyr stories, faded in intensity. Donatists quickly learned that persecution by Christians was a different beast from the oppression of the pre-Constantinian era. Hence, it required a different biblically based defense. Military metaphors for the endurance of persecution, which had supported fidelity in crisis, still persisted; however, they were transformed from the promise of imminent victory to support for the endurance of continual strife.[24] Nowhere in this period was the heavenly inheritance as heavily stressed as it had been in the pre-Donatist period. On the few occasions when it was mentioned, it was expressed in political and military metaphors, such as reigning with Christ or never being overcome by the foe.[25] This closeness to God was never an end in itself, nor was it achieved only in a soon-to-be-experienced heaven. This association was, on the contrary, the component of everyday life which made endurance possible.

Although the Donatists may have seen themselves as close to God, the theme of love and unity within the Christian community that was so strong in the pre-Donatist martyr stories was now fading. In its place was the converse, division.

Even in the earliest of the stories, unity reflected badly on outsiders. The first of the stories, the *Acts of the Abitinian Martyrs*, does contain biblical materials devoted to affirming the unity of

Christians. In this story, the governor Anulinus offered to release the young confessor Victoria to the custody of her brother, who was at least temporarily estranged from Christian practices. She chose to remain in prison because she preferred her true family, and her views were expressed in biblical language: "My brothers and sisters are those who keep the commands of God."[26]

In the second of the stories, *The Passio Ss. Maximae, Donatillae et Secundae,* Secunda, like Victoria of Abitina, preferred her "sisters" in faith to her natural family. When the other two martyrs tried to persuade her to save herself and think of her family, she did not express her opinion demurely, as did Victoria. This young woman used biblical language to threaten the vengeance of God on anyone who would impede her on her road to martyrdom.[27] In both cases, positive biblically based statements of Church unity came at the expense of others. The third of the stories, the *Sermo de passione Ss. Donati et Advocati,* contains no material advocating unity. By the time it was written, the emperor had issued an edict of unity and the word itself had become anathema to Donatists. In response, the *Sermo* explicitly lambasted Catholic cooperation in the subjection of Donatists.[28]

A large percentage of scriptural material in these stories was devoted to direct condemnation of Catholics and the legitimacy of separation from them. The opponents of the Abitinian martyrs were anointed scribes and Pharisees, people whose sacrifices were rejected as unclean.[29] Alliances with such unclean people as these were as unthinkable as a confederacy between light and darkness, the true temple and idols, or between Christ and the Devil. Those who persecuted the saints were to be excommunicated and they could expect no share in the life to come.[30]

Maxima, Secunda, and Donatilla were coincidentally praised when the Catholics who sacrificed to the genius of the emperor were likened to those who worshiped the statue of Nebuchadnezzar in the book of Daniel.[31] When Maxima's interrogation manifested her imitation of Christ, it simultaneously cast Anulinus, her judge, as Caiaphas.[32]

The *Sermo de passione Donati et Advocati* was filled with scriptural material supportive of the theme of negative example and the justification of separation from enemies. Opponents of the Donatists became Judas, pseudochrists and pseudoprophets, false prophets in sheep's clothing, and trees bearing only bad fruit.[33] Their thoughts and ways were not God's thoughts and ways. Their practices were exposed when they themselves were revealed as the People of the Lie.[34]

With the change from credal formulae to law as the measure of the true Christian and the turn from an imminent *eschaton* to continual struggle, the Donatists were forced to find a new way to envision their community. Their characterizations of their enemies and the deep divisions between them and other Christians provided the groundwork for the exploration of models for the community.

The idea of Church as simply the holy company of martyrs did not perdure in Donatism because it could not support them in the long-term, low-level conflict to which they were subject. In their search for a new identity they turned to the Bible, the Law of God. Not only was the figure of Law uppermost in their confessions, but adherence to the Law of God also structured their whole self-image. Where the earlier martyr stories had found their references to law in the moral codes of the New Testament, Donatist references to law (in the *Acts of the Abitinian Martyrs* and the *Passio Ss. Maximae, Donatillae et Secundae*) were based almost entirely on Old Testament texts.[35] Consequently, their most powerful typological description was also expressed in an Old Testament idiom: they described themselves as the *collecta*, the assembly of Israel.[36] This metaphor demonstrates that Donatists were beginning to think of themselves not so much as people at war with an oppressor as the people of God travelling in a strange land in which they were tempted to idolatry. They were not anticipating a single and final victory over their enemy but continued warfare, in which the ability to draw boundaries between genuine and pseudo-Christians was the critical issue.[37]

In line with the adoption of the *collecta* as the typological image of the Church, Donatists tried on the cloaks of biblical figures to see which ones fit their new identity. Narration of the torture of Donatist champions provided occasions for reflecting on the torments of those who had suffered for their faith in the past, especially during times when Israel was subject to foreign domination. In all of the Donatist martyr stories, a significant number of the biblical quotations and allusions address the theme of Donatist martyrs' imitation of earlier saints.

In populating their typological world, Donatists portrayed their martyrs as triumphing because they were intimates of God. The motif of closeness to God, taken together with the theme of the imitation of divinely sanctioned figures of the past, comprise the largest group of biblical references in all Donatist martyr stories.

Indeed, in the *Acts of the Abitinian Martyrs*, no other theme received more attention than the familiarity of the martyrs with God. The martyrs could even use the words of the Bible to formulate their own prayers:[38] they asked God not to hold their persecutors liable for the sin they were committing just as Stephen, the first martyr, had. The Psalms and the words of the prophets became their prayer book as they voiced their trust in God and their desire not to be put to shame. They used Paul's advice to the Corinthians, "Do not be yoked to unbelievers," to justify their own holiness.

Eleazar and the Maccabees were the paradigms for the Abitinians.[39] They were common models of perseverance in the early Church but were especially apt among the Donatists since these models lived, like the Donatists, in a time of foreign occupation and, like the Donatists, they were tempted to assimilation. As the persecuted Christians of Abitina had taken up the mantle of the old man and the seven brothers, the Donatists could read the *Acts of the Abitinian Martyrs* and cast themselves in the roles of the Abitinians. Next they could clothe their own opponents, the laxist Catholics, in the same robes as the Abitinians had cloaked their persecutors, those of the assimilating Jews who assisted Antiochus, the tyrant, and all his minions. The Donatists echoed their models in being "mindful of the dignity of old age," in calling their persecutor "tyrant" and "murderer," and in pronouncing the ultimate curse: "For you there will be no resurrection to life."[40]

In the *Passio Ss. Maximae, Donatillae et Secundae*, one sees the three protagonists' closeness to God manifested in their confidence in their trials; they believed that it was the hand of God that comforted them and allowed them to say with the Psalmist, "We have passed through fire and water, and we arrived at a place of refreshment."[41]

The *passio* of Maxima and her companions makes much of their youth, allowing them to take on the roles of the three youths in the Book of Daniel who refuse to commit idolatry in Babylon even when Jewish elders and all about them apostatized. In this respect, they were perfect foils for the cowardly failure of the elderly Catholic hierarchy of their own time who did not, in Donatist eyes, adhere to sound Christian teaching.

In a striking novelty, their passion was modelled on that of Christ, a literary move almost never made in the pre-Donatist period. Their persecutors interrogated them with the identical words: "By the living God, I charge you to say. . . ." These words showed that the persecutor of the young women was Caiaphas *revivus*. In addition, soldiers offered both Christ and these young women sour wine and gall.[42] The motif of "the hour," the time of Jesus' passion in John's gospel, colored the account of their suffering.[43]

Here one finds that there was no sexual discrimination among Donatists in the area of who could imitate Christ. There were no particularly "masculine" (strong and active) or "feminine" (passive) virtues. On the contrary, women could be examples for men of courage in the time of persecution. Whereas the pre-Donatist Perpetua had bemoaned the suffering her martyrdom caused her family, Secunda, the youngest of the three martyrs in the *Passio Maximae*, paid no heed to the call that she, an only child, should stay home to care for her father.[44]

The *Sermo de passione Ss. Donati et Advocati* also exhibits new models for martyrs. The bishop Honoratus of Sciliba was persecuted because those who were chosen by Jesus and served him could expect nothing less than the treatment meted out to their master.[45] The holiness of the martyrs in this story allowed for the modeling of their passion not only on the prophets but also on Jesus and his disciples. The bloody slaughter of righteous Donatists within the walls of their basilica was described in biblical terms. In that place, all the innocents from Abel to the prophet Zaccharias provided as a group the types for the bishop slain before the altar when "the priest of God was cut down before the altar of the holy Name."[46] Jesus' prediction about his own passion and the scattering of his disciples was turned on its head as the place of the assassination of the Donatist bishop became the site of the gathering (and massacre) of his congregation: "Where the shepherd lies struck down, the flock of sheep gathers around that place of suffering."[47] There the faithful Donatists imitated their Lord, commending their souls into the hands of God.[48]

Summary

The major themes of the Donatist martyr stories under Constantine were related to, but different from, their predecessors. Although confessions of belief were made, they were minimal by comparison or else they were changed to support specifically Donatist interpretations of Christianity. Eschatology and martyrs' rewards in the hereafter were minimized so as not to raise false expectations of imminent relief. The motif of love and unity, so prominent in the pre-Constantinian stories, is beginning to be replaced with language of division and scriptural quotations and allusions supporting negative character judgments. Finally, in a bold and creative move, Donatists identified themselves with the *collecta,* the assembly of Israel on pilgrimage to the promised land, tempted in the midst of idolatrous nations. This identity was revolutionary, for it provided a model not only for justifying death but also for enduring long-term persecution at the hands of those who held power. It licensed the Donatists to characterize their martyrs as the champions of a faithful minority of innocent people. In death—and, more importantly, in life—they became Isaac, the prophets, Eleazar and the Maccabees, and, finally, Christ. Their typology not only provided them with an identity but it also furnished one for those who harassed them. Their persecutors were rendered the murderers of the prophets, the vicious pagan rulers Nebuchadnezzar and Antiochus, and the persecutors of Jesus.[49] Thus the identification of their persecutors with biblical types built on and strengthened their own identification as righteous.

On the whole, the Donatists' use of the Bible during the persecutions under Constantine shows the Donatists moving away from a reliance on the texts and themes used in the martyr stories of the third century, stories that emphasized martyrdom per se. This period of persecution under a "Christian" emperor had forced them to rethink their self-perception as Christian Church against pagan state. Through their use of the Bible we can see them opting for a new identity to support themselves in the long-term struggle against a state that was in league with "nominal" Christians. To maintain unity and to promote endurance, they took on the biblical identity of those who resisted assimilation to the idolaters. The *collecta* was once again on pilgrimage through the land of apostates.

A Peaceful Interlude

In 321, faced with the failure of the campaign and more pressing military concerns, Constantine suspended the laws against the Donatists. During the next quarter century Donatists and Catholics achieved a modus vivendi. Some areas were primarily Catholic, others Donatist. Occasionally both parties lived and prayed side by side in the same towns, with one church for each group. Double lines of bishops succeeded one another with only occasional quarrels. During the period of 321 through 346, Donatists increased in number, especially in Numidia. They sent bishops to Rome to head an existing congregation and they established themselves in Spain.[50] Donatism grew without significant state interference until 346.

Persecution Returns, 346 through 348

In 346, the Catholic bishop of Carthage died. Following a thirty-year-old protocol, Donatus, leader of the Donatist congregations in the capital city, should have been recognized as head of the diocese. He appealed to the emperor for recognition as sole bishop of Carthage.

In response, the emperor Constans sent military officials Paul and Macarius, with their troops, to investigate and to make peace. Prejudiced by Hosius, religious adviser to the emperors Constantine and Constans, they attempted to enforce an edict of unity under Catholic leadership. The civil authorities even offered financial incentives for conversion. Donatus encouraged Donatists to reject such bribery and few, if any, converted.[51] When persuasion and bribery failed, the government resorted to force. For two years, from 346 through 348, the military persecuted Donatists both in the coastal areas around Carthage and in the foothills of Numidia, where they probably formed a substantial majority. The result of their campaign was the renewal of sectarian strife, the creation of a new crop of martyrs, and the composition of new martyr stories different in style not only from those written before Constantine but also from the stories of the first wave of persecution of Donatists before 321.[52]

The Stories

Two martyr stories survive from this period. The first, the *Sermo de passione Maximiani et Isaac,* narrates the events of late August 347, in which Maximian was executed and his companion Isaac died in prison. It is attributed to Macrobius, a Donatist bishop known to have been residing at Rome (perhaps in exile from Carthage) as late as 366.[53]

This *sermo* also includes the remarkable story of how the prison authorities endeavored to keep the execution of Donatist martyrs from exciting public opinion and providing relics to be honored. In it we find a focus on care for the confessors similar to that in the *Acts of the Abitinian Martyrs.* But instead of a Christian bishop interdicting supplies for the bodies of living Christians, this story tells of the removal of the suffering confessors from the reach of the supporting community.

This time, prison guards prepared a ship and loaded it with imprisoned Donatists *vivi pariter cum defunctis,* as well as with common criminals. Then they weighted the bodies of the Christians with casks full of sand and dumped the bodies of all the prisoners together into the sea. The jailers thought none of the bodies of the martyrs would wash up on the shore. Even if some of the bodies did, they reasoned, how could the Christians tell the water-logged and disfigured bodies of the martyrs from those of criminals?

But Nature itself cooperated to frustrate the wicked jailers, and the waves separated the bodies of the martyrs from those of the criminals, returning the bodies of the saints to the shore.[54] As in the *Passio Ss. Maximae, Donatillae et Secundae*, in which a bear recognized the holiness inherent in the flesh of the martyrs, so here the ocean depths venerate the bodies of the holy ones.[55]

The other story, the *Passio Benedicti Martyris Marculi*, describes in detail the torture and execution of Marculus, a Donatist bishop from Numidia, who died at Nova Petra in late 347.[56] Its author is unknown, but it was probably written close in time to the events it narrates.

This is a magnificently crafted tale of suspense. First the audience listens to the story of the bishop's early life and his episcopal career. After a reminder of the genesis of the persecution, the narrative recalls how Marculus had been the most prominent member of a delegation sent to reason with Macarius and to intercede with him on behalf of the Donatists. But Macarius would have none of their protestations and ordered the members of the delegation to be beaten. The story continues with a focus on Marculus. The soldiers tortured him in various ways, but when they could not break his body or his spirit, they dragged him through the countryside from city to city as a public spectacle. Then his torturers taunted him for his Donatist affiliation. In a parody of the rumors that Donatists martyred themselves by jumping off mountainsides, the soldiers decided to throw Marculus from a high cliff. So he was pushed over the edge of the precipice. As the readers eagerly anticipate the gruesome results of his headlong fall, the author ever so slowly and carefully describes the beginning of the descent, the body that cuts the liquid air by its fall and the billowing clothes of the martyr. With the spectators, the audience follows the course of his fall, anticipating the horrible sight of Marculus' body being shattered on the rocks below. They follow the path of the soldiers and faithful friends of the bishop as they travelled from the place they were watching to the foot of the precipice, expecting a frightful scene of carnage. But, like the bear who refused to attack Maximae, Donatilla, and Secunda and the sea that cared for the corpses of the martyrs in the story of Maximian and Isaac, the rocks recognized the holiness of the blessed martyr Marculus. They refused to desecrate the mortal remains of the saint by piercing and ripping his body as it fell on them. So when the soldiers and followers of the holy bishop arrived at the base of the cliff, they found no body. In the moment of wonder, the shocked bystanders looked heavenward and saw Marculus' silhouette on the clouds. Later, members of his household found not a battered body but his perfectly preserved corpse resting peacefully not far from the bluff.

Martyrdom by precipitation was ridiculed by Catholics. They claimed that when pagan persecutions ceased, Donatists were frustrated in their attempts to achieve their martyr's crowns and so Marculus and others had simply committed suicide. Whether Marculus committed suicide or was murdered, the Donatists treasured the *passio* within their community.[57]

These stories from the later period of persecution present differences not only from pre-Donatist martyr stories but also from the Donatist martyr stories of the previous generation. We shall see how they chart the constantly evolving self-identity of the Donatist movement.

Analysis

In this second set of Donatist martyr stories, we can see an evolution in self-identity. Themes that were prominent in the pre-Donatist period and appear in softened form in the early Donatist stories have no place in this period. Confessional statements disappear entirely, and the martyrs are transformed from models of dying to exemplars of self-segregation, intimates of God even in this life. As expectations for a swift end to the world faded, danger came not so much from those who would break the will of Donatists in torture as from those who would seduce them into assimilation to Catholics. The transformation of biblically based themes thus provides a window onto the transformation of the

Donatist worldview and self-identity during the period of 346 through 348.

The first of the changes is that, unlike the stories of the first period, these contain no confessional statements. Such statements were missing for two reasons: genre and audience. The literary genre of these pieces is that of a sermon with a passion narrative embedded in it. Consequently, there are no formal trial scenes in which to situate confessional statements. Second, there was within the sermons no non-Christian audience before which to confess. The judges of these martyrs were Christians—of a sort. As such they allowed little room for dialogue of any kind. The audience to whom these sermons were preached were likewise Christians, and their troubles with other Christians did not include conflicts over basic Christian doctrines. Consequently, they did not need instruction in the art of apologetics through martyr stories.

However, although the Bible was used as an authority in this intra-Christian conflict, there was a marked contrast between this period and the era of Constantinian persecution a generation earlier. During the first period, Donatists defended and appealed to the Scriptures as a whole, as a book to be guarded against sacrilege by non-Christians and as a tradition to be adhered to in the face of Catholic opposition. During that time, there was not yet a consensus on how Donatist interpretation had to differ from that of Catholics. However, a generation later Donatists had achieved some accord on key biblical texts and could use specific texts in arguments with Catholics.

One example comes from the *Sermo de passione Maximiani et Isaac.* When this story was written, not all Donatists were executed and achieved the crown of martyrdom. Some had suffered longer than others under Roman persecution. So the question arose as to whether the duration or the intensity of torture mattered more in terms of a heavenly reward. By this time, Donatists had learned to use the gospel story of the laborers in the vineyard (Matt. 20:1–16) to prove that all who suffer for the sake of the truth are equal in God's eyes.[58]

The lack of confessional statements and the use of proof texts were not the only novelties. During this second period of Donatist persecution, these stories' authors were still interested in the sufferings of the saints and how those afflictions could comfort and inspire Donatist congregations; but the political situation had changed from concerted attacks on Donatists to lower level harassment. By this time, it must have been clear to the Donatists that the state had been and was going to continue to be allied with the Catholic party for some time to come. Under these circumstances, it is no wonder that eschatology played an even smaller role in the Donatist stories of 346 through 348 than it had in the period leading up to 321. Unlike the stories from the earlier part of the century, these did not present models of suffering and death or of champions who looked forward to the Last Days. Instead, the martyrs of these stories acted as paradigms for standing firm in persecution, for keeping oneself from giving in to the world. They were not models for dying the noble death but for living a long and segregated and, therefore, pure life.

Only once in the *Passio Maximiani et Isaac* does eschatological language emerge. Three times Isaac cries out in the words of Revelation: "Woe to you, o world, for you are perishing."[59] The battle is almost over for this one martyr. His world is passing away, but he is an anomaly in this period. For all the rest, their part in the battle may be over, but the war continues. The battles of the Donatists were not a once-and-for-all conflict; like Israel surrounded by the nations and undergoing trials, Donatists expected continual strife and the temptation to apostasy.

Conversely, the theme of the martyrs as intimates of God grew even stronger in this post-Constantinian period of persecution, for it was the affirmation of intimacy that carried the Donatists through periods of alienation from Catholic and imperial authority. In the *passiones* of Maximian and Isaac and that of Marculus, the themes of intimacy and imitation provide a majority of the uses of Scripture. The *Passio Marculi* proclaimed its subject "praelectus et praedestinatus a Domino."[60] Marculus, like the Apostle Paul, was already so closely joined to Christ that he longed for death: "It would be better to depart and to be with Christ." But Donatists knew that Paul did not die immediately but continued his evangelistic endeavors. The author of the *Passio* also appropriated the *nunc dimittis* of Simeon in the Gospel of Luke as his own expression of delight in approaching death.[61] But if the heavenly reward was presented in mildly militaristic terms during the first period, when Donatists were actively being persecuted, the second period represents a marked contrast. Later stories provided even more pacific images, such as this dismissal or entering into the vineyard of the Lord, having one's thirst satisfied or finding a treasure or tranquillity. These rewards could be enjoyed not only after a swift death but also in this life, and were anticipated especially in the course of torture, but also in the daily life of harassment that these later Donatists lived.[62]

These *passiones* also repelled any attempt to divide Donatists among themselves. Thus they could use the same text of the laborers in the vineyard to reassure themselves that those who endured persecution (though perhaps not death) were no less dear to God than the martyrs who died in the earlier period.

The stories of the martyrs during this period took their patterns from the stories of those in the *collecta* of Israel who had suffered innocently. The character of Isaac provided a model for his namesake in the *Passio Maximiani et Isaac*. It is ironically appropriate that Isaac was the model for the Donatists, for although the biblical Isaac once approached a sort of martyrdom in the *Akeda*, the majority of biblical stories of Isaac tell of his survival and his role as progenitor of the tribes of Israel. So also could the Donatists take Isaac as the model for providential care that promoted survival and for their role in establishing this new Israel, the *collecta*, which was surrounded by latter-day idolaters.

The Canticle of Canticles provided Isaac the Donatist with the words to describe his own ability to dissociate his mind from the pain inflicted on his body: "He says, 'I sleep while my heart keeps watch.'"[63] Indeed, the Donatists had to keep careful watch against the encroachments of their enemies as both sides looted each other's churches and harassed their ecclesiastical officers.[64]

When it came to the characterizations of their opponents, these later Donatists needed to be even more careful. They had to separate themselves and their communities from people who were at least nominally Christian. So their persecutors took their roles from Jews who had cooperated with idolaters. Using the vocabulary of the influential *Acts of the Abitinian Martyrs,* they applied to their Catholic persecutors the epithets *carnifex* and *tyrannus,* the names given to the torturer of the Maccabees who, like the Donatists, resisted assimilation into the idolatrous majority. Since the *collecta* was also the Church, the true body of Christ, those who persecuted the Donatists became the embodiments of Caiaphas in addition to that of the torturers of the faithful of the Old Testament.[65] No longer would negative characterization do; invective was piled higher and higher.

CONCLUSION

In this latter period of persecution, Donatist martyr stories became stories not of one-time confession and perseverance to the end but of holding out for a long duration against persecutors who did not kill but who tempted faithful Donatists to come over to the side of the Catholics. In the face of low-level warfare rather than outright persecution, Donatists used biblical texts to emphasize boundaries between Donatist orthopraxis and Catholic infidelity. They portrayed themselves as members of the *collecta,* tempted to apostasy in the midst of assimilationists. Their closeness to God allowed them to survive through temptations as the end receded into the distant future.

This chapter has surveyed the prime literature of the Donatist movement, the stories of its martyrs. It has shown how the Donatists survived when they could no longer claim that they were the church of the martyrs. Transformations in the use of biblical materials *in the martyr stories themselves* promoted the transformation of the church of the martyrs into the new *collecta* of the true Israel. No longer need a Christian be distinguished by professing faith in the face of death. If martyrdom was no longer possible, the new hallmark of the true Church was separatism. It would be well to look at other genres to see if they too provide corroboration of Donatist self-identity in flux between the tumultuous days of the birth of the movement and its retreat into the shadows of the Vandal conquest.

CHAPTER 3

Donatists in Controversy

THE LITERARY WORKS considered in the previous chapter are all narratives directed to nominally united audiences. Their authors aimed at encouraging an already hardy faith and at solving the problems that surfaced in a community under the threat of annihilation. This chapter concerns, in contrast, the literature of pastoral care. In these pieces, the Donatist authors and their congregations share an overarching construal of the world, but differ in details, in the application of Donatist biblical principles to contemporary problems. Material discussed in this chapter is varied in form and style, but all of the works treated here presented to their original audiences arguments designed to reshape the opponents' worlds to that of Donatist orthodoxy. These are the texts of controversy.

This chapter deals with works written between 320 and 362. The works are the *Gesta apud Zenophilum*, the record of a bishop's trial as *traditor*; *De singularitate clericorum*, a pastoral letter on celibate clergy living with women who likewise are vowed celibates; and the *Sermo in natali sanctorum innocentium*, a sermon for the Christmas season. Not all will use biblical verses in the same ways as the martyr stories, that is, to create a world, to populate it, and to provide messages. One or another of these functions may predominate. Even though these works differ in genre and style, a relatively uniform approach to the texts will be profitable. For each document, the important considerations will be the selection of scriptural verses and their use in the texts. The ways the authors deploy biblical verses in building their arguments can be analyzed to reveal what they believed about the Scriptures and the nature of life patterned on the Bible.

All of these texts come from situations in which persecution was not imminent, in which martyrdom was not the first option for dealing with the world. The Bible was no longer used to spur people toward a good death. Consequently, the types that served to encourage martyrdom—Jesus suffering on the cross and the Maccabees tortured to death—faded as patterns for Donatists. The new task was living in the midst of a world populated not only by unfriendly non-Christians but also by hostile Christians who, in Donatist eyes, were apostates. The contemporary challenge was fidelity to God and God's Law in the face of persistent temptation to defection from true Christianity to a Christianity compromised by its association with the world, that is, to Catholicism.

Under those circumstances, Donatist use of the Bible changed in two ways. First, since their trials and tribulations were not brief and intense but long term, the biblical type that provided support for them became the faithful of Israel, led by their prophets. The *collecta* of Israel continued to function as the model for the Donatist Church, as it had in the *Acts of the Abitinian Martyrs*. Second, their dispute was no longer with those outside Christianity. Their quarrels were with Donatists who read the same precious Bible they did. Hence, they had to be more concerned with the exact wording of the texts, and tendencies toward a literal interpretation, especially of biblical commands, came to the fore.

GESTA APUD ZENOPHILUM

The first of these texts is the *Gesta apud Zenophilum*.[1] It is the truncated record of a trial that took place in 320 in the city of Thamugadi, before Zenophilus, the Roman *consularis* of Numidia.

This is a period during which Christianity, both Donatist and Catholic, had joined the ranks of other state-supported religions. In some areas where there were insoluble differences between

Catholics and Donatists, Constantine's troops persecuted the latter. However, there were places, especially in Numidia, where Donatism was the only viable option. There imperial officials treated Donatists as the only representatives of Christianity.

In his capacity as emperor, Constantine felt it his obligation to support divine worship by freeing Christian priests from mandatory service on town councils so they could spend their time, energy, and money on Christian liturgy. In addition, he provided direct monetary subsidies to Christian communities, at least those he and his subordinates deemed orthodox. He also considered it his duty to keep peace between warring religious factions.[2] Hence a Roman magistrate acted as arbiter between Donatists over ecclesiastical affairs.

Zenophilus heard charges that Silvanus, the Donatist bishop of Cirta (ordained at the end of the Council of Cirta in 305), had obtained his office by a combination of simony and mob agitation. Silvanus was castigated for the rocky relationship he had with his clergy. He was also accused of alienating church property and of being a *traditor*, one who handed over the Scriptures to the Romans during persecution. The inquiry over which Zenophilus presided considered Silvanus as Christian, not as Donatist or non-Catholic. It considered all the evidence. The verdict is lacking in the manuscripts, but the remarks of the *consularis* leave little doubt that, no matter what the facts of the matter were, Silvanus was found guilty.

Although witnesses at the trial did not quote Scripture, five letters introduced as evidence against Silvanus are saturated with biblical verses. The use of Scripture in these letters provides some insight into how their authors, all Donatists, interpreted the Bible and used it to sustain the Donatist Church under the new, nominally Christian regime.

The most important of these materials is the letter to Silvanus from Sabinus, another Numidian bishop. After Silvanus had stripped his deacon Nundinarius of his clerical status, Nundinarius had come to Sabinus with his account of the division in Silvanus' diocese over the question of whether he was a *traditor*. Nundinarius' story had convinced Sabinus that his brother bishop needed some friendly advice. So Sabinus then wrote to Silvanus, exhorting him to restore Nundinarius to the clerical state and to bring peace to his diocese.

Sabinus rebuked his fellow bishop with the words of Scripture: "I will destroy the wisdom of the wise" (1 Cor. 1:19) and "People preferred darkness rather than light" (John 3:19).[3] These quotations demonstrated that the Bible, when it was written, encapsulated what would eventually come to pass, because it provided the appropriate words for the situation at hand. Both the biblical and contemporary situations were those in which people who were exposed to the truth, who should have known better, refused to see the light. Indeed, Sabinus had found the texts that sarcastically affirmed Silvanus' worldly wisdom. At the same time, the verses Sabinus chose condemned Silvanus for not choosing the wiser spiritual course but the worse in his conduct both during Diocletian's persecution and in administering his diocese. The way Sabinus read the Bible had saved him from any shock or surprise at Silvanus' conduct during persecution, for the Scriptures had predicted what would come to pass in the life of the North African church. Sabinus' prophetic view of Scripture allowed him to use the words of the Bible, "Expel evil from your hearts" (Isa. 1:16) and "Throw out evil from your midst" (1 Cor. 5:13), to encourage bishop Silvanus to fulfill the prophecies of Scripture in his own person by coming to terms with his Christian accusers.[4] In this letter, the Bible provided a world and messages appropriate to that world, not one in which outsiders persecuted Christians but one in which some Christians had lost their way.

Other letters are not quite so transparent, but they do reveal their authors' interpretive tactics. Nundinarius the deacon had also visited Purpurius, bishop of Limata (the murderer-bishop from the Council of Cirta), and told him of the dissension at Cirta. Purpurius wrote to the clerics and *seniores* of Cirta exhorting them to be evenhanded in their judgment of the situation and to do their best to restore harmony in the community.[5] Purpurius used typology to show his readers what they ought to do. Capitalizing on the Donatist perception of themselves as the *collecta*, the community of Israel, as found in the *Acts of the Abitinian Martyrs*, Purpurius used the harmonious relationship of the leader of the *collecta*, Moses, and the elders of Israel as a model. In concert they had proclaimed legislation for their people and they provided the God-given paradigm for the functioning of ecclesiastical authority. Purpurius likened the community of Cirta to the children of Israel in the desert. He appropriated for Silvanus, the religious leader of Cirta, the mantle of Moses and attempted to convince the *seniores* that they should come to terms with their bishop in the management of the affairs of their diocese. Here typology was Purpurius' chief interpretive device. It influenced all three functions of the biblical verses: it provided a world (Israel under Moses); it populated it (the bishop as Moses, his clergy as the elders); and it licensed a directive (Be reconciled).

In Bishop Fortis' letters to Silvanus and to his clergy, he used the Bible to provide words of warning. Fortis exhorted Silvanus not to delay the reconciliation with his clergy: "Take care, lest while you are nipping at one another and wrangling, you annihilate each other" (Gal. 5:5).[6] The attempt of the clergy to subject their bishop to proceedings in a civil court received the same treatment from Fortis that Paul had provided to the divided Christian community at Corinth: "Is there not a wise person anywhere among you who can adjudicate between Christians? Must it be that a brother goes to law with another, and in the court of unbelievers at that?" (1 Cor. 6:5-6).[7] One can take these sorts of citations merely as coincidentally convenient words that Fortis happened to find in the Bible, or, as the Donatists did, as typology, the words of the Lord written to a first-century Christian community but also meant for the guidance of the contemporary, divided Church. Again, the biblical verse sets up a world (the church of Corinth as paradigmatic for the church of Cirta), populates it (Corinthians as models for the people of Cirta), and licenses a message (Settle out of court).

The Donatists often took the words of the Bible literally, but these letters show how they occasionally interpreted them ironically. Verses of consolation and praise were sometimes transmuted into words of challenge and condemnation. "My peace I give you" (John 14:27), which Jesus spoke to his inner circle, was used to castigate an opponent and to illustrate just how lacking in true peace its addressee was.[8] All of the quotations in these letters show that the Donatist bishops believed that the Bible spoke authoritatively and that it was written as a guide for the solution of present problems. Thus, in dealing with fellow bishops, that is, other Christians, Donatists used biblical language culled from stories of division within Israel or within a New Testament community. They did not confuse insiders with outsiders, even in their anger. They had inherited from their predecessors the tradition of drawing lines in the sand. Now they added the custom of circling the wagons.

DE SINGULARITATE CLERICORUM

The second of the Donatist works is a pastoral letter, *De singularitate clericorum*, composed about 350 by Macrobius, the Donatist bishop of Rome.[9]

The sermon was written after the point at which Catholics and Donatists had come to a modus vivendi that sustained their relationship in North Africa from 321 to 346. During this time, towns often had two bishops and two churches, one for each party. Even Rome had its Catholic and Donatist bishops and congregations. This time of peace was, of course, disrupted in North Africa during the Macarian persecutions of 346 through 348.[10] However, there are no indications that the persecution profiled in the last chapter affected Donatists elsewhere. There were rivalry and enmity between groups outside of North Africa, but not to the same degree as in North Africa. Macrobius would have known of the North African situation, but his own circumstances were not nearly so acute; he pastored his flock at Rome on a parallel track to Julius I, the Catholic bishop of Rome.

In this sermon, Macrobius wrote to warn his clergy of the dangers of spiritual marriage, an arrangement in which two members of the opposite sex, vowed to celibacy, shared the same home and sometimes the same bed.[11]

This is an amazing letter for its surfeit of scriptural material. In its forty-six short paragraphs there are one hundred forty quotations and sixteen allusions. The majority come from Wisdom literature, the Corinthian correspondence, and the Pastorals, all of which are concerned with the upright life, with personal conduct and its effect on others.

The quotations at first appear to be simply phrases or sentences that coincidentally suited Macrobius' situation. However, the simple utility of the words should not obscure Macrobius' deliberate use, which he himself described in a statement of purpose at the beginning of the letter: "We add the strength of Scripture, so that all might know how to obey the revelation of the Lord even in this matter."[12] Macrobius added quotations from the Bible to his own arguments so that his clergy might understand how to obey the general revelation of the Lord with respect to the specific question of spiritual marriage. The Roman situation presumed agreement on the state of the world and the identity of those who inhabited it, so Macrobius' biblical verses are primarily those of command.

Macrobius mined the books of Proverbs and Sirach for their rich trove of misogynist texts, which he then forged as his tool for probing male-female relationships and warning against the untenable position of the man in a spiritual marriage; for example,

> Who will bind fire to his chest and not burn his clothes? Or who will walk on the embers of a fire and not scorch his feet? That's the way it is with anyone who goes in to the wife of his neighbor. He will not be spared if he touches her (Prov. 6:27).[13]

> Hell, the love of a woman, the parched earth, and fire never say, "Enough" (Prov. 30:16).[14]

From Wisdom literature and the letters to the Corinthians, he chose quotations that illustrated the paradoxical simultaneous weakness in strength and strength in weakness exposed by challenges to the moral life: "Out of fear a wise person turns from evil; a self-confident fool gets mixed up in evil" (Prov. 14:16), and "Will your weak brother for whom Christ died perish on account of your knowledge?" (1 Cor. 8:11–12).[15] Through these and similar quotations, he hoped to dissuade his clergy from placing themselves in the proximate occasion of sin and from providing malignant example and scandal to the local church and the broader community. This application of the texts of the Bible to his contemporary situation demonstrates Macrobius' belief that what was written in Scripture was addressed to, and therefore useful in, the present.

But Macrobius was not naive. Like his predecessors and colleagues in North Africa, he did not believe that every text spoke to every situation. According to Macrobius, when Paul quoted Jesus' command "Bear one another's burdens," he had in mind burdens other than celibacy. Macrobius also alluded to several Bible stories used by the proponents of spiritual marriage to support the legitimacy of their chosen way of life. The examples he cited included Elisha lodging at the home of the Shunamitess, the Apostles travelling in the company of women, the disciple John taking the mother of Jesus into his home, and Jesus himself staying beneath the roof of his friend Martha, speaking with the Samaritan woman, and being touched by the woman who wept at his feet. Macrobius rejected all these examples as evidence of logical fallacy on the part of his opponents.[16] He countered each of them by showing how they illustrated only transient associations with women or ones that were commanded by God. They failed to provide a precedent for continued and self-chosen cohabitation.[17] These examples reveal that Macrobius was aware that the context of a particular quotation in its story was vital to the exegesis of the verse and to its consequent use in exhortation.

Macrobius had no illusions that, even when the surrounding story was provided, his opponents would understand the falsity of their scripturally based arguments. Unfortunately, their evil minds had blinded them to the true interpretation of Scripture.[18] Scripture may, indeed, have spoken to the present, but only those with ears to hear could hear it.[19]

From Macrobius then one learns that the Bible spoke to the present, making clear God's will about specific situations. The Bible, however, had to be interpreted with care, taking into consideration the historical context of the words spoken by Jesus and the events narrated as patterns for action. Finally, the Bible was not open to all, but only to those whose hearts were not blinded by adherence to evil.

Spiritual marriage was a problem beyond the confines of the Donatist communities. An examination of how a non-Donatist author used the Bible in his preaching against the practice helps to highlight what is specifically Donatist in Macrobius' letter. John Chrysostom preached two sermons on spiritual marriage, one to men and another to women.[20] Though Macrobius antedates Chrysostom by about two generations, there are no indications of dependence. However, the similarities and differences between the two sermons written to men point to Macrobius' distinctively Donatist style.

Like Macrobius, Chrysostom relied on the Bible for reasons his clergy ought to avoid living with celibate women. Both authors availed themselves of the New Testament for approximately two-thirds of their biblical materials. Both derived a large block of their verses from the Corinthian correspondence. Some were the same citations, specifically the materials on whether the unmarried ought to wed and on whether one might eat idol meat.[21] Finally, both used "Let your light shine" to encourage virtue in their audiences.[22] In the biblical material they chose, both authors focused not so much on the state of the soul of the *individual* as on the *social* implications of spiritual marriage.

Beyond their general selection and use of these verses, they had little in common either materially or methodologically. Macrobius drew the preponderance of the rest of his quotations from Wisdom literature, a genre Chrysostom ignored. Macrobius' work was thoroughly biblical, whereas the patriarch of Constantinople took his guidance only partially from the Bible. Chrysostom's delicately sketched portrait of the emasculated celibate was as potent a part of his subtle argumentation against unholy wedlock as philosophy or history.

Chrysostom's cajolery stands in stark contrast to Macrobius' deadly solemnity. For Macrobius, the Bible was the primary locus of guidance for a Christian. For even the most sophisticated Donatist, there was no more powerful warrant for any action than the command of Scripture, and no other one necessary. History and philosophy were superfluous because Donatists lived and died by drawing lines between themselves and others, between the Church and the world. They had taken to heart the axiom of their predecessor Tertullian: "Quid ergo Athenis et Hierosolymis?"[23] Thus Macrobius' sermon demonstrates continuity in Donatist rhetoric: whether in times of warfare and persecution or in periods of peace, Donatist Christianity defines itself by rejection of the world and its ways.

SERMO IN NATALI SANCTORUM INNOCENTIUM

The third work in this collection of Donatist texts is the anonymous *Sermo in natali sanctorum innocentium*.[24] When it was discovered at the beginning of the twentieth century, it was immediately attributed to Optatus of Milevis (*fl.* 370), because it was found in the same manuscript with his writings against the Donatists. Very quickly, though, scholars recognized its Donatist provenance. Although they were unable to agree on assigning it to any particular author, their consensus is that the sermon is a Donatist product of the second half of the fourth century.[25]

More precision may be possible. Reference to exile would place the sermon after 347, when the Edict of Unity forced some Donatist bishops into exile. The *terminus ante quem* for the letter would be the promulgation of Julian's rescript allowing the return of those bishops in 362.[26]

This work provides a good example of what it meant for Donatists to embody the Bible in the way they lived their lives. To illustrate and encourage this personification of the Scriptures, the author of the sermon utilized the story of the Holy Innocents and the Magi of Matt. 2:1–23. The key elements of the narrative were divided into two groups in the sermon. In the first half, the preacher concentrated on Herod's attempt on the life of the child Jesus and the slaughter of the baby boys. These incidents enabled the preacher to construct a world in which he commanded his own audience to stand firm in persecution. The second half of the sermon reflected on the Magi's presentation of their gifts of gold, incense, and myrrh, and their return to their home by an alternate route. These incidents provided a biblical lesson on asceticism and the reformed life. Crucial to the use of both elements of the story were the presuppositions of the incarnation of Christ as the mixture of God with humanity, and of the Church as the body of that God-man *extended through time*. The author of the sermon presented Christological and ecclesiological doctrines as the basis for a correct understanding of the story of Herod and the Magi when he wrote: "For the Lord Christ is born, a human being joined with God, who joins the Church to God in himself and provides an example to Christians who follow him."[27]

Thus, the typological identification was not with the Holy Innocents who shed their blood as true protomartyrs but with Christ, who, like the Donatist bishops, endured exile patiently. This *imitatio Christi* informed all of the first half of the sermon. Herod not only persecuted the child Jesus but also the Church of the author's time: "The devil who has been cast out of heaven harries the Church through Herod."[28] Attention to the details of the Gospel of Matthew confirmed this. Both Herod and the fourth-century persecutors of true Christians pretended to worship Christ. Both were the cause of exile, one of Christ and the other of the Donatist bishops. Upon the death of Herod, the angel addressed Joseph with the message that those who persecuted the Child were dead. So a message would ultimately come to the Donatist bishops in exile also. Perhaps they anticipated Julian's religious policies.

The reference to persecutors in the plural was key for the author of this sermon, for it confirmed his belief that the Scriptures were written to explicate the sufferings of his Church:

> O mystic account containing the examples for all time within it! Although only Herod the persecutor died, it says that *many* died at his death. It says, "Those who sought the life of the child are dead." What is it that "many" reveals except that in Herod the persecutor all the persecutors of subsequent times died? For in the Lord is exemplified a figure of the whole Church, and in Herod the evil of all persecutors is condemned. Thus, therefore, in the Lord the whole body of the Church everywhere is affected by the persecution of his enemies and the suffering of everyone of conforming faith is revealed.[29]

In this scheme of events, all innocents were persecuted, from Abel and the prophets to the Holy Innocents and the Donatists. The sermon notes that this eternal warfare between evil and good was predicted from the very beginning, when God addressed the

Serpent in the Garden: "I will place enmity between your descendants and those of the woman" (Gen. 3:15).[30] After their suffering, however, the persecuted will all reign with Christ (Rev. 20:6) and the Church itself will treat its persecutors with derision: "Virgin daughter of Zion, it makes you laugh; it makes you shake your head, virgin daughter Jerusalem."[31]

The two halves of the sermon hinge on the admonition "Be of sound mind and committed faith, and anticipate help."[32] Although this counsel was not appropriate to a situation in which one anticipated death, it did provide models for heroic and patient suffering at the hands of the enemy. It also served to introduce the ascetic lessons to be learned from the gifts of the Magi and their return to the East by a different route. This lesson also involved an appeal to the audience to model their lives on a biblical image. But this time the rhetoric is not typological; Christians were not asked to put themselves in the place of the persecuted children, offering a one-time sacrifice of their lives. This time the appeal was allegorical and tropological; they were to become the gifts of the Magi, as well as following the path of the Magi.

The gifts of the Magi became virtues in the moral life. Their presents were, according to Francesco Scorza Barcellona, spiritualized. Instead of being concrete, palpable presents in a biblical story, they became incorporeal gifts of the believer. Those who could not give gold, incense, and myrrh could give the gift of a holy life. They could practice various virtues. Thus the sermon's concentration on the presents of the Magi provided an opportunity to discuss an alternative model for the *imitatio Christi*—not the death of the martyr, but the life of the ascetic.[33] As in the stories of Donatist martyrs, biblical quotations armed people for the long struggle, one in which they faced not only real personal enemies, but also, to an even greater degree, internal adversaries in the life of virtue.

In the *Sermo*, the gold represented faith and evangelical poverty, the incense a holy and peaceful life, and the myrrh suffering.[34] This incense and myrrh provided a sweet odor of sacrifice, a life of good works, and endurance to the end, even if that end was not a death at the hands of persecutors but one at the end of a life of self-persecution through asceticism. With this sweet odor, the Christian was to imitate Christ, who offered the most accep-table sacrifice.[35]

The author of the *Sermo* exploited the final element of the story of the Magi, their return to their homeland by another route. He used this change in itinerary to exhort his audience to change their own lives, to take on the life of virtue. Then they would truly seek, find, and adore Christ, unlike the duplicitous Herod. Then they would imitate the patient and long-suffering Christ in exile in Egypt.[36] In this section of the sermon, the author combined the typological, allegorical, and tropological senses of the story of the Magi.

In the *Sermo in natali sanctorum innocentium,* the anonymous Donatist preacher offered a hermeneutic similar to that of the North Africans already reviewed. The author relied on the Bible for guidance in day-to-day living. The people who heard this ser-mon were expected to pattern their lives on the lessons of the Bible. They were to apply Scripture typologically to their own lives and to model themselves on the characters in the story of the Magi. But those who died, the Holy Innocents, were not invoked as models. Their deaths were almost ignored. Instead, Donatists were told they could expect persecution like Christ's, not the Christ of the cross but the Christ of exile in Egypt.

Conformation of life extended beyond the typology that thus far has been common to Donatism. The unique contribution of this author to Donatist exegetical practice is the inclusion of alle-gorical and tropological interpretations through his use of the ele-ments of the three gifts and the theme of the "return by another way." Yet even these reinforced the message that the Bible is the pattern not just for death, but also for life. Donatists were still being taught to find the way they ought to live in the paradigm provided in the Bible. But now the Bible provided guidance for a life in which persecution was far less likely.

CONCLUSION

Donatist pastoral literature betrays many of the same attitudes toward the Bible as did the stories of the martyrs. First, God spoke to contemporary communities through the Scriptures. The Bible was a guide to conduct in the present. When one considered the message of God for the present, one found that the Donatist construction of the biblical message was still very practical. Pragmatism was brought to bear on new challenges. No longer was the issue martyrdom. The questions were not how to suffer and when to submit to execution. The issue was how to survive as a pure and spotless Church in a world filled with sinful Christians. The questions included: how ought a bishop to deal with the clergy; could a priest share a hearth, home, and even bed with a woman to whom he was not married; and what virtues ought the ascetic cultivate. In every case, the answer was separation from sinners.

Like the communities of the martyrs, the fourth-century authors and exegetes were discriminating about the applicability of various texts. Attention to the context of biblical quotations diminished the opportunities for proof-texting, although it did not eliminate it entirely. Donatists like Macrobius enlisted the context of a verse as a weapon against adversaries who had tried to use the text against them. Typology still reigned as the dominant mode of interpretation but allegory made its appearance.

Yet Donatist controversial literature was different from its predecessors on two accounts: the range of texts and an attitude toward tradition.

Donatist authors represented in this chapter used a greater number and variety of verses for two reasons. First, the issues themselves were less restricted in compass. There was more to talk about than simply martyrdom and the temptations to defection. Second, the genres of this chapter also presupposed some conversation between Christian opponents, people who knew and cherished the Bible. Thus Donatists did not simply advance their favorite texts, as they had been able to do in the face of a non-Christian audience. They also had to counter the scriptural citations and interpretations of their opponents. They accomplished this either by reinterpreting the verses used against them or by culling evidence of their own viewpoint from other parts of the Bible. Anyone who failed to agree with the interpretations of the Donatists was simply blinded by the depravity of sin.

But there is another difference between the pastoral works and the martyr stories. The martyrs had found their typological models in the prophets, the Maccabees, and occasionally Jesus. In the controversial literature of the Donatist movement, Jesus and the Maccabees gradually lost their place as models (except for the infant Jesus, in the *Sermo in natali sanctorum innocentium*). In *De singularitate clericorum*, Jesus is explicitly rejected as a type for Donatists. Aside from Jesus' parables and statements on the world in the Gospel of John, one reads very little about Jesus, the Apostles, or early Christianity, even about the martyrs themselves. Instead one finds that the Donatists took as their typological models the people of Israel and their elders, especially under the aspect of their fidelity to the Law. This adherence to Old Testament types had become the standard for Donatist typology.

The cause of this change in typological models is important. But searching for the genesis of this modification in the area of church-state relations is not fruitful. Lack of intense state persecution is not sufficient to account for this change. After all, Donatists of Africa Proconsularis were still being harassed by the state. It is true that the oppression they suffered was intermittent, but that had been the pattern of persecution throughout the history of Christianity. Their relation to the state was not entirely different from that of the Catholics, in most respects. Both groups had appealed to the imperial government to settle disputes between and within parties.[37] Finally, the Donatists could always wish that a new emperor might recognize them as the true Christians, or at least might stop the confiscation of property and restore what the Catholics had seized. There were ample precedents to nourish the hope that one emperor could reverse the policy of his predecessor.

The important difference lies not in Donatist or Catholic relations to the state so much as in the issues that differentiated Christians among themselves. The literature of controversy that this chapter examined brings to the fore that essential distinction. Throughout these works, the crucial point was not remaining a Christian, but remaining distinct from another particular part of the Christian population and not dividing one's own party. The texts chosen by the Donatists, especially in the case of Macrobius, attack those departing from group norms. In both the letters of the *Gesta apud Zenophilum* and in Macrobius, the situation of the divided community at Corinth in the New Testament provided biblical warrants for reconciliation. Finally, the texts promoting asceticism in the sermon on the Holy Innocents showed how to maintain one's Christian identity and progress in virtue. All of the documents focused on the maintenance of small group identity in the face of possible assimilation into a larger group characterized as sinful and impure. There were various sorts of sins and sinners: the sins of the *traditores*, the sins of those corrupting the community by the scandal of spiritual marriage, the deliberate courting of temptations against chastity, and despair of God's eventual help. In each case, the focal point was the choice between identity as true Christians and assimilation to the sinful standards of nominal Christians.

The issues of sin and assimilation were the same ones that had faced not Jesus but Paul's Christians at Corinth and the people of postexilic Israel. This is why advice from 1 Corinthians and the Wisdom literature was so attractive to the Donatists. Consequently, the types of martyr, prophet, and the faithful people in the midst of the nations were temporarily eclipsed by Old and New Testament communities striving for harmony.

Yet the use of the Bible in the controversial literature of the Donatist movement exhibits the same hermeneutic as the literature of the martyr stories. The Bible was the voice of God, giving instruction in the details of daily living. It was expressed typologically, as usual, and now allegorically and tropologically too. The main difference between the typology of the martyr stories and later Donatist controversial literature was the use to which the technique was put. Typology in the first sort of literature differentiated Christian from non-Christian and encouraged perseverance in the hour of death. In the latter works, it separated Donatist Christians from Catholics, and encouraged daily maintenance of the identity of the Donatist church as the harmonious community, united in love.

CHAPTER 4

New Times, New Ecclesiologies
Parmenian and Tyconius

IN THE LAST THIRD of the fourth century, Donatists were adapting to a new stage in their history. In the previous half-century they had moved from persecuted faction to separatist church. They had already learned that separation was the sine qua non of survival as a church. At first, the empire and the Catholics had enforced that separation by their persecution of Donatists. Then, when exterior forces no longer drew the line between the church of the martyrs and the church of the *traditores*, Donatists had been forced to draw their own lines between themselves and the Catholics by refusing state support and encouraging a separatist mentality.[1] However, during the latter part of the century, up to the 390s, circumstances changed considerably: the emperor Julian turned against Catholic Christians and brought Donatist bishops back to North Africa from exile. He provided a time of peace and respectability for the Donatists. Donatism became an acceptable church. It grew larger and more diverse. Donatism constituted the majority religion in most, if not all, of North Africa. When even government officials joined it, the Donatist Church had to redefine itself again.

The situation was especially acute when this popular movement spawned its own schisms. The Donatist church could no longer be the church of the martyrs or even the church of the outsiders. Donatists no longer felt any impetus to look for a speedy end to the history of the world as relief or vindication. Yet they had to deal with a tradition that had taught that the separatist Church was a pure church and had, at least initially, fostered millennarianism. This chapter describes in detail the ways in which the Donatists' use of the Bible reveals their tactics for coping with a change in status from a persecuted minority, to a solid separatist movement, to an internally divided community, during the time from the reign of Julian to the 390s. This situation of radical change called for a response to bridge the gap between an ecclesiology that valorized purity and promoted separation to one that could deal with evil within the Church and foster integration.

The political background for the Donatist schism of the late fourth century is the transition from Julian's pro-Donatist stance to the less supportive and occasionally pro forma hostile attitude of subsequent emperors.[2] When Julian's successors, Valentinian and Valens, took office in 364, they were not as well disposed toward Donatism as Julian had been; however, they were not openly hostile to the Donatist church. They sent new officials to the provinces, men who would enforce the status quo *ante* Julian. This should not be interpreted solely or even primarily as a religious response. The larger issue was the rigorous collection of taxes.

The emperors' deputy in North Africa was the *comes* Romanus. The reaction to Romanus' campaign to enforce taxation regulations was a revolt in Mauretania Caesariensis led by Firmus, a local leader and perhaps a relative of the last independent king of Mauretania. The rebellion was joined by many Circumcellions, religiously conservative migrant agricultural laborers who were usually, although not always, Donatist supporters.[3]

The Mauretanian-Circumcellion-Donatist alliance against onerous taxation was harshly repressed by Romanus. Understandably detested by the local populace, he was, according to Ammianus Marcellinus, not very popular with the troops and finally failed to win even imperial favor when his policy of underreporting casualties was discovered.[4] The fighting was largely over by 373, when the Roman military had to turn its interest to more pressing concerns, the defense of the *limes*. In the decade that followed, Roman officials made attempts to enforce fiscal obligations. In addition, there was some lip service paid to the religious issues. The emperors had promulgated a few measures against heretics that included issues relevant to Donatism. They forbade the rebaptism of Catholic converts to Donatism and they issued orders for the destruction of Donatist sanctuaries.[5] But this legislation was largely ignored by authorities in North Africa. This may have been due, at least in part, to Valentinian's persistent refusal to be drawn into doctrinal disputes as an active participant.[6] But even after the accession of the more religiously aggressive Gratian, Catholics could not expect much help from Roman authorities. In fact, Flavian, the *comes Africae* in 376/377, was a member of the Donatist church, and Gildo, Firmus' brother, was back in power as *comes* in 385.[7] Neither could have been expected to enforce legislation against their own power bases.

Although Donatists did not need to worry about active religious persecution in the period from Julian to the 390s, the circumstances of the relaxation of exterior pressure brought to the fore internal dissension issuing in schisms. There were many such schisms, some smaller, some larger, some short-lived, others longer lasting. For the sake of this narrative, the largest of the schisms before 390, that of the Rogatists, will serve as example.

The Rogatists' was the earliest major schism. It began during the original backlash against the enforcement of taxation rules by Romanus. At that time, some groups of North Africans had taken up arms. But a minority of Donatists objected to both the militant attitude of their neighbors and to what they claimed was a misuse of church property by drunken Circumcellions. Prime among the disaffected was Bishop Rogatus of Cartenna. He and nine of his Mauretanian colleagues broke communion with the rest of the Donatists over the issue of armed resistance. The group separated from the main Donatist movement, forming their own ultrapure and pacifist church. Although it remained small and restricted to Mauretania and was persecuted by Firmus, it lasted over half a century, disappearing from history only after 420.[8]

With the centripetal force of separation from the *traditores* of the Catholics no longer necessary or helpful, Donatists needed some mechanism to work against centrifugal forces, such as the Rogatist schism, that were fragmenting their church. Now that the Donatists were a majority religion, they no longer needed to draw lines of exclusion in the sand to maintain group identity. Instead they needed to draw lines of inclusion to promote group solidarity.

Two of the Donatist authors who bridged the gap between separatist sect and majority church were Parmenian and Tyconius. Both wrote their major works beginning around the reign of Julian. Both formulated their ecclesiologies at a time when Donatists had respite from persecution and enjoyed government support. During the period when persecution had ceased and the emperor was on their side, Donatists began to develop an ecclesiology, or rather a variety of ecclesiologies, to suit their new situation. Both of the authors examined in this chapter wrote on the question of the identity of the Church. Both came to shape their ecclesiologies differently. In fact, as bishop of Carthage, Parmenian eventually excommunicated Tyconius, a lay theologian in his diocese. In the end, however, it was Tyconius whose ecclesiology would make the larger impact on Donatist and Catholic theology. But in examining the work of these two writers one can see how Donatism used the Bible to survive the transition from united minority to fractious majority.

PARMENIAN

Parmenian, the first of the two bridge-builders, was the most famous Donatist writer of his day. He had come from Spain or Gaul to succeed Donatus as bishop of Carthage in 362. He began his episcopate during a period when the government supported and encouraged Donatism. Even after the death of Julian, his diplomatic and pastoral style of leadership promoted the Donatist cause for an entire generation. At Parmenian's death *ca.* 391, Donatism still held the allegiance of many Christians even in the area of Carthage.

Parmenian's primary work, *Adversus ecclesiam traditorum* (*ca.* 362), has been lost, but his arguments survive, and one may extract them from the writings of Optatus of Milevis and Augustine of Hippo. Because the distillation of a theologian's work from the polemical tract of his opponent is an exercise with numerous pitfalls, it is important to be clear about the method used before the material extracted is examined.

The first consideration in assessing the material of Parmenian embedded in Optatus and Augustine is the fact that every author, including Optatus and Augustine, writes from a particular perspective. Geographical and social location, sex, religion, education, and political affiliation enhance or limit possibilities for hearing, seeing, and understanding one's environment. Second, in addition to limiting what an author can understand, these factors may influence what an author is allowed—by self, others, or genre—to say. So the reader needs to be attentive to the biographical context of the work. Adequately understanding the content and force of the statements communicated by an author in a specific work presupposes a familiarity with the person and situation of the author. Therefore, Optatus' and Augustine's own life stories are important.

Optatus was born in the wake of the first major anti-Donatist campaign (*ca.* 320). He came from a non-Christian family of indeterminate social status.[9] His own baptism initiated him not simply into Christianity, but into Catholic Christianity, an embattled minority in Donatist-dominated Numidia. By the 360s, he had become bishop of Milevis, his place of birth. His elevation to the episcopacy may even have taken place during the reign of Julian (361–63). This emperor had suspended all anti-Donatist regulations. He had allowed the return of bishops exiled by Constantius in 347 as well as the restoration of the property seized during the enforcement of the edict of unity under Paul and Macarius in 346 through 348.[10] Thus, Optatus the bishop was not only confronted with Donatist congregations forming a majority in the area around his city, but also faced at least one rival Donatist bishop.[11] He resorted to both arms and pen in the defense of his adopted religion.[12]

Optatus' only surviving work, an unnamed treatise, provides the only contemporary view of the work of Parmenian, bishop of Carthage. Optatus' first edition was a work of six books written between 366 and 370. It was published during a period when Catholics were still recovering from the shock and the horror of Julian's reversal of the religious policy of Constantine and his sons favoring their party. A second edition with a seventh book appeared in 390.[13] Parmenian had written about the nature of the Church and how to identify the true Church in an effort to vindicate Donatism. Optatus' work did not directly refute Parmenian's ecclesiology, but it attacked Parmenian and capitalized on the seeming inconsistency in Donatist policies on rebaptism. Donatists baptized those who had come to them from the Catholic party because the Donatists viewed Catholic baptism as invalid. In Donatist eyes, it had been administered by *traditores*, who by their sin had lost the Spirit and placed themselves outside the Church. However, they did not rebaptize those returning to the fold from groups they considered schismatic (not heretical). Donatists would have seen them as descendants of true Christians, that is, of those who were not *traditores*. Therefore, in Donatist eyes, their Baptism had been valid. Optatus, and Augustine after him, for their own reasons, will not admit the difference among these various converts and will accuse Donatists of inconsistency.[14]

Optatus' reply to Parmenian shows that he was primarily a historian rather than a theologian. He began and ended in the history of the Donatist movement, showing how Donatists had been obtuse, self-willed sinners from the beginning of their troubles with the Catholics. He asserted that the Donatists could not possibly possess the truth about anything, for their way of life failed to correspond to their vision of the Church as pure and spotless. He hoped that this ad hominem argument would meet some success among ordinary Donatists. With their own church, its bishops, and its people convicted, they could not possibly be the true Church. Hence their church, not the Catholic church, was the imposter, and it would behoove them to join Optatus and his congregation.

With a work written under these circumstances, the reader must beware of two hermeneutical issues: the fragmentary nature of the materials presented and the partiality of the author.

First, Optatus presented only a portion of what he read and knew of Donatist practice and their writing and preaching on the Bible. He did not offer to his readers a systematic presentation of Donatist teachings. At times he was self-contradictory.[15] Still less did he present what was central or distinctive. Rather, he exposed what, from his Catholic viewpoint, he found eccentric and objectionable. Because of this bias, anyone trying to disentangle Parmenian's teaching from Optatus must view his presentation with some suspicion. His tract must be checked for internal consistency as well as for coherence with what has been discovered independently.

Second, Optatus was not presenting Donatist teaching for its own sake. Because of his position as pastor and teacher of an embattled minority congregation, his exposition of Donatism was the by-product of his desire to refute teachings he considered unorthodox. In such polemical circumstances, there were always opportunities to misunderstand the Donatists and temptations to make Donatist teaching and practice as unattractive as possible. Even when he knew or wrote of material that might be used in their defense, he construed it in the most negative manner possible. One must read Optatus with great care if the goal is understanding Donatist history, not a contemporary hostile reaction to the movement as a whole, from the inside.

However, even when drained in the sieve of skepticism, Optatus does provide solid evidence of Donatist ecclesiology. In his failure to address Parmenian's ecclesiology directly and his attempt to use the Donatist bishop's theory of the Church wholesale against the Donatists, Optatus had to provide an explication of Donatist belief that would be credible not only to Catholics but also to Donatists. Without at least some verisimilitude of Donatist theology—and both Donatists and Catholics knew what was credible because they lived in close and open proximity—his work would have been less than successful. Although not all of Optatus' testimony can be accounted accurate, when compared with what is already known of Donatism and in view of the situation of Donatism after 360, Optatus' work does provide some valuable evidence about what Donatists did indeed believe, what Parmenian most probably wrote, and how the Donatist movement adjusted to its majority position.

Augustine is the other major source for material about Parmenian. Augustine's biography is so well known as to need little rehearsal.[16] By his own admission, his information on the early history of Donatism largely reproduces what is in Optatus' work.[17] But as a pastor in a largely Donatist area, a frequent visitor to Carthage, and a good friend of its bishop Aurelius (bishop *ca.* 391–429), his own observations supplement this information. One must observe the same caveats as those mentioned for the writings of Optatus. The reader should remember that Augustine's advanced Christian education was not North African and that he was a *Catholic* bishop, as Optatus was.[18] His *Contra Epistulam Parmenian* provides some evidence of Parmenian's theology. However, it should be noted that Parmenian's theology was not uppermost in Augustine's mind as he wrote. The purpose of the treatise was not the refutation of Parmenian's theology generally. The treatise was written *ca.* 400, that is, after Parmenian had died.[19] Couched as a defense of some of Tyconius' teachings (those against which Parmenian had written), Augustine's treatise is really directed at undermining the Donatists in their struggle with dissident Maximianists in the early years of the fifth century. Hence, the treatise is only of limited value for a consideration of Donatism in the period before 390. Much more will be mined from it in the next chapter.

Now that we have surveyed our principal sources and their liabilities, we can proceed to Parmenian's contributions to Donatist survival.

The main practical issue Parmenian faced as bishop of Carthage was whether to baptize those who entered the Donatist church if they had already undergone a baptismal ceremony while attached to another Christian congregation. Augustine described Parmenian as a moderate who did not rebaptize all converts.[20] However, Parmenian believed that converts from the Catholic party were required to be baptized, because Catholicism was not the true and only church of God; it was the party of the *traditores*. Catholic bishops held no communion with Donatism, the true Church. Schismatics such as the Rogatists (and later the Maximianists) were another case. They had been baptized as Donatists, that is, as members of the true Church, before their separation; their priests and bishops had been ordained in a line of bishops traceable to the those who had not been *traditores*. Pastoral practice and Parmenian's own ecclesiology contraindicated a second baptism in these cases. In his own work, Optatus related Parmenian's defense of Donatist ecclesiology supporting this nuanced answer.

Parmenian, like the majority of his North African predecessors, believed that there was but one true Church that could administer the sacraments.[21] But Parmenian knew that Catholics attacked this reply. They turned the Donatist adage "You can't give what you don't have" against Donatist ministers of the sacrament when those ministers did not live sinless lives. The Catholics construed Donatist sacramental theology to teach that if Donatist or Catholic ministers were sinful, they did not have the Spirit. If they did not have the Spirit, their baptism would be useless.[22] Augustine quotes Parmenian as saying that the dead could not give life, the wounded cure, the blind give light, the naked dress others, and the unclean make others clean—a string of phrases surely reminiscent of the Abitinian martyrs' condemnation of the members of the Caecilianist party.[23]

The Catholic attacks by Optatus and Augustine were popular ones designed to inflame old antipathies. Their construction of the Donatist position remains a popular reading of Donatist sacramental theology to this day. But it does not reflect what Donatists actually taught and practiced. Donatists had not claimed that their priests were sinless. Even Augustine knew that.[24] North Africans had, in fact, debated the issue of the relationship between the personal purity or impurity of the minister and the validity of the sacrament as early as 305 at the Council of Cirta, when they had to decide who was worthy to consecrate a new bishop. They allowed Purpurius of Limata, a self-confessed

murderer, to participate in the elevation of the new bishop of
Cirta. Following this precedent, the issue for Donatists was not
personal sin but *ecclesial affiliation*. Since Purpurius had not been a
traditor, nor had he been consecrated by a *traditor,* he was still a
member—albeit a sinful member—of the true Church. His private affairs, even murder, were no bar to his participation in the
ritual of consecration. His affiliation with the true Church was
what mattered. So the answer in 305 and in Parmenian's day was
the same: not the holiness of the priest but the holiness of the
Church with which one was affiliated made the difference.

With two parties claiming the title of true Church, the
believer seeking Baptism needed a test to distinguish the true from
the false. Parmenian proposed a test, which Optatus described:
the true Church has the *dotes* or gifts that God gave the true
Church. Although this test may seem to be an exercise in circular
reasoning, it was convincing enough that Optatus could not refute
its premises.

The *dotes* were the gifts or ornaments God bestowed only on
the one and true Church. The Donatist church's possession of the
dotes was the key to Parmenian's ecclesiology and sacramental
theology. Only the Church that had the *dotes* could confer Baptism. They were: the *cathedra,* or authority of the Church; the
angel, variously interpreted as a rightly consecrated bishop or
guardians of the churches like the angels in Revelation; the Spirit,
the fountain (of true Baptism); the seal of the fountain; and
finally, the *umbilicus,* the navel or central focus of worship, a properly consecrated altar.[25] Members of the church possessing the
dotes could baptize *no matter what the state of their personal sanctity.*
Baptism belonged to the true Church, not to any specific member. Baptism belonged *only* to the true Church, and to no other
community, because there was only one Holy Spirit, and that
Spirit had a unique relationship with the Church.[26] Consequently,
Baptism belonged to the Church not because the minister of the
sacrament or the individuals within the Church were holy, but
because God endowed the Church with the gifts or *dotes* requisite
for the administration of the sacraments. Thus, if a holy person
administered a sacrament, well and good; it was a true sacrament

because of the minister's membership in the Church. If a sinful person administered the same sacrament, there was no problem, because the *dotes* of the Church, not the spiritual gifts of the individual member, were what was needed. The same sacrament was administered.

Lest there be any confusion at this point, one should note that Parmenian's stand was not that of Augustine, who, in his search for the power of the sacrament, would move it even farther from the individual minister of the sacrament. Augustine would locate the power to administer a sacrament not in the minister or even in the Church, with its *dotes*, but directly in God.[27] As the power to administer the sacraments was not a function of the possession of the *dotes* in Augustine's sacramental theology, he would be able to bypass the Church and say that even those outside the Church could baptize. He even affirmed baptism by schismatics. On this basis, he defended the Catholic practice of not administering Baptism to those already initiated by Donatists. Even the schismatic status of the Donatists could not impede the power of God.[28]

In reading Optatus and Augustine, then, Parmenian's approach appears as a very high ecclesiology. The Church was gifted by God and provided the sacraments to its adherents through its priests. The moral status of the minister was not of serious consequence; he may even have been a murderer. However, the proper ecclesial status of the priest was essential; only those in communion with the true and gifted Church could administer the sacraments.

The replies of both Optatus and Augustine to the Donatists included many quotations from the Bible. Many of these were verses they chose as ammunition against their opponents. But examining the use of the biblical verses they attributed to Parmenian and the Donatists will reinforce our general perceptions of Donatist ecclesiology and show how the Donatists responded to changing times through their use of the Bible. Here, as in the preceding chapters, typology and the application of commands in the Bible to the situation of Donatist-Catholic rivalry will be the most important characteristics of Donatist method.

The *dotes* of Parmenian, as they were explained in Optatus, presupposed a typological reading of several verses from the Canticle of Canticles:

> An enclosed garden is my sister, my bride, a sealed fountain. Your shoots are an orchard of pomegranates with all the trees of incense . . . a cistern of living water (Cant. 4:12–13, 16a).

> One is my dove, my perfect one, the only one of her mother, the chosen of the one who bore her (Cant. 6:8).

> Your navel is a finely wrought bowl which never lacks its drink (Cant. 7:2).

Here one finds three of the *dotes* named: the sealed fountain, the seal affixed to it, and the navel or altar. Optatus' report of Parmenian's explanation of the first two of the *dotes* is congruent with Donatist use of these passages before and after Parmenian. The godfather of Donatism, Cyprian of Carthage, equated the garden and the one dove with the Church as spotless bride.[29] Later, Donatists at the Conference of Carthage will use another part of this same Canticle in a similar way. Canticle 4:7 says, "You are beautiful, sister, and there is no fault in you." To this they would join the favorite Cyprianic and Donatist epithet, Eph. 2:27, "the church not having stain or blemish."[30] The Canticle joined with the text from Ephesians embodied a solidly established complex of verses in North Africa, especially among Donatists. Thus Optatus' presentation of a typological exegesis of the Canticle as *dotes* is consonant with and ought to be taken as a fair representation of Donatist usage, and not as a creation of Optatus.

The importance of the altar as the navel of the Church in Parmenian's writing is rendered credible by Optatus' concentration not only on the typological exegesis itself, which he accepts, but on the question of whether the navel can be one of the ornaments or *dotes* of the Church or must be considered a body part. According to Optatus, if it were a body part rather than ornament, Parmenian should not have counted it on his list of *dotes*. The significance of the altar is corroborated by the long-standing Donatist devotion to regular celebration of the Eucharist, even during persecution, and to their interest in the altar in narratives about martyrs.[31]

Optatus' discussions of the *cathedra* and of the Spirit did not focus on specific uses of Scripture by Parmenian. However, in his treatment of the angel, Optatus hinted at one interpretation. He mentioned the angel stirring the waters of Baptism. For him, this was a reference to the story in John 5:4, the cure of the paralytic at the pool of Bethsaida.[32] If the angel is simply an agent of God in the preparation of the baptismal water, Parmenian has adopted the angelology of Tertullian with which the Donatists would have been familiar. Tertullian has both an angel and the Spirit operative in different ways in the sacrament of Baptism. The angel prepared the way for the Spirit who sanctified the water.[33] In this case, the angel was simply a deputy of God. This was a very old interpretation, one shared by Augustine.[34] If any other interpretation is feasible, it is that the angel was a guardian of the community. This places the Donatists at Carthage on a par with the churches of Revelation, each with its own angel. In fact, Optatus spoke of the angel not being in communion with the angels of the other churches, a likely interpretation only for Catholics who regularly charged the Donatists with separatism.

The comment about communion has led O. R. Vassall-Phillips to construe the angel as a type of the local bishop.[35] There is no direct testimony in Optatus that Parmenian interpreted the angel thus. Angels do not figure as types of bishops or of anyone or anything else in Donatist materials. They are simply deputies of God who assist the saints. At the least, it is unclear whether Parmenian would have utilized such a typology. On the other hand, it provided a very convenient ground for attack by Optatus. He linked the lack of a proper *cathedra* to the lack of an angel, impugning Donatist claims to be the true Church. Because of the polemical role of this interpretation, it is suspect. Consequently, one cannot make a firm commitment to the angel as a type of the bishop in the work of Parmenian; it is more likely an affirmation of the nobility of the Donatist church, which had its own angel, like the churches of the Apocalypse.

An examination of Optatus' writings on Parmenian's *dotes*,

then, provides evidence of a typology in continuity with Tertullian and Cyprian and with the exegesis of the communities that produced the martyr stories. This typology allowed for the interpretation of the Church as a closed community and for Baptism as the property of the one true Church, that of the Donatists. The application of the texts to the Church of the present demonstrates that Parmenian, like other Donatists, thought the Bible spoke to the present for guidance in the practical issue of trying to decide where one ought to be baptized and whether one ought to repeat the ceremony when transferring one's allegiance to a different community. So one sees that, in contrast to the picture normally presented of Donatists, Parmenian was no millennialist. The significant advance Parmenian made was to provide in a well-articulated form what had been heretofore only latent in Donatist ecclesiology, that is, it is not the personal holiness but the ecclesial affiliation of the minister of the sacrament that is necessary for validity.

Elsewhere, Optatus discussed Donatist use of material from the Canticle. In his first book, he spoke sarcastically of Donatist exclusivity:

> Rightly hast thou closed the Garden to heretics, rightly hast thou claimed the Keys for Peter, rightly hast thou denied the right of cultivating young trees to those who are certainly shut out from the garden and from the paradise [the *paradisus*, i.e., orchard] of God; rightly hast thou withdrawn the Ring from those to whom it is not allowed to open the Fountain.[36]

This portrayal of Donatist exclusivity appears to license Donatists to shut people out of their community and, in the context of the controversy, this is just the impression Optatus wished to evoke, for he wanted to portray the Donatists as a church that by excluding everyone, excluded themselves.[37] This he will immediately contrast with Catholic expansiveness.

If one is to use this quotation from Optatus to provide any information about Donatist practice, it needs to be read in light of what is already known about Donatist use of the Canticle. When studied in that context, the exclusivity is not that of the Donatists keeping others out—in fact, they welcomed those returning from the Catholics—but of keeping Baptism in, in the sealed fountain, inside the enclosed garden, that is, the exclusive property of the Donatist church. To be saved, one must come *into that garden.* Here Parmenian was showing Donatists how to use the Bible, not for a separatist but for an inclusivist tradition.

The urgency of inclusion is amply demonstrated in Optatus' discussion of Parmenian's work. Optatus repeatedly uses references to Donatist exegesis to show their transformation of eschatological texts into texts that counsel the urgency of the present. Besides employing material on the garden from the Canticle, Optatus cited a Donatist use of Scripture that capitalized on another piece of typology related to horticulture, more precisely, the viticulture well known in Numidia. He claimed that the Donatists used the parable of the vine and the branches (John 15:1–8) against the Catholics:

> Amongst other things you have said that the schismatics have been cut off, like branches, from the Vine, and that they have been reserved, marked off for punishment, like dried wood, for the fires of Hell.[38]

Catholics associated this reference to hell with the end of the world and the results of the Final Judgment.[39] There is no independent verification of any use of this passage among the Donatists, much less of such an interpretation. Rather, Donatists were known to interpret passages as applicable to the present, whereas Catholics heard the words as speaking of the end of the world. Augustine is ample witness to the dispute on the correct time to which to apply parables of separation, the time of the discovery of the sin or the end of the world,[40] and he specifically supported a Tyconian interpretation of the Church not as static bride "not having stain or blemish" but as an entity in process, one that was growing and evolving.[41]

Although we cannot independently verify Donatist use of John 15:1–8 by Parmenian, Optatus' accusation that Parmenian used this passage (in some manner or another) ought not be dismissed for two reasons. First, the Donatists were not habitually

biblical atomists. Rather, they often used many verses from the
same part of the Bible as part of a sustained argument, and they
also recognized that the context of the verse affected the proper
interpretation of a passage.[42] The similitude of the vine and the
branches comes from Jesus' discourse at the Last Supper in the
Gospel of John. Donatists were very familiar with this sermon and
regularly used other parts of it in anti-Catholic propaganda.[43]
Thus Parmenian may, indeed, have used it in reference to his opponents.

If Parmenian had indeed employed the passage about the vine
and the branches, the rhetorical force of the use would be the
important issue. If it were not about a future judgment and punishment, a Donatist author might well have used it to demonstrate
the seriousness of the evil of adhering to a dead Catholic branch
instead of the living vine of Christ and the true, that is, Donatist,
Church. This once again provides reason to believe that Donatism
was not an intransigent millennialist movement. Both Donatists
and Catholics transformed texts of the End Time. Whereas
Catholics pushed the End far into the future, Donatists transformed the eschatological urgency of the future into a warning for
the present.

The next time Optatus used this verse was in the context of a
discussion on the difference between schismatics, who were not
cut off, and heretics, who were. He claimed that Donatists made
no such distinction and, therefore, any claims Parmenian made
about folks who were cut off from the body of the Church might
be applied to Donatists. He said, "Now do you see, my brother
Parmenian, now do you recognize, now do you understand, that
by your arguments you have fought against yourself?"[44]

But this is not an accurate representation of the Donatist position on schismatics and heretics. In fact, Donatists "rebaptized"
only those whom they considered ecclesiological heretics, that
is, the lineal religious descendants of *traditores*. Although such
rebaptism was practiced fairly regularly in Numidia, Optatus'
area, it was not always done and, in fact, rarely done in Mauretania to the west, an area about which Optatus does have information.[45] Thus, Donatists did recognize the difference between

heretics and schismatics and Optatus was obscuring that fact for the sake of his own argument. So Parmenian must have been using the verses for another purpose than to wholeheartedly condemn all non-Donatists. One possibility is that he was condemning Catholics only, not Rogatists, whom Donatists did not rebaptize. Another, more probable possibility is that he was interpreting Scripture in a very Donatist way, using the language of eschatological terror to apply to the present. The threat of being cut off and then burned, even if in the near future, was uttered to prompt change in the present. Such an interpretive tactic is consonant with the accusations Optatus made against Parmenian elsewhere.

In addition, Optatus was unhappy with the Donatist interpretation of the parable of the wedding feast (Matt. 22:1–14).[46] Here he candidly accused Parmenian of applying it to the wrong time, the present, instead of to the end of the world. Optatus is credible here, as this will be the same interpretation put on the passage by the Donatists themselves at the Conference of Carthage.[47]

Donatists used not only texts about the future but texts about the past to give urgency to their efforts to bring Catholic and Rogatist converts into the Donatist fold. Three examples from Optatus and Augustine illustrate the Donatist hermeneutic, which applied a maximum number of texts to the present.

One passage was Ps. 140:5, "Let not the oil of the sinner anoint my head."[48] According to Optatus, it could not apply to David, its author, because at the time of its composition David was already king. Having been anointed by Samuel years before, he had no need of a second anointing. Thus it must have applied to someone else. In the Cyprianic tradition, Optatus interpreted this verse Christologically. It was an expression of desire on the part of Jesus, who disdained any human anointing or validation of his work. The Donatists, said Optatus, were wrong to interpret this as a command and to apply it to themselves, refusing a baptismal anointing by Catholics.

Augustine, too, had the Donatists using this text to apply to their present controversy with the Catholics. Whether he received his information from Optatus only or heard it in his own situation years later, he offered his own rebuttal. He asked how the Donatists could use such a verse to avoid participation in Catholic sacraments when one of their own bishops, Optatus of Thamugadi, had been a notorious sinner.[49]

Although the surviving Donatist works do not make any reference to this verse, the exegesis Optatus and Augustine cite is certainly in line with the Donatist treatment of a similar verse. At the Conference of Carthage, they will take a comparable passage as a command. They will interpret Ps. 1:1, in which the psalmist's goodness is confirmed by not sitting with the wicked, as barring them from being seated in the presence of the Catholic bishops.[50] More importantly, it accords with the reports of Donatist lack of respect for Catholic anointing. Optatus mentioned this in connection with Donatist abuses of Catholics and their ritual objects. He charged that Donatists had scraped Catholic altars and the heads of Catholic clerics before reanointing them and that Donatists had thrown out the window a vial of chrism consecrated by a Catholic bishop.[51] Given Donatist concern with ritual pollution, one may count the interpretation offered by Optatus as faithful to Donatist exegetical and ritual practice.

The second of the passages about the past that the Donatists also applied to the present is the combination of Wis. 3:16 with 4:3, a condemnation of the offspring of illicit unions: "the children of adulterers do not grow up . . . false shoots cannot strike deep roots." Apparently, Donatists had taken it to apply to Catholics. Optatus objected that if one took it figuratively, one excused literal adulterers. But he granted that one could take it in that manner. In that case, the referent should not be Catholics but rather Valentinus, the second-century gnostic heretic whose sacraments were like invalid marriage spawning illegitimate birth.[52]

While previous and contemporary Donatist materials do not record the use of these specific verses, the example Optatus reported followed an exegetical strategy identical to that of the Donatist bishops at the Conference of Carthage, when they employed Hos. 2:4–5, another condemnation of the children of adultery, to characterize the Catholics.[53]

A third text urging immediate incorporation into the Donatist church rounds out a consideration of Donatist use of the Bible. It is Jer. 2:13, the condemnation of those who forsake the fountain and dig broken cisterns for themselves.[54] Again, Optatus' objection dealt with chronology. He insisted that the passage should have been applied to the group Jeremiah addressed, idolatrous Jews, and not to anyone else.

The exegesis of Jer. 2:13 is not found in other Donatist material up to this time, although Augustine rebuts what he claims is Parmenian's use of it.[55] But such an interpretation would have suited the Donatist point quite well. They often used anti-idolatry texts to condemn the Catholics. Optatus was even aware of one of the reasons. He himself recorded that Donatists accused Catholics of idolatry when the Catholics reportedly set a bust of Constantine on the altar during services in the presence of the imperial commissioners Paul and Macarius.[56] Based on the surrounding rhetoric in Optatus and the coherence of this use with the Donatist program, there is no reason to believe that this verse was not part of their repertoire.

Although Optatus and Augustine are not perfect mirrors of Parmenian, they do provide some insights into a period of change in the movement. They show how Parmenian provided ways in which Donatism could cope with its change from minority to majority religion. First, Parmenian provided a way to deflect charges of immorality among the clergy from any attack on the validity of its sacraments. A small church might strictly control its members, expelling sinners, but with Donatism growing in Mauretania, Numidia, and even Africa Proconsularis, such strong control was no longer feasible, if it had ever been desirable. By attributing the power of the sacraments to the Church, endowed with its holiness by God through the *dotes*, he preserved the validity of the sacraments for a church in which individual ministers could not avoid the label of "sinner."

Second, Parmenian supplied a reason why people should join the growing Donatist movement *immediately*. Although Catholics pushed judgment and, consequently, the hour of decision far into the future, to the end of the world, whenever that might be, under

Parmenian, Donatists insisted that the present was of prime importance by applying eschatological texts to the present. Lest Christians grow lax in their attention to decisions about affiliation with the correct Christian community, Parmenian and his followers provided them with encouragement, verse after biblical verse, to join their church without delay.

Based on a careful analysis of Optatus and Augustine, one can see that Parmenian provided Donatists with some mechanisms to meet the challenge of being the majority Church in a period of schism. First, Parmenian showed how a church with sinners in it could still be the true Church. He accomplished this by focusing on the Church itself as pure. In a sense, then, he could sweep nonecclesiological sin and individual sinners under the Church's rug. In this endeavor, he used biblical texts primarily from the Canticle of Canticles, long a North African favorite. Second, he provided an impetus for an immediate choice of Donatism in his use of prophetic texts of warning and condemnation. In both cases, typology functioned as the prime hermeneutical tool. Types from the past were applied either to the Catholics as a faithless group or to the Donatists as a faithful institution.

What Parmenian and his opponent shared is a dichotomous treatment of their churches. Each treats his own church as a singular and pure institution. Each treats his adversary's church as a collection of sinful individuals. Such a stalemate would have left both sides permanently vulnerable to attack. The stalemate was broken by one of Parmenian's own communicants, Tyconius.

TYCONIUS

Tyconius provided a revolutionary alternative to the bickering between the Catholic and Donatist parties. He was successful in putting to rest any residual millennarianism within Donatism. He also offered Donatists a novel ecclesiology to cope with schism and evil inside the church of the pure. Unlike Parmenian, he did not minimize evil in the Church. His own interpretation of the

Bible furnished a way to conceive of evil and evildoers as constitutive elements within the Church *on the basis of the Bible itself.*

Tyconius lived from *ca.* 330 to *ca.* 390.[57] He grew to adulthood during the second period of Donatist repression, the time of the Macarian persecution. But much of his early adult life was spent in the years when both Catholics and Donatists were settling down into a routine of mutual toleration. He was about thirty-two when Parmenian became bishop of Carthage. His literary works spanned the years 370 to 385, a period of a modus vivendi between Catholics and Donatists but also a period of Donatist schisms. The earlier of his works, *De bello intestino* (*ca.* 370) and *Expositiones diversarum causarum* (*ca.* 375), although now both lost, appear to have been explanations of the internecine warfare between North African Christians and his apology for his own party.[58] It is unclear whether these works were meant to describe disputes between Donatists and Catholics or among dissident Donatist groups.

At any rate, these writings were meant as apologetics. So they had to be accessible and inviting to every interested party. However, Tyconius' arguments were apparently misunderstood by Donatists in general or they did not meet the standards of orthodoxy for the rigorists among the Donatists, for he was condemned by a Donatist council of Carthage (380) presided over by his own bishop Parmenian.

The records of the council do not survive. Our only evidence comes from Augustine, who claimed that Tyconius was excommunicated, first, because he maintained that the Church was diffused throughout the whole world, and, second, because he taught that no one could be stained by the sin of another.[59] This explanation by Augustine reflects Catholic polemic against Donatists more than Donatist theology. Donatists before and after Tyconius' excommunication had been able to maintain the first of these tenets, that Donatism was diffused throughout the whole world, without being excommunicated.[60] In fact, Donatists had communities in Spain and Rome—Bishop Parmenian himself was not from North Africa—and they had a history of amicable correspondence with non-Donatists in Asia Minor who recognized

them as the true Church.[61] Even when Donatists rejected particular Christian communities overseas that kept communion with
Catholics, Augustine knew they never categorically denied the
possibility of orthodox churches outside Africa.[62] So the accuracy
of this first charge is suspect. The second of the accusations would
have been the more dangerous, for the Donatist view of sin as contagion was deeply rooted in their tradition. It certainly applied in
the situation of ordination by *traditores,* though there is no reason
to think that it applied in any area other than ecclesiology.
Although Augustine does not mention it, Tyconius' *Liber Regularum* (*ca.* 382) contains an even more significant cause for condemnation: the assertion that the very constitution of the Church
as body of the Lord admitted the presence of sinners.

Although excommunicated by the Donatists as a disciplinary
tactic, Tyconius never rejected his roots and by joining the flock of
their adversaries.[63] He could not, for his theology was thoroughly
Donatist. First, he was obsessed even more than other Donatists
with the presence of evil in the Church. Second, he was
uncompromising in his belief that the present time was the period
of the revelation of the division between good and evil, this when
Catholics were highlighting the importance of the Last Judgment.[64] Finally, as Robert Markus suggests, Tyconius never could
have made peace with the post-Constantinian Catholic church,
with a church that made its peace with the world.[65] In short,
although Tyconius' beliefs on evil in the Church would have been
too Catholic for the Donatists, the urgency with which he advocated repentance would have been too Donatist for the Catholics.

Tyconius is important for this study because he exemplifies
the transitions Donatists had to make to survive as a religious
movement. As a theoretician, he codified Donatist use of typology
and offered rules for the interpretation of the Bible, far more
explicit and detailed and yet more flexible than the authors previously considered here. First, he provided a definite role for both
the Spirit of God and for human reason, thus helping Donatists to
avoid the Scylla of a charismatic, martyrdom-loving movement
hurrying to its own suicide and the Charybdis of inflexibility that

would have locked the movement into a program with no con-temporary appeal. Second, he furnished a way for Donatists to justify the application to the present of texts that their opponents would relegate to the end of the world. He kept the movement from falling over the flat edge of the world of millennialism. Finally, he provided an interpretation of the Church as the body of the Lord that challenged at least some Donatists to admit the presence of evil within the Church. Breaking down Donatist sep-aratism allowed the movement to proselytize and to maintain its position as majority church, if not in Carthage, at least in Numidia.

After his excommunication, Tyconius wrote two other works, the *Liber Regularum* (*ca.* 382) and the *Commentary on the Apoca-lypse* (*ca.* 385), now lost.[66] It is the *Liber Regularum* that survives and shows how Tyconius assisted Donatists in becoming a church whose internal dynamism sustained itself well beyond even the time of Augustine.

The *Liber Regularum* is the first systematic attempt to treat hermeneutics in Latin Christianity.[67] It is not a handbook of rules, as Augustine expected.[68] In Tyconius' scheme, the *regulae* are not rules to be imposed from without. Rather, they arise organically from the text of Scripture itself.

The mystic nature of the rules simultaneously reveals and hides the secrets of the Law. The reasonable character of the rules makes them accessible to those with the right disposition, those who see the Bible and life typologically.

Tyconius' mystical rules provided an explanation of the unity not only of Old and New Testaments, but also of the Bible and the world. In the *Liber Regularum*, the internal unity of the Bible and the unity of the Bible with current events were played out on three planes or three periods in history. The first was the period of Abra-ham and his seed, a period of promise; the second was the period of Israel with the Law; the third was the age of Christ, when the promise is fulfilled and the Law ended.[69] The Church itself existed in all three periods, and everything written in any part of the Bible was typological for the events of the Church of the present. In this respect, his work was in continuity with his predecessors.

This reinforcement of the unity of the Bible and the world was in direct opposition to the distancing of the Scriptures from current events that was happening on the Catholic side. Augustine, their mentor, believed that nothing significant had happened since the Incarnation.[70] Tyconius believed that not only were the incidents of the past at one with the events of the present, but also that the words of the Scripture directly addressed Christians in the present. However, the message of the Scriptures was addressed only to a particular audience. Although all within the Church, both the just and those in need of repentance, could hear the powerful words, none outside who refused the call to reform could understand the Bible. The mystic rules revealed by the Bible spoke to the faithful for their edification, and to repentant sinners to exhort them to conversion.[71]

However, Tyconius knew that not all would respond, for those same mystic rules rendered the treasures of the truth invisible to some. Those who did not respond were deliberately spiritually blind to the truth.[72] Thus Donatists would deprive Catholics of the right to use Scripture in their own defense, unless, of course, they were willing to join the Donatist Church.[73] Again, Tyconius' work would be appealing to the most intransigent Donatists.

Those who were able to understand the Scriptures did so through reason, aided by God's action through the Holy Spirit.[74] By "reason" Tyconius meant a kind of common sense informed by and in tune with the rules themselves. Reason allowed the Bible reader to apply the rules that Tyconius had deduced from the text.

To understand Tyconius' hermeneutic and how it functioned in the Donatist community of the 390s, one needs to examine the rules. His seven rules were concerned above all else with a typological interpretation of Scripture. Such a construction of the text would for the first time explain the presence of evil *within* the Christian Church. Accounting for the presence of evil was a leitmotif of his entire text.[75]

In the explication of six of his seven rules, Tyconius employed different verses from and allusions to 2 Thess. 2:3–4, 6–9 to provide the organizational pattern for his book.[76] The passage predicts events that will transpire before the Day of the Lord, including division and the revelation of evil. The author comforts the readers but warns that the mystery is already at work in the present:

> Lest anyone lead you astray in any way, the schism must come first so that the man of sin, the son of destruction, may be revealed. He sets himself up in opposition and is exalted over all who call him God and he is worshiped when he sits in the temple of God pretending that he is God. . . . And you know what holds him back now so that he will be revealed in his proper time. The mystery of evil is already at work. He delays for a while until he comes out in the open. Then that ungodly one will be revealed and the Lord Christ will kill him with the breath of his mouth. . . . His arrival will be assisted by the work of Satan in all power with false signs and omens.[77]

The importance of these verses is illustrated by their crucial positioning, often linking one rule to the next.[78] The passage offered to Tyconius' readers his understanding of the Donatist-Catholic schism in North Africa. The present was the predicted time of trial in which the man of sin, the son of destruction, evil itself, was being revealed. Although Tyconius used the verses that revealed the warning signs, significantly, he never referred to verse 10, which ends this apocalyptic section: "because they would not tolerate the love of the truth so that they might be saved." Thus adumbrated, the verses stood as a admonition and a call to repentance in the present, not as a final condemnation. Like Parmenian, Tyconius did not close the door on Catholics or Rogatists; he invited them urgently to repent and thus to enter the true Church. Significantly, though, he exhorted even Donatists to repentance. Unlike Parmenian, Tyconius did not sweep the evil of the true Church under the rug of the pure Church.

Except for Deuteronomy and Hebrews, Tyconius used all of the more popular liturgical texts of his day.[79] Just as other Donatists had done and would do, Tyconius subsumed all of Scripture under the rubric "Law." However, "the immense forest of prophecy" was the prime area in which he exercised the art of interpretation. Of the four hundred fifty-three citations in the

Liber, the largest portion, 30 percent, are from the prophets. A similarly large share, 28 percent, come from the Pauline corpus.[80]

A survey of his seven rules will show how he uses his interpretation of prophecy to modify the Donatist tradition and thus to contribute to its long-term survival.

The first rule, *De Domini et corpore eius,* enunciates a guiding principle of Tyconius' hermeneutics: reason aided by the Holy Spirit is capable of discerning whether the Bible speaks of the Lord or of his body, the Church.[81] The rule presumes by metonymy the biblical identification of Christ (as head) with the Church (as his body) and the consequent possibility of confusion in the applicability of texts. It also takes for granted a Christological interpretation of the Old Testament. Thus Tyconius amalgamated Christology and ecclesiology, making possible an ecclesiological interpretation of all of the Old Testament as well as the New. In his first rule, Tyconius applied material from the Suffering Servant in Isaiah to the Church of his own day, harassed by the Roman authorities (albeit under consultation with other Christians): "It says in Isaiah: 'He bore our sins and suffered on our behalf. . . . And God wished to purify him by affliction'" (1 Pet. 3:24).[82] Although Jesus is a model of suffering, he is never a model of dying. This recalls the tentative moves away from martyrdom made by the anonymous Christmas sermon. There, it was the suffering—not the dying—Jesus who was to be the model for Donatists.[83]

Reason assisted the interpreter by taking note of the number and gender of words. These grammatical attributes helped to distinguish the referent of the text, Christ or the Church. Christ as head was presumed when the words were masculine singular, while his body, which was composed of many members, might be referred to simultaneously by both masculine and feminine terms; for example, the quotations referring to both bride and bridegroom in the same clause pertained to the Church, whereas those mentioning only the groom represented Christ, the head of the Church.[84]

Single feminine references were usually to the Church as bride, sister, or holy virgin. When the Church was represented as a pregnant woman, her single personality stood for her unity; in the second rule, her dual offspring will exemplify the good and bad within the Church. Singular male referents, where they did stand for the Church, did so under the aspect of fratricide and rebellion, representing both good and bad people within a single entity, like Jacob, who stole the blessing of his brother Esau.[85] Recognizing these grammatical points in the texts was reason's contribution to their exegesis, but was also a way to admit there might be evil within the Church.

Reason also noticed finality and ongoing processes when it attempted to interpret the Bible. Thus Tyconius could divide closely linked verses such as Dan. 2:34–35. In v. 34, a stone was cut from a rock and broke an idol into pieces. In v. 35, the stone is filling up the whole earth. The finality of the action in the first verse betokened its referent, Christ; the failure of the second to be accomplished as yet (the rock is still growing) meant that it pointed to the Church, an organism still in process.[86] The idea that the Church was still on the journey of faith allowed for turns into unproductive paths and temporary setbacks, a concept hardly possible when the Church was Christ's one beloved, his only and spotless bride.

The discussion of the process by which the rock was filling the earth opened the way for Tyconius to discuss his second rule, *De Domini corpore bipertito*. The second rule was framed in a way similar to the first: just as reason helped the reader discriminate between Christ and the Church, so reason would also help to distinguish between the right and left sides of that body.[87] The use of the Church as the bipartite body of Christ was Tyconius' way of reconciling in a reasonable manner seemingly contradictory statements in the Bible, namely, declarations of approbation and salvation or assertions of condemnation and damnation, which all seemed to have the same entity or people as addressee. In one instance, he inquired how God could say to Israel, "I will open invisible treasures to you, that you may know that I am God," and also state, "You have not known me." At another point, he questioned how Solomon could call the Church both dark and beautiful.[88] These negative and positive statements must both be directed to the same Church, but they had as their respective addressees those on the right and left sides of the Church, in the first instance, and vice versa in the second.

The Bible testified to the bipartite nature of the single body of the Lord, the Church. As examples, Tyconius told the story of the seed (singular) of Abraham that became both Isaac and Ishmael, and he recounted the episode of Jacob and Esau battling within the one womb of Rachel.[89] These texts reconciled the reality of the unity of the Church with the internecine struggles of Donatism itself. Thus the Church, which might have spot and wrinkle in the present, might still be the true Church.

This rule was even more complex than it first appeared. Not only could two people in the same circumstances represent the right and left sides of the Church, but often a single individual or entity could represent both sides simultaneously. Isaac, although not the firstborn, came by fraud and trickery to inherit the blessing, thus manifesting the left side by his cunning and the right by claiming what God had meant for him.[90] From the prophets, Tyconius chose texts that promised both prosperity and obliteration to Jerusalem.[91] Even Nineveh and Egypt as units could respectively represent the left and the right in the Church.[92] Tyre represented both the opposition between the world and the Church and the left and right within the Church.[93] Thus, by using single figures, Tyconius preserved the unity of a Church that, albeit temporarily, included both bad and good, left and right.

Reconciling texts that speak of the unity and duality of the Church allowed Tyconius to resolve the apparent opposition between passages that implied divine foreknowledge and others that seemed to posit free will.[94] His third rule, *De promissis et lege,* helps him deal with conditional and unconditional covenantal statements that seem to be at odds with one another. Interpreting Scripture by Scripture (primarily Isaiah, Romans, and Galatians), he takes unconditional and the conditional covenants literally, while using typology (based on the first two rules) to apply them to the Church. As he had previously differentiated the left and right sides of the Church as addressees, he harmonized the promises through their application to different groups. If the addressee belonged to the right side of the Church, the unconditional covenants applied. The Law held no sway over the people of the right side, for they had the Spirit of God within them and of their own free will did whatever that Law required, even in the absence of the Law. So the Law ruled the just neither before nor after Christ. Conditional promises directed to the Church applied only to the left side, to those who were sinners. The conditional promises manifested not only the powerlessness of the Law to save but also the inherent inability of those on the left side to keep the Law. Uttering conditional commands, God showed the incapacity of those on the left to survive without grace, thus implicitly condemning those who would not fly to God's mercy.[95]

If the Bible spoke to the present, as Tyconius contended, one had to determine whether the words of Scripture addressed the present by direct commands or indirectly through types from the past. The fourth rule, *De specie et genere*, was his attempt to specify how one might determine in what manner the Scriptures spoke.

Using the tenses of verbs, the geographical and temporal spread of referents, and quotations about unity and duality, Tyconius differentiated two types of biblical passages by the use of the terms "genus" and "species."[96] His only definition of these terms was a negative one. Genus and species, in his *Liber Regularum,* did not represent the same concepts that one found in rhetoric, so they were not terms representing sets and subsets.[97]

But Tyconius revealed the meaning of the rule through its use, that is, by examples. Species passages referred to specific events of the past that described particular situations in the present; for example, the historic fact of Israel's infidelity described in Ezek. 36:16–21 provided a type for the faithlessness of Christians in Tyconius' time.[98] Genus passages referred to events of the past or future that served as types for the continuing history of the Church; for example, Nathan spoke to David in 2 Sam. 7:13a, promising him an everlasting throne. Since David and even Solomon had died (and there was no king in Israel in Tyconius' time), this passage had to refer to the Church that had existed from the beginning and will exist forever.[99]

In every case, whether genus or species, there was some reference to current events. The most important implication of this rule for Donatist survival was that even future events described in eschatological passages had contemporary antitypes, for, as Tyconius said, "What Daniel said [concerning the Son of Man] is happening in Africa now."[100] Thus the apocalyptic Son of Man was de-eschatologized and functioned as a figure of the contemporary Church.[101] Even when he spoke of the final resurrection, Tyconius could not omit a reference to the resurrection within the contemporary life of the Church, that of Baptism.[102] He was interested in present applicability of the Scriptures and the development of the Church within time rather than the end of that growth in the eschaton.

Here Tyconius influenced Donatist interpretation at a critical point: no longer did an event have to have occurred already, that is, to have been a historical event, for it to provide guidance for the present. This flew directly in the face of early North African tradition. Tertullian had deliberately limited typological referents to past events in history to prevent the use of figures as the basis for allegory by the Marcionites.[103] Tyconius' freedom also opposed Catholic exegesis, which sought to distance the future from the present as much as possible.

Tyconius' fourth rule would seem to provide grist for the Catholic mill that accused Donatists of being millennialists. But Tyconius was no millennialist, first, because his fourth rule did not look to the future for fulfillment but to the present. Second, he took the favorite texts of millennialists and applied his fifth rule, *De temporibus*.

This rule was devoted to an explicit discussion of the biblical use of numbers both for counting objects and, more importantly, for telling time. Tyconius used synecdoche, the part for the whole or the whole for the part, to diffuse any residual millennialism.[104]

According to this rule, one measure of time might substitute for a similar number of different units, either larger or smaller. This biblical tradition was already active in the *Vita Cypriani*, in which one day was equated with one year.[105] Tyconius used this form of synecdoche to show that the idea of the ten-month pregnancy of Wis. 7:2 could not be falsified. The tenth month was simply equated with a single day.[106] So also could the six days of creation become the six-thousand-year history of the world.[107]

In Tyconius' system, numbers could also lose their ability to represent discrete units and instead serve to represent particular qualities. Thus, seven, ten, twelve, and their multiples represented not specific numbers of items but the concept of perfection.[108] On that logic, six might indicate imperfection and the number of the beast, 666, would indicate radical evil. Similarly, there was no contradiction between the three servants in Matthew's parable of the talents and the ten in Luke's version. Both represented a full complement.[109] Also, one indefinite number might serve to exemplify any other indefinite length of time, such as the final hour, the day of salvation or tribulation, or an acceptable year.[110]

Consequently, for Tyconius, in line with the other Donatist authors, numbers in apocalyptic literature provided no basis for the prediction of the timing of future events, not even the End Time. Rather, they focused attention on the moral exigencies of the present moment. This use of numbers substantiates Tyconius' lack of interest in eschatological exegesis. The way later commentators treated Tyconius' numerology confirms his focus on the present. Only those attempting to make him more orthodox emphasized passages that might be taken in an eschatological sense. None of those who condemned him attacked him as a millennialist.[111] Thus Tyconius provided Donatism with a way to be faithful to its biblical heritage, to take numbers in the Bible seriously, yet to dodge the charge of being a millennialist movement. When distressing low-level persecution of schismatic movements continues for weeks, months, and years, there was no loss of face for Donatism. One had to be vigilant continuously because the fulfillment of time would happen, but only on God's terms.

Since Tyconius counted time literally and by synecdoche, the past and future as revealed in the Bible were both very important to him. In his sixth rule, *De recapitulatione*, he explained how both history as recorded in Scriptures and the incidents prophesied for the future could illuminate present events.

It had been a commonplace in early Christianity that the

words of the prophets helped Christians to understand the sufferings of Jesus. But, for Tyconius, the words of Jesus himself provided the warrant for the use of biblical verses as an interpretive
lens for the present history of the Church. Jesus had said that the
conduct of humanity in the days of Noah and at Lot's departure
from Sodom manifested the manner of the return of the Son of
Man.[112] Tyconius asserted that the present was the time of which
Jesus spoke.[113]

For years, Donatists had been reading martyr stories in such
a way as to cast the oppression of their own era in terms of the persecution of the prophets, the martyrdom of the Maccabees, and
the passion of Jesus. Finally, it was Tyconius who provided the
exegetical warrant through the mouth of Jesus, as well as the technical terminology for this hermeneutic. Tyconius called it
recapitulation.

Christian use of recapitulation had already provided for the
illumination of the present by the past. Paul and Irenaeus looked
to the figure of Adam in the Book of Genesis as a model for the
sinfulness of humanity, and, using Adam as a type of either
humanity or Jesus, they explained the work of Christ.[114] In the
Liber regularum, recapitulation also utilized events that the Scriptures projected onto the distant future to clarify the meaning of
the present. The book of Daniel, traditionally the revelation of the
End Time, was the prime example: "What Daniel said is happening in Africa now, not at the end of time."[115] The special focus of
this revelation was the identity of evil as it existed in the world and
as it was foreseen in the Bible: "the schism must come first"
(2 Thess. 2:3).[116] Thus Tyconius could use the disputed parable of
the wheat and the tares (Matt. 13:24–30) to drive home his point
in a way that would cause contention between Catholics and
Donatists after Tyconius' death. Tyconius used the parable to
expose the presence of good and bad within the Church, discom-
fiting the Donatists, who claimed the Church was pure. He emphasized the present as the time of exposure, alienating Catholics
who pushed the discernment of evil to the end of time.[117]

But what ought one do when various parties applied the rules
differently? To answer this question, Tyconius used the advice

given to a church split by schism even before the close of New Testament times, the community of the Johannine church. Tyconius uses the words of the first letter of John:

> Many false prophets have gone out into this world. In this recognize the Spirit of God: every spirit which dismisses Jesus and denies that he has come in the flesh has not come from God, but from the antichrist. This is the one you heard was coming and is now present in this world (1 John 4:1–3).[118]

By warning against listening to any interpreter of the Bible who denied that Jesus had come from God in the flesh, Tyconius denied interpretive authority to anyone who refused his own hermeneutical rules, beginning from the first, the identification of the body of Christ with the Church. These people were to be recognized by the same criteria that John had given his own community: failure to keep the commandments and hatred of other members of the Church.[119] This was perfectly congruent with the already well-established Donatist descriptions of Catholics, down to the word *pseudoprophetae*, false prophets. They failed to keep the Law by handing over the Bible during persecution. They persecuted the true Church, the Donatist communion, when they repeatedly called on imperial authority to seize Donatist property, to exile Donatist bishops, and to torture the Donatist faithful.

All of this carnage and persecution of Donatists by Catholics had been undertaken to ensure an outer conformity: attendance at Catholic altars. Tyconius had to face opponents among Catholics who justified this repression in the interest of the spread of Christianity and defended Catholic sacraments by quoting the Bible: "What does it matter, but that in every manner whether out of expediency or the truth, Christ is preached" (Phil. 1:18).[120] His reply came from the Johannine letter: "Children, keep yourselves from pretense." In his words "Filioli, abstinete uos a simulacris," Tyconius has the last word, for the same term, "simulacris," serves both for pretense and for false gods, the idols against which the prophets preached.[121]

This accent on the Catholics and their relationship with idolatry would have satisfied hard-line Donatists and, in fact, this sort of interpretation will become a major focus for exegesis in the writings of Tyconius' successors.[122] However, like the Gospels themselves, Tyconius' attack on pretense will become a two-edged sword, cutting into the most intransigent Donatists with his seventh rule.

To give the lie to all pretense, Tyconius advanced the seventh and last of his rules, *De diabolo et corpore eius*. As reason helped to distinguish the Lord and his body in the first rule so also does it assist the reader in distinguishing the Devil and his body.[123] Again, grammatical number and geographic spread helped one discern the referent. As in his first rule, plural nouns, when treated collectively, betokened the body of the Devil. Individuals might represent the head of the body.[124] Oppositions between the mountains of the North and the South, between Israel and Seir, indicated opposition between the body of the Lord and the body of the Devil, and helped distinguish the two.[125]

Yet a simple North-South division was not adequate, for the Church itself was bipartite, having both North and South within it. Thus the reader would have to take care in noticing the exact technical terms for the mountains and for the North and South used by the Bible, for example, *Sion, Seir, septrionalis, meriodionalis, Auster, Aquilo*. Comparing the ambiguous use of these terms with verses that were more straightforward, one could attempt to determine whether a term, in conjunction with other indicators, stood for the body of the Lord, its right side or left side, or the body of the Devil.[126]

But even when these techniques were employed, one could build no firm partition between the body of the Devil and the left side of the Church. Thus, reason and the Bible itself led Tyconius to an inescapable conclusion. Both the body of the Lord and the body of the Devil were spread throughout the world.[127] The warnings that God uttered offering an opportunity for repentance applied both to the body of the Devil and to the left side of the Church. So it was that the logical, rational, Spirit-directed approach to the Scriptures revealed the mystery of iniquity of 2 Thess. 2:3–9: the man of sin, the son of destruction, the mystery of evil was at work *within the Church*. The King of Tyre was also a good example for Tyconius because, like the Devil, he had been created pure by God. Only after the discovery of subsequent iniquities was he forced out of the sphere of goodness.[128] Now if what was happening in the Scriptures revealed the truth about current events, who was the King of Tyre in Tyconius' time, if not the Church? Initially pure, its members had committed iniquities. Even Parmenian could admit this. But this entity could not be the Catholic church for, according to Donatist ecclesiology, it was not the true Church. The figure of the king who fell from grace and needed to repent somehow indicated Donatism itself!

Although Tyconius was excommunicated by the Donatists, he does manifest one point on the trajectory of Donatist interpretation that is in harmony with the larger movement. The Donatists had faced evil in their midst before and would again after Tyconius. From the Council of Cirta, with the murderous Purpurius of Limata, to the Conference of Carthage, with its debate over dealing with hidden and obvious sin, the Donatists had never denied the presence of evil within the Church. They had, however, maintained that it was exposed in the present and had to be and could be dealt with. Indeed, it was their contention, against the Catholics, that the ability to deal with evil in an appropriate and timely fashion was a mark of the true Church. Whereas Catholics pushed off judgment to the end of time, Donatists reinterpreted eschatological verses to apply to the present, allowing the constant purging of evil from the Church, keeping her as the pure bride of Christ.

However, the implication of Tyconius' *Liber Regularum* that the Scriptures showed evil as a constituent part of the Church was beyond the pale of Donatist orthodoxy.[129] Repeatedly in his answer to Parmenian's attack on Tyconius, Augustine quoted Parmenian's uses of biblical verses, which Parmenian had hoped would bring Tyconius to his senses. Those selections included all of the classic Donatist repertoire. It was essential that Tyconius cease his flirtation with evil, with the idea that evil was part of the Church. For if God spoke the same word to those inside and outside the Church, in the true Church—the Donatist community— confusion reigned. Donatists perceived the wall between good and bad, in and out, Donatist and Catholic, as being dissolved. The sacrifices of the martyrs now seemed to have been in vain and the struggle with the both the Catholics and with the Roman state was evacuated of any rationale.

History has not recorded the specific reason that Tyconius was excommunicated by the Donatists. He was already excluded from their communion before he published the *Liber regularum*, so it was not the novelty of this conclusion in 382, when the *Liber* was published. Perhaps this had been part of his earlier works. Had Tyconius not already been excluded from the Donatist communion, his call to repentance to those within the true Church would have been more than sufficient cause for his excommunication.

CONCLUSION

The two Donatist authors reviewed in this chapter show the Donatist movement adapting to its newfound strength in a period of relative freedom from imperial harassment. The controversies of the past over which church, the Catholic or the Donatist, was the true Church faded in importance as Donatists realized the diversity of their own movement and began to cope with disagreement in their own ranks. The various schisms of the late fourth century challenged Donatism to develop a coherent ecclesiology that took seriously the presence of sin in the Church. The Donatist bishop Parmenian had proposed one answer with his doctrine of the *dotes,* or gifts of the Church. It was not the moral state of the individual minister of a sacrament that guaranteed the validity of a sacrament but the holiness of the Church as institution.

Tyconius proposed a more radical solution that allowed that personal evil might be—indeed, according to the Scriptures, had to be—found within the Church. This devastating discovery was balanced, again on biblical grounds, with an urgent call for repentance of all wrongdoers.

Whichever solution Donatists of the late fourth century chose, they could be assured that their church was the true

Church and that they could deal with Catholic charges that their church included evil. In both cases, the impact of evil was minimized. In Parmenian's theology, the misdeeds of individuals did not invalidate the acts of the Church as institution; she still remained the pure, spotless dove of God. Only the Donatist church was endowed with the special gifts necessary for the proper administration of the life-giving sacraments. In Tyconius' scenario, evil within the Church was already known and allowed for in God's eternal plan. Its existence was a mystery. However, the Donatist response was to deal with evil through urgent preaching of immediate repentance. Thus those who were to be saved through the Church would be, as they learned to interpret the Scriptures that would bring them to repent. In either case, the Donatist church and only that church could claim the title of the true Church.

CHAPTER 5

Harassment and Persecution Again

I N THE YEARS leading up to the 390s, Donatists and Catholics lived side by side, often with two bishops and two churches in the same city, and generally without rancor.[1] However, as the 390s unfolded the situation changed, and with the transformation came another phase in the evolution of Donatist use of the Bible. This chapter will sketch the political, social, and religious changes in North Africa during this period and show how corresponding changes in the Donatist use of the Bible helped the community to re-form its identity and to survive these new circumstances.

The 380s had been a time for Donatists and Catholics to find a way to live together. Imperial leadership was congenial to the idea. If there were any major religious concerns in the western half of the empire, they were not with Donatists but with the practitioners of traditional Roman religion and with Arians. Theodosius evenhandedly persecuted both.[2]

During this time Africa was largely in the hands of those who would not persecute Donatists. Nichomachus Flavian, reputed to be a Donatist, was the imperial vicar in Africa beginning in 376. The *comes Africae* Gildo was a man who was both loyal to Rome (at least for the time being) and who, as a member of the household of the last independent rulers in Mauretania, had the respect of the African provincials.

The circumstances of ecclesiastical leadership had also promoted a modus vivendi. On the Donatist side, from the consecration of Donatus the Great as bishop of Carthage between 313 and 315 to the death of Parmenian in 392, the Donatist majority had enjoyed a time of capable and stable leadership. The charismatic and sometimes abrasive—at least to the Catholics—Donatus the Great enjoyed a long and popular tenure. He was succeeded in 362 by Parmenian, an able and amicable personality who promoted Donatist coexistence, if not cooperation, with the Roman state. This long tenure was conducive to great stability, although, as W. H. C. Frend notes, it was "not conducive to theological innovation; particularly since the conservative and largely rural province of Numidia soon became the heartland of the Church."[3]

Meanwhile, on the side of the Catholic minority, the succession of bishops had been undistinguished. Mensurius, elected by a rump session of bishops from Africa Proconsularis in 311, had not been able to hold his church together or to exert much influence outside his city. The sole monument to his successor Gratus is the record of largely ineffectual disciplinary councils held during Gratus' tenure. Little is known of his successor Restitutus save that he was attacked for his Arian tendencies by both Athanasius of Alexandria and Damasus I of Rome. Summoned to Rome on suspicion of heresy, he dropped out of sight about 378. Following Restitutus, Genethelius presided over Carthage until 393. According to Frend, he was not a strong figure. His main ambition seemed to have been to avoid strife between Catholics and Donatists. He may even have been at least partially responsible for the lack of enforcement of anti-Donatist legislation during the 380s and early 390s.[4] With Catholics lacking the leadership to rouse their number, much less civil authority, there was no concentrated anti-Donatist campaign.

This is not to say that all was quiet. Occasional complaints came to the attention of the authorities and even to the notice of the imperial court. However, legislation promulgated in the 380s betrayed the interest of the emperors in civil order, not religious issues.[5] In general, as long as Catholics and Donatists had their own modus vivendi, imperial and provincial officials would not be active in moderating religious strife, except when such issues were well defined in civil law, such as property rights or disturbing the peace.

During the 390s, the situation and the cast of characters began to shift. Provincial loyalties began to turn, at least in part, from the empire to local leaders. At the beginning of the decade, Theodosius was in full control of the empire. His borders were largely secure since he had an amicable relationship with the Goths. In Africa he felt assured he could have confidence in his appointees. When Firmus had revolted in the 380s, Firmus' brother Gildo had remained loyal to his Roman master over his own brother. Although he had momentarily chosen the wrong side when Magnus Maximus had been proclaimed emperor by the troops in Britain in 387, he was obviously forgiven, for his daughter later married into the imperial family. Gildo, promoted to *magister utriusque militiae*, was the emperor's loyal servant. Even in 392 through 394, when Eugenius, aided by the Frankish leader Arbogast, had challenged Theodosius' authority, Gildo remained loyal. However, after the death of Theodosius in 395, he seemed to have neither respect for nor fear of the emperor's young sons Honorius and Arcadius. As the Visigoths entered the empire in the East and the Vandals crossed into the empire in the North, and the sons of Theodosius quarreled over jurisdictional lines, Gildo saw his chance to restore North Africa to its former glory: he began to try to control Africa for himself.[6] This attempt was one factor that upset the balance of power in Africa.

In response, the Honorius appointed Christians loyal to himself and to Catholic Christianity to positions of power in North Africa.[7] After the revolt of Gildo, never again would native military leaders hold the command of Roman troops in North Africa, nor would officials with North African—and Donatist—sympathies be sent from the emperor.

The second factor in the change in the North African setting was the transformation in ecclesiastical leadership. The Donatist side saw the rise of several new bishops, men both blunt and strict.[8] Facing off against them were new Catholic leaders far more capable and aggressive than their predecessors. Donatist leadership matched burgeoning Catholic aggression. A roll call of leadership on both sides illustrates the changing tenor of the times to which Donatist scriptural interpretation responded.

On the Donatist side, the de facto primate of Africa was Petilian of Cirta (then Constantine). He was born into a Catholic family. After a career as a lawyer he was, perhaps persuasively, perhaps forcibly, converted to Donatism. He served his native city, presiding over this important see, one of the earliest sites of Donatist sentiment, with the zeal of a true convert, writing numerous pamphlets against the Catholics from about 395 until around 420.

The de jure *primus inter pares* among Donatists was Primian, elected bishop of Carthage in 391/392. He was a talented orator and gifted theologian. Unfortunately, this was not enough to counterbalance his lack of pastoral sensitivity.[9] Within a year of his election, he had alienated the *seniores* (lay administrators) of his diocese and excommunicated four of the senior deacons. One of these men was Maximian, a relative of Donatus the Great.[10] Primian's conduct brought on Donatism's greatest split, the Maximianist schism, when some Donatist bishops assembled and excommunicated him and elected his rival Maximian bishop of Carthage and primate of North Africa.[11]

Primian and his supporters retaliated at their own council at Bagaï on April 24, 394. They promulgated a sentence of excommunication against Maximian and his consecrators and gave the Maximianist bishops until Christmas to return to the larger Donatist fold, laity until the following Easter. If they delayed, they would be subject to canonical penance on their return.

Most Donatists supported Primian, except in Byzacena and a few scattered areas. He had powerful allies in bishop Optatus of Thamugadi and the *comes* Gildo, who by 397 was in open revolt against Rome. Once the deadlines established at Bagaï passed, Primianists invoked civil law, numerous times and successfully, for the recovery of church property occupied by Maximianists.[12]

Although Primian seems to have been victorious, he never

regained either the popularity or strong control of his initial months as bishop, but seems to have been eclipsed by the bishop of Thamugadi, who had arranged the return of many Maximianist bishops to the Primianist fold. More dangerously, he and his supporters were perceived as allies of Gildo, a revolutionary.[13] Neither his pride nor the unity of his church ever fully recovered. After the Edicts of Unity in 405, he was deprived of his see, but he had regained it and primatial status among Donatists before 411. He disappeared from history in the aftermath of persecution after 412.

Farther west, in Mauretania, was Emeritus of Caesarea, a talented orator with a good mind for legal nuances. He was born around 350 and was the principal architect of the Donatist Council of Bagaï in 394, which condemned Primian and tried to keep the Donatists united. Evidence of his abilities is abundant in the proceedings of the Conference of Carthage in 411. Even Augustine paid tribute to his exegetical skills and debated him publicly.[14] Exiled in 405 as a result of the Edict of Unity, he reappeared at the Conference of Carthage. Although dispossessed of his diocese after the Conference, he continued tenaciously preaching and writing in defense of Donatism until he disappeared from history about 420.

Leading the Donatist church in Numidia was one of the most famous (or infamous) of the Donatist bishops, Optatus of Thamugadi, who was active from 388 until his execution in *ca.* 398, shortly after Gildo's fall.[15] Optatus presided over the Donatist church nestled in the foothills of Numidia. The area was a crucial one for anti-Roman sentiment and it constituted the heartland of Donatist strength. Optatus allied himself with Gildo in Gildo's revolt against imperial authority. He was also a strong supporter of Primian in his disputes with the Maximianists. The Catholic minority and nonconformist Donatists were caught up in the military exploits of Gildo, which simultaneously served the desires of Primian and Optatus. Yet even the Catholics admitted that Optatus was gracious in his exercise of power. When the Maximianists of his diocese belatedly sought reentry into the Primianist church, he mitigated the harsh provisions the Council of Bagaï had set for their readmission. No doubt Catholics would consider him lenient, for although Donatists considered Maximianists to be schismatics, Catholics considered them heretics.[16]

Succeeding Optatus at Thamugadi in 398 was Gaudentius. He was much less aggressive than his predecessor and lived amicably with Faustinus, his Catholic rival in the city, until dispossessed of his see in the aftermath of the edict of union of January 30, 412.[17] Seven years later, the tribune Dulcitius attempted to enforce the harshest of edicts against the Donatists. When the tribune entered his city in 420 to attempt the forcible conversion of Gaudentius' congregation, he came out of hiding, barricaded himself and his communicants in the cathedral, and threatened to set fire to the entire lot. Correspondence with Augustine postponed the day of conflagration. Whether it eventually took place is unknown, but the very fact that it was seriously proposed gives us a clue to the tenor of the times, so different from the period between Julian and the late 380s.

During the 390s, Donatists were preoccupied with internal struggles and beleaguered by imperial repression. Rebels had to be brought to heel by the imperial government because of the strategic importance of North Africa as the breadbasket of the city of Rome. Meanwhile, the Catholic side made strides in leadership. Augustine was ordained to the presbyterate in 391 and would soon begin his active campaign against Donatism. In 393, the lackluster Genethelius, bishop of Carthage, was succeeded by the able orator and theologian Aurelius. Three years later, Augustine joined his friend in the episcopate as bishop of Hippo Regius. Both of these men, together with Alypius of Thagaste, an old friend of Augustine, would enjoy long tenures, providing stability that matched that of Donatism in the earlier period. Taking advantage of the strength that leadership afforded the Catholics, they repeatedly sent embassies to the imperial court to persuade the emperors to promulgate new legislation or to renew old laws against the Donatists.[18] Augustine and his allies took advantage of Donatist disunity. They exploited the Donatists' reputation as associates of the rebel Gildo and the Circumcellions, the migrant agricultural workers who aided him.[19] A prime strategic maneuver was to speak of the Donatists not as schismatics but as heretics, so that antiheretical legislation already promulgated against others such as Arians and Manichaeans could be used against them.[20]

With strong personalities arrayed on both sides, changes could be expected in the old amicable modus vivendi. Increased legal and polemical action fostered a hardening of attitudes and violence on both sides.[21] Beginning in 392, mostly at Catholic behest, Donatists were the object of imperial legislation. In that first year, they were subject to fines and threatened with deportation for disrupting Catholic ecclesiastical life.[22] Two years later, the state struck at their institutional life.[23] First they were forbidden to ordain new bishops,[24] then to assemble, ordain lower clergy, or teach.[25] The next year, cult was under attack as the emperors forbade the Donatists to gather for any rituals.[26]

Although friction increased, neither side wanted a repetition of the age of martyrs. When the emperors confirmed all previous anti-Donatist legislation in 395, they also sent word to the proconsul to moderate any excessive zeal in the enforcement of the laws.[27] On the other side, Donatist bishops met the next year and cautioned against voluntary martyrdom.[28]

Yet beginning in 397 the situation grew more grave. As Gildo declared his independence from the empire, the emperors reasserted their authority. Heretics were not only heretics but were more like revolutionaries if they were receiving help from Gildo.[29] At the turn of the century, the property of Gildonian supporters and of Donatist bishops was being confiscated.[30] Catholics expected even more help when, in July of 401, Bathanarius, a Catholic sympathizer and brother-in-law of Stilicho (the *magister militum*), became *comes Africae*.[31]

The Catholic-imperial response consisted of three measures promulgated in early 405, known collectively as the Edict of Unity.[32] Although designed to force Donatists into the realm of Catholic authority, the measures were unevenly applied, exacerbating the situation.[33] The fall of the pro-Catholic Stilicho and the recall of Bathanarius in 408 further frustrated Catholic hopes. But Catholics kept up their pressure on the imperial court, so that over the first decade of the fourth century the general trend was for more legislation, including financial and civic penalties for adherence to Donatism.[34] Although the death penalty was available in this period, there is no indication any Donatist was executed for adherence to Donatism.[35]

Finally, in 410, the emperors Honorius and Arcadius sent a new *comes* to Africa, Flavius Marcellinus. In response to Catholic requests, this pious Catholic came with instructions to convoke a conference of Catholics and Donatists. The meeting was to put an end, once and for all, to the religious and political unrest in the provinces of North Africa. Following the Conference of Carthage in 411, imperial legislation was promulgated time after time against the Donatists.[36] Although the emperor made provision again in 415 for the death penalty, no one seemed to force the issue; neither Catholics nor Donatists wanted any more martyrs.[37] This is the way events continued until the Vandals made their way through Roman North Africa.

With Catholics newly ascendent and enjoying imperial favor, and Donatists harassed, sporadic violence broke out again between the factions—violence of words and deeds. Able writers on both sides engaged in a pamphlet war, producing much of the material used in this chapter.

As in previous chapters, Donatist materials reveal the world the Donatists erected through their scriptural texts, the characters who populated that world, and, finally, the biblical messages issued to those characters. The final section of the chapter is devoted to the hermeneutics that underlie the Donatists' use of Scripture in the Augustinian period and that make possible the application of the Bible as Law to Donatist life.

SOURCES AND METHODOLOGICAL CONCERNS

Since much of the Donatist material in this chapter is extracted from the works of their opponent, Augustine, it is worthwhile to raise some methodological concerns. Surely the caveats of chapter 4 on the works of Optatus and Augustine against Parmenian still apply,[38] but the reader also needs to be aware that Augustine's attitude toward the Donatists, and especially toward the use of imperial force against them, hardened over the years between 393 and 413.[39] At the beginning of his pastoral career, he thought that persuasive teaching in catechetics or debate might be effective in converting Donatists from the error of their ways, but after the violence of 397 through 399 (the end of the Gildonian revolt) and the Edicts of Unity (405) he turned toward the use of legal constraints—although not martyrdom—to force their submission to the authority of the Catholic church.[40] Augustine's writings, therefore, need to be read with an eye toward his changing attitude.

Over the course of his episcopate, Augustine wrote several works that provide information about Donatist exegesis not found in materials considered in previous chapters. These are: *Contra litteras Petiliani*, in opposition to one of the most forceful and talented of Augustine's Donatist opponents (400–403); *Epistula ad Catholicos de secta donatistarum*, also known as *De unitate ecclesiae*, an exposition of Donatist crimes (401); *Contra Cresconium grammaticum donatistam*, an answer to an opponent who sought to defend Petilian (405); *Liber de unico baptismo*, probably against Petilian (410/411); and *Contra Gaudentium*, a response to the Donatist bishop of Thamugadi on the issue of using force against schismatics.[41] Many of Augustine's letters, sermons, and other works contain references to the Donatists. Chief among them is *Ep.* 185, *De correctione Donatistarum*, an exposition of their nefarious beliefs and way of life.[42]

Augustinian works present the same sort of problems the material from Optatus did. I have tried to differentiate reports of Donatist exegesis from extrapolations, that is, to divide "You say . . ." from "You would say. . . ." The latter class is not entirely useless but must be evaluated in terms of Augustine's prejudices. The texts surviving this process of discrimination are introduced as evidence of Donatist exegesis. Still, the reader must exercise a caution similar to that employed when reading Optatus. One must be especially alert in analyzing the works in which Augustine's real preoccupation was with a subject other than the Donatists. In those cases, his comments on the Donatists may be distorted by his current interest in those other problems.[43]

Although one needs to be suspicious about many statements by Augustine, it is clear that several of Augustine's anti-Donatist works were direct responses to already well-known Donatist tracts. He wrote these works with Donatist pamphlets in front of him and quoted the Donatists before adding his own comments. So extensive were his quotations of the Donatist tracts that Paul Monceaux has been able to reconstruct the texts of the Donatist works behind *Contra litteras Petiliani*, *Contra Gaudentium*, and the pseudo-Augustinian *Contra Fulgentium*. They are, respectively, *Petiliani epistula ad presbyteros et diaconos*, *Gaudentii epistulae duo ad Dulcitium*, and *Fulgentii Donatistae libellus de baptismo*.[44] Augustine wrote *Contra epistulam Parmeniani* to reply very precisely to specific Donatist claims. Although Monceaux did not reconstruct Parmenian's text, one can find such lengthy parts of that letter in Augustine's work that it is possible to use those quotations to assist in the analysis of Donatist hermeneutics. Happily, then, readers of Augustine are in a better position to extract Donatist exegesis from the bulk of Augustine's anti-Donatist corpus than they were when faced with the work of Optatus.

In addition to the Donatist materials in the Augustinian works, there are three Donatist works to round out the picture. They are the *Liber Genealogicus*, the *Gesta* of the Conference of Carthage, and the *Contra Fulgentium*. After describing these three works, the chapter will analyze the way they and the Augustinian materials reveal how the Donatists used the Bible to construct their religious world, to populate that world with good and evil characters, and to extract from the Bible verses that licensed or condemned actions taken by the people populating that world.

The first document, the *Liber Genealogicus*, is of the genre *chronology*. It is a list of events in chronological order, stretching from the creation of Adam and Eve to the fifth century.[45] This list combines genealogical materials from the Bible and stories from apocryphal works with lists of Persian rulers and Roman kings, dictators, and emperors. Generally the entries are very short, but occasionally the compiler provides details or a brief narrative or added clarifications.

Chronologies represent a common form of literature in the ancient world. The simplest were those that merely listed the occupants of political and/or religious offices, such as the registers of priests, consuls, or urban prefects. The more complex form the basis for historical narratives. The compiler of each chronicle decided which facts available from earlier sources were important for providing a "correct" view of the world and which were irrelevant, trivial, or meaningless.

The *Liber Genealogicus* was composed in North Africa between 405 and 411. Donatists issued editions in 427, 438, and 455. In many sections the compiler simply reproduced the sources, especially genealogies of rulers and biblical figures.[46] Occasionally, the chronicler added explanatory comments. Later Donatist editors thought it important to highlight biblical texts or events in world history that were especially interesting to their partisans. They took over a preexisting chronicle and retold the events to shape the audience's understanding of the history of the world, adding sections to suit sectarian purposes. They tried to show that what was happening in Africa had been predicted in the Bible. Since the *Liber* went through several editions, it is especially helpful in showing changes in Donatist interpretive strategies.

There are also the minutes, or *Gesta,* of the Conference of Carthage in 411. This was the conference called under Marcellinus, a friend of Augustine and pious Catholic. The purpose of the meeting was to debate the differences between the Donatist and Catholic parties and to arrive at the truth. The resolution of the issues would, in theory, put an end to theological controversy and civil strife. That the outcome of the Conference was the vindication of Catholicism was a foregone conclusion from the opening of the first session. However, the transcript of the stenographic record that details the debates and records the documents read into the record remains a precious resource for a reconstruction of Donatist beliefs in this period.

Finally, we will examine an anonymous work, once attributed to Augustine, called *Contra Fulgentium.*[47] Written between 412 and 420, it attacks the Donatist teaching on Baptism and, through its replies to Donatist tenets, provides a good indication of how Donatists used the Bible to maintain their identity and advance their program.

In this chapter, we shall see how Donatists used their biblical heritage to sustain themselves. During the last decade of the fourth century and the first quarter of the fifth, Donatists were subject to harassment, fines, confiscation, and exile. However, unlike in previous periods of persecution, there was little opportunity for the glories of martyrdom or, in many cases, even for being the only congregation in town. Thus some of the texts popular in earlier persecutions could not be used. Others had to be reinterpreted to suit new times. Finally, new modes of interpretation and new verses will provide support for the continued existence of the Donatist church.

Texts and techniques are analyzed in a manner similar to that in previous chapters. The biblical material is divided into three categories. The first consists of texts the Donatists used to describe the world in which they found themselves, that is, texts that construct their world. The texts provide a key to a Donatist understanding of the environment in which their controversies with Augustine and the other Catholics take place. The second group of quotations serves to populate the world the Donatists constructed for themselves. There are, of course, two sets of characters: Donatists are the protagonists and Catholics are the villains. The last group of biblical materials contains the messages the authors intended for their audiences, both Catholic and Donatists.

THE DONATIST WORLD

In a world of persecution and harassment—although not of death—Donatists chose from their arsenal of Scriptures with great discrimination. Their challenge was to keep Donatists from being pressured to join the Catholics. The pressures to do so were not threats of martyrdom; they were financial, legal, and social. In their quest to ensure group solidarity, bishops and orators used biblical materials to create a world and to harness the energy of the martyrs without endorsing their deaths as models for contemporary believers.

The Donatists employed biblical verses in a variety of ways. Many verses at first seem to be mere reports of the state of affairs, whether of the Donatist community or of the Catholics. The words in the Bible match the situations as perceived by the Donatists. But these are not simple descriptive sentences with words convenient to the speakers. Instead, their function is more complex. In their context of controversy, these quotations (and those used by the Catholics) might well have been prefaced each time with the introduction, "This is the way the world, the Church, or life is. This is the way I want you to think about it, and you will, if you accept God's words. I know I'm right because what I say matches what the Bible says. And we all know the Bible is true." So each of these descriptions is an attempt to mold the world to the speaker's likes and dislikes, to bend the mind of the listener to a new perception of reality, to provide commands a right-thinking person would have to obey. Thus the quotation of 1 Tim. 3:2, "The bishop ought to be above reproach," described an ideal bishop, proclaimed a rule, and, when applied by the Donatists to the Catholic bishop, Caecilian, showed how far from being a real bishop he was.[48]

The world-construction of the Donatists has three important features that demonstrate their survival tactics in a world including harassment but without the officially sanctioned shedding of blood. These are the Donatist constructions of time, their image of a separatist community, and, finally, their circumscribed concern with the location of the true and pure Church.

The construction of time as an element of world-construction is the first feature. Here Augustine's comments in the *Breviculus collationis* are helpful. He claimed that the Donatists divided history into two periods: the present, in which saints *and Christ* die, and the future, in which both the holy ones and their Lord will rise.[49] Although this does not match Tyconius' clearly stated partition of time into three periods, Abrahamic, Mosaic, and Christian, there is no reason to doubt that what Augustine claimed did indeed reflect general Donatist exegetical practice. This apportionment of time provided the same opportunities for typology with respect to the persecution of the Donatist church that Tyconius' divisions did; that is, it allowed Donatists to identify their own times and troubles with those of the martyrs and the prophets. All lived in the same time frame and died for the same cause.

This division of time, as reported by Augustine, is far from the pre-Donatist treatment of time that tended to collapse the immediate pre-eschatological period into the present.[50] Rather, the content of the report more closely resembles the chronological partition by the Donatist martyrs who saw the present as a continuing battle between God and the Devil.[51] But by this time, the battle was no longer cosmic but personal. The opposition was between Jesus and Judas or between the prophets and their supporters, as well as the false priests and their followers, and not so much between God and the Devil. The time of trial now stretched from the past through the present into the indefinite future.

Although Augustine also divided time into two parts, he did so for purposes that ran counter to those of the Donatists. He parted the ages by discerning the differing relationships of civil authority to true believers. The first period was that of infidel rulers who persecuted the faithful; the second was the age in which impious subjects suffered the wrath of faithful rulers. Accepting Augustine's division of time obviously renders the Donatists impious, because the emperors of Augustine's day were good Christians.[52]

The Donatists, however, maintained their own twofold construction of time, the time of suffering and the time of glory, in the construction of their world. This division made it easy for them to see themselves as the *collecta*, the assembly of Israel. Like Israel in the desert, they were on pilgrimage. Like Israel in Canaan, they were faithful to God and God's Law in the midst of the faithless Catholic tribes, who like the inhabitants of Canaan, succumbed to the temptation of apostasy and idolatry.[53]

The *Liber Genealogicus* provides especially important evidence of the Donatist construction of time. Its pages called the roll of martyrs from the protomartyr Abel to Perpetua and Felicity, all the way to the Abitinians. The *Liber* then brought the chronology to an abrupt end with a summary of the earliest Donatist case against the Catholics. It accused Mensurius, the bishop of Carthage at the time of the Abitinians, as well as his deacons, Strathon, Cassian, and Caecelian, of having publicly burned the books of the Gospels. All that preceded this section, the references to fratricide and civil war as well as to the beast of the Apocalypse, have their import spelled out here. Christians made war against each other while the representative of evil approached. Nothing new had happened since the Bible was written or at least since the time of Mensurius. All of the events of history followed the same pattern. The editor could, therefore, pass over everything that happened from the time of Mensurius to the contemporary period. All the events between the early fourth century and the fifth were simply repetitions of the events predicted in the Bible. What happened in the past was happening all over again: the fratricide, the division of the united kingdom, and the persecution of the prophets.[54]

The omission of any explicit reference to the Macarian persecution of 346 through 348, with its martyrs, and the harassment of 404 through 405 is significant. The elision of these events into the category of "nothing new" is indeed something new. It indicates that during the period from 405 to the Vandal invasion, Donatist chroniclers could differentiate "real persecution," the formative events of their history, from later oppression. There should be no mistake: the recording of *current* events as the precursors of the eschaton was definitely over. Even in the face of imperial proscription under the Edicts of Unity in 405, amid the persecution after the Conference of Carthage, and in the face of the Vandal invasion, the editors did not add to the horrors of the chronicle nor did they succumb to the temptation of apocalyptic millennialism.

Victorinus of Pettau (d. *ca.* 303) was one of the sources of the *Liber Genealogicus*. He had offered its editors some very real temptations to a millenarian interpretation of Scripture and the events of history, including mention of the new prophecies presaging the end of the world,[55] a scenario mentioned in one of the most popular North African martyrologies, *The Passion of Saints Perpetua and Felicity*. The earliest editors resisted and simply copied Victorinus' information on Nero as the Antichrist. But they did not apply this material typologically to their own situation.

Instead, the Donatist quest for survival cast a new light on martyrdom and the divisions of time. The Catholics had realized that the bloody persecution of the Donatists had been and would still be counterproductive. If the Donatist church were to be a church of the martyrs in any sense, at the turn of the fifth century it could not look forward to martyrdom. The Antichrist and the apocalyptic End Time were not on the horizon. Without the impetus or pressure of the End Time, how did Donatists maintain their world and solidarity within it? The answer is that instead of looking *forward* to martyrdom, they looked *back*. By constructing time so that they were part of the same block of history with Jesus and the early martyrs, they did not need new and contemporary ones. Hence, their "nothing new" attitude toward the Macarian persecution.

The second world-construction issue for Donatism in this period is separatism. If the time of the earliest Donatist persecutions was one with the present, it is no wonder that the cry of the Abitinian martyrs echoes through the Donatist literature with as much value as that of anyone recently tortured:

> If anyone has fellowship with the traitors, that person will have no part with us in the heavenly kingdom. . . . Do not join yourself with non-believers, for what sharing is there between justice and injustice and what fellowship has light with darkness, what bond has a faithful person with an infidel, what agreement between the temple of God and idols? (2 Cor. 6:14–16)[56]

Separatism was the order of the day. At the Conference of Carthage, Donatists opposed the indiscriminate mixing of the Church with the sinful world. To counter the Catholic association of the Church and the world, they used the most positive biblical language about the Church and the most derogatory about the world. The Church was the pure one, without spot or wrinkle, the redeemed daughter of Sion, the beautiful sister, the holy virgin. None of the unclean or uncircumcised would enter it. When Catholics used John 3:17, "He sent his son not to judge the world but that it might be saved through him," to support their contention that God was saving the world, that is, that both the good and the bad mixed in the Church in that world,[57] Donatists used material from Romans and the Johannine corpus to show that the world was stained with guilt and that the world neither knew nor loved God, but rejected those who belonged to God.[58]

Although typology had up to now been the primary Donatist hermeneutical tool to warrant separation, their bishops occasionally employed allegorical interpretation. In each case, however, these Donatist allegories were provoked by Catholic allegorizing. Donatists then used the Catholic train of thought to support their contention that the true Church, that is, that of the Donatists, separated itself from sinners. In these cases of separation, the focus was not on the Final Judgment, as it was for Catholics, but on the present—again, a strategy for world-construction and the maintenance of solidarity in the here and now.

The first case of allegory involved the parable of the dragnet.[59] Catholic interpretation of this parable focused on the time that the fish spent together in the net and the delay of separation until the boat reached land, the *finis maris*. In the years previous to the Conference, Augustine, for example, had allegorized this as the *finis saeculi*, the end of the world.[60] The Donatists in their allegorical reconstruction of the parable interpreted the people hauling in the nets as being the priests of the Church. The net was still the Church, as it was in Augustine's interpretation. However, the focus was not on the length of time the good and bad fishes swam around together, but on the fact that the fish in the net were still swimming below the level of the water. Hence, their goodness or badness was hidden from the sight of those hauling in the nets. However, as soon as the nets were hauled out of the water and the nature of the individual fish was known, the sorting process began. For Donatists, then, the allegorical interpretation of the parable focused on the details of fish hidden below the surface of the water and *immediate* separation once their identity was known. That time of division was not the Final Judgment, as the Catholics would have it, but the present. Therefore, the parable justified separation and exclusion in the present, and, in the Donatist interpretation, laid the responsibility for separation at the feet of the bishops, the fishing crew of Christ. Thus Donatist bishops were faithful disciples who immediately separated good from evil, whereas the Catholic bishops were derelict in their duty.

The second instance of allegory involved the parable of the wedding garment (Matt. 22:13–14).[61] When the king came into the room and saw the guest without the proper garment, he ordered his ministers to expel the guest. As one would expect, Catholic interpretation focused on the guest without the wedding garment remaining at the party, eating and drinking, *until the arrival of the king.* Catholics such as Augustine could interpret the parable as allowing the mixture of good and bad until the second coming of Christ.[62] On the other hand, the Donatists focused on the command of the king to his ministers that they should expel the guest. Since the priests of the Church were the ministers of the eternal king, they were licensed to exclude those who were sinners, *as soon as they knew their condition.* Again, allegory justified timely action by the priests of the Donatists and excoriated Catholic priests lax in their duties.

Immediate separation from the *traditores,* that is, the Catholics, was the faithful response to the commands of the Bible, and this evolving interpretation of Scripture guaranteed group cohesion. It built a wall between the impure, traitorous Catholic community and the pure and faithful Donatist church.

Separation implies a sense of place, of geographic location, in world-construction. Although Donatists had communities in various locations around the Mediterranean, Donatist space was pre-eminently North Africa, and especially the congregations of believers who lived there. They did not indeed condemn the rest of the Church, that is, true believers outside Africa who were not Donatists, although they surely had unpleasant things to say about "the world" in the Johannine sense.[63] They were in communion with congregations outside Africa. But the only group they ever condemned were Catholic congregations *in Africa*.[64] Their concerns were eminently provincial.

One way to ensure that the use of biblical material is accessible to the project of world-construction under the aspect of space or location is to show how the authors of the Bible were attuned to North Africa and the situation at the turn of the fifth century. The *Liber Genealogicus* provides an example. Its editor attempted to place North Africa center stage in world history. This was no mean feat, as Carthage is not mentioned in the Bible. However, in the discussion of the descendants of Noah, the editor noted that they were the people who settled the biblical city of Tyre. Mention of Tyre and its colony at Carthage in a source the compiler of the *Liber* used allowed the original editor the opportunity to comment on the North African city, adding details from the *Aeneid* on its foundation.[65] Thus, although Carthage is not mentioned in the Bible, its establishment and history found a place in the scriptural sequence. Thus Donatists found in their Bible reason to believe that God cared about their situation.

The Donatist claim that God cared for North Africa would have been one with which most Catholics could agree. However, exclusivity was one of the aspects of Donatist theology that angered Augustine and his cohorts. But surely, exclusivity had been licensed by pre-Donatist interpretations of the enclosed garden of Cant. 4:12, which was part of the Catholic heritage.[66] An exclusionary interpretation of one verse inspired and licensed the same sort of exegesis with other texts, such as Cant. 1:6: "Tell me, O you whom my soul has loved, where do you graze your flock, where do you make it lie down *in meridie*?"[67] Catholics such as Augustine interpreted the final phrase to mean "at midday," an obvious time for the animals to rest from the intense heat of the North African sun. On the other hand, Donatists thought that the phrase could only mean "in the south." The flock of the Lord could be restricted to a particular location in the south of some definite place.[68] Augustine claimed that Donatists answered the Catholic interpretation by locating the true Church in the south, that is, in their stronghold in Numidia. It would then be the Donatists and no one else who were the flock of the Lord.

But did the Donatists themselves really use Cant. 1:6 to bolster their claim? Augustine offered various geographical, grammatical, historical, and biblical objections to the Donatist appropriation of the verse in the construction of their world.[69] The strenuousness and regularity with which his objections were advanced would lead one to believe that this quotation was actually used by the Donatists to confirm their title as the beloved of the Lord, although Donatists would not disclaim their adherents who lived in the north. After all, they did have congregations in the northern part of Africa, including Augustine's own diocese, as well as farther north in the city of Rome.

But Donatists did have precedent in using Cant. 1:6 to foster exclusivity. There were, after all, loyal followers of Cyprian who taught that outside the Church—the ark, the sealed garden— there was no salvation.[70] If the Church was the flock of the Lord and it pastured among the Donatists, it could have been a logical conclusion that outside the Donatists there was no salvation. However, the Donatists did not claim to be the whole Church. In fact, they professed themselves to be in communion with churches outside North Africa. Thus the use of Cant. 1:6, the separatism and attendant condemnation, would have applied only against North African Catholics and would not have been applicable to the churches overseas. For except when questioned specifically about their affiliation with overseas churches, Donatists were concerned only with the North African situation. The Catholic response, then, that the Donatists condemned the entire world would have been a polemically useful overstatement. But it did reflect the provincial attitude of the Donatists.

Only in the *Contra Cresconium* did Augustine claim to be quoting a person who provided direct evidence that the Donatists indeed thought few were to be saved. He based his statement on Cresconius' use of Luke 13:23: "There are few who are saved."[71] Augustine replied to Cresconius' charges that the world is full of heresy and that few retained the truth. He admitted that, yes indeed, there were heresies, but there were also texts that used the word "many" when talking about the number in the kingdom of heaven. His real interest, here as in other texts written after the Conference, lay in the question of the mixing of the good and bad within the Church. Augustine never seemed to address the issue of the number saved, except to attack the Donatist use of the term "few." Given Donatist exclusivity, they may indeed have taught their doctrine in the biblical words "There are few who are saved." But also given their provinciality, the meaning of those words would have been this: there are many Catholics in North Africa who won't be saved, and we Donatists who are, in comparison, few in number, will be saved.[72]

In his *Epistula ad Catholicos,* written in 401, Augustine highlighted the differences between Catholic and Donatist senses of place as they referred to the universal spread of the Church. Augustine claimed that Donatists did not deny the veracity of biblical statements on the subject but only their present applicability.[73] The division of time between the age of suffering and the age of glory made this possible. The Church was not spread through the whole world during the time when the holy ones were dying, but would reach the ends of the earth in the age to come. This certainly was in harmony with the teaching of Tyconius, who stressed the development and eventual perfection of the Church as the body of the Lord. The Law described the Church as the last will and testament of God, and it would be promulgated in its fullness with only Donatists as legatees.[74]

Augustine attributed the Donatists' attempt to deny the geographic universality of the Church in the present world to their firm belief in free will. Augustine asserted that Donatists maintained that the Church had not spread because people did not wish to believe.[75] Certainly such a report would place the Donatists in a bad light in Augustine's eyes. His own developing theology of grace and free will was moving in the opposite direction.[76] Although we cannot know if this indeed was the Donatist view pure and simple, whatever they taught would have seemed far from fatalism in Augustine's eyes.

Augustine cited other verses of Scripture that he claimed the Donatists used to support their exclusionary conception of the

Church. Petilian was supposed to have employed biblical passages about the righteousness of Enoch, Noah, and Lot, and the per-durance of two of the twelve tribes as models for their Donatist exclusivity. Even the seventy-two disciples were thought to have apostatized, leaving only the Twelve.[77] The narrow gate of Matt. 7:13–14 was supposed to be a watchword among Donatists.[78] Yet this language of righteous men of old is found nowhere in any of the texts in which Augustine was closely following the pamphlet of any other Donatist author, nor has it been part of the Donatist documents studied in previous chapters. One needs to look else-where for affirmation or negation of the genuineness of this sort of interpretation.

In sum, then, the world the Donatists constructed was simul-taneously broad and narrow. Its breadth was temporal. Donatists were not descendants of but sisters and brothers in faith to all of the holy ones of the past. Donatists lived in their biblically based world. At the same time, the Donatist world was geographically narrow. Their concerns were circumscribed by the boundaries of the Donatist-Catholic controversy, that is, by the geographic boundaries of North Africa, from Mauretania in the west to Byza-cena in the southeast. Since the Bible was their world, the Bible referred to the events of North Africa. Tyconius had already pro-vided them with the watchword with which they could justify the construction of their world: What Daniel said is going on in Africa *now*.[79]

The People of the Donatist World

The second set of scriptural verses considered in this chapter are those that populated the Donatist world with its particular char-acters.

In Augustine's time, as in the past, the Donatist world was inhabited by true believers and apostates, by those on the inside and those on the outside—that is, by Donatists and Catholics. The Bible was the tool used to distinguish the two groups. The Donatists could be recognized as true believers because they were persecuted and because they were holy and faithful to God's Law.

Their opponents, on the other hand, were to be condemned because the Bible showed them to be unfaithful, impure, and violent oppressors of God's people. This section of the chapter focuses on these aspects of Donatist and Catholic identity.

The first attribute that distinguished the Donatists was their persecution. Persecution had always been a popular motif in Donatist literature, beginning, of course, with the martyr stories. The *Liber Genealogicus* provided typological clues for the present. The original text of the *Liber,* composed about 405, mentions the fratricidal conflict of Cain and Abel, but it is only in the editions published after 412, when conflict between Catholics and Donatists grew more intense, that Donatist revisions speak of Abel as the first martyr.[80] His brother Cain was the founder of a city named Enos. In his status as founder, he was the type of all those who oppressed the faithful in every age:

> This is the city of blood which even now sheds Christian blood.
> This city built in the land of Nod was examined and still exists.
> This place is interpreted as the one which until the end of time
> persecutes Christians who are called the faithful.[81]

Division in the kingdom of Israel provided an opportunity for the writer to interpret the contemporary North African situation in terms of the past. After a reference to rival altars in Samaria and Israel, Donatist editors expanded this section with this analysis:

> There was a schism between Rehoboam the son of Solomon,
> and Jeroboam the son of Nebat, and they waged war all the
> days of their lives, just as it now happens between true Christians and false Catholics.[82]

Fratricide and civil strife were not the only violence recorded in the Bible. The Scriptures also recorded the persecution of the prophets and the just. But the Bible did not merely record past events. It also prophesied the future. Enoch and Elijah were supposed to have predicted the oppression of Christians under Nero.[83]

Although the Bible was purported to have foretold certain future events with great precision, Donatist editors of the *Liber* were cautious about the accuracy of their sources. Their successive editions show Donatist creativity in biblical interpretations as a survival tactic. Comments on the reign of the emperor Nero are a case in point. In this entry, the editors acknowledged that they were relying on Victorinus of Pettau whose *Scholia in Apocalypsim* taught that the Bible showed that Nero was the Antichrist.[84] The editor of the edition of 438 challenged the accuracy of the numerology that had led Victorinus to this conclusion. This person noticed that the aggregate of the letter values of A-N-T-I-C-H-R-I-S-T-U-S multiplied by four, the number of letters in Nero's name, did not equal the number of the beast, 666 (Rev. 13:18).[85] This later editor took more seriously Victorinus' other possible referents for the beast, including Antemus, perhaps a Romanized version of Anthemios, the praetorian prefect who persecuted John Chrysostom; and Genseric, that is, Gaiseric, the leader of the Vandals. Since the Vandals were moving across Mauretania and Numidia toward Carthage as the text was being re-edited, the interpretation was a most attractive one. Even the Catholics might have resorted to millennialist interpretations of the invasion. Later editions, produced while Genseric was reigning at Carthage, prudently omitted these sections.[86] The final edition of 455 reflects the fall of Rome to the Vandals. The recently deceased Valentinian III is likened to the state with the feet of clay in Dan. 2:31–35.[87] Such a reference would have been safe, even prudent, under Vandal rule. Again, there is evidence that Donatists took care for the long-term preservation of their church through their recognition of political realities.

Up to the end of the third quarter of the fourth century, Donatist materials had all used biblical verses that stressed faithfulness in the face of bitter persecution. The most popular were the stories of Eleazar and the Maccabee brothers (2 Macc. 6–7) and of Daniel's three young companions (Dan. 3), all people who were tortured by their persecutors. In the latter part of the fourth century and the beginning of the fifth, the reader finds even more verses. In these materials, Donatists presented their stance as supported by the suffering of their people, who were tested like gold in fire.[88] Classic verses about persecution called them blessed, told them to turn the other cheek, and utilized the words of Jesus that those who persecuted the Donatists would think they were doing God a favor.[89] Not only was suffering historically inevitable, but it was ontologically necessary, for, as Jesus had told his faithful followers in North Africa, the grain of wheat must die to yield its fruit. Paul too preached that anyone who wished to live in Christ had to suffer.[90] However, these materials reveal that although persecution was still a central motif, death was not.

Another change was, paradoxically, that Jesus had become more a model. The anonymous *Sermo in natali* pioneered the appropriation of the suffering child Jesus persecuted by Herod.[91] But it is a part of Petilian's own spirituality, for it surfaces primarily in his speeches in the *Gesta*, his *Epistula ad presbyteros et diaconos*. Petilian was the only Donatist of this period who exploited the model of the persecuted infant Jesus,[92] but he and those dependent on him expanded their use of the model with materials from the other end of Jesus' life, either from the Gospels directly or from the portrait of Jesus dimly reflected in the stories of the martyrs.[93] With Petilian, Gaudentius and Fulgentius knew they could expect persecution, because no disciple was greater than the Master (Matt. 10:24).[94] If the world hated Jesus, it would equally despise them (John 15:18–20).[95] Evil kings had persecuted the Maccabees, the three youths, and Daniel, as well as the child Jesus (Matt. 2:16). Like those innocents, the Donatists were persecuted by an oppressive ruler.[96] Like all the disciples, the Donatists professed their willingness to be baptized in the baptism of suffering (Matt. 10:35–39).[97]

The Donatist texts provided a second exemplar besides Jesus for the suffering Donatists, the Apostle Paul. His call, "Be imitators of me," and his recital of his afflictions provided Donatists with another hero for emulation.[98] The appearance of Paul as model should occasion no surprise. Both Donatists and Catholics in North Africa were increasingly interested in Paul at the end of the fourth and the beginning of the fifth centuries. Marius Victorinus produced his commentaries on Ephesians, Galatians, and Philippians beginning in 362; Tyconius, writing between 380 and 382, had centered his whole *Liber Regularum* on texts from the

Thessalonian correspondence; Augustine himself began his life-long writings on Paul in 395 with *Ad Simplicianum*.[99] The corpus of Donatist writings in this period is littered with references to Paul in a way heretofore unknown.[100] So it is no wonder that renewed exegetical interest in Paul would have issued in preaching that in turn would make Paul's sufferings available as a model for the Donatists.

Being the good people persecuted by the evil ones, then, was a hallmark of Donatist self-identity in this period no less than in previous years. However, there are differences from the past. In the fifth century, Jesus, who had not been the major figure of suffering in the martyr stories, became a more important model owing to the influence of Petilian. Paul, in his sufferings and patience, joins Jesus as a figure for Donatists to emulate.

Besides being the people who suffered persecution, the second mark of Donatist identity reinforced by their reading of the Bible was their fidelity to the Scriptures as Law. In the *Gesta of the Conference of Carthage* in 411, the Donatist bishops referred to the Bible primarily as the Law or divine testimony, in contrast to the Catholics who regularly referred to specific types of literature contained within the Bible, for example, gospels, apostolic letters, etc.[101] Donatists conceived of the whole Bible as Law. Gaudentius repeatedly referred to the Bible in juridical terms, as commandments and as the Law.[102] Petilian used his discussion of Law that was composed of the commandments and the beatitudes to show how Donatists were and Catholics were not the true Church.[103]

This reliance on Scripture as Law cohered well with the Donatist perception of themselves as the *collecta*, the community of the Old Testament. This third aspect of Donatist identity cast them as the people who had originally received and cherished the Law. This was the self-understanding of the community of the *Acts of the Abitinian Martyrs*. The Donatist bishops introduced this account of martyrdom into the Conference records and relied on it for a number of their biblical citations during the debate.[104] As one might expect from the date of the Conference of Carthage, Donatist use of Scripture reveals a preoccupation with the self-preservation of a minority, not one persecuted but one subjected to seduction and to pressure in their daily living amid those who believed wrongly.

One way of keeping the community separate and preserving its identity was to deny those on the outside the right to interpret the Law or Christian Scriptures. According to Augustine, Cresconius claimed that as Ezekiel and the other prophets came only to the house of Israel, so the Bible, the words of the prophets, were to be interpreted only by the true Church.[105]

There is nothing unusual about this interpretation. From the beginning of Christianity, its adherents have advocated the view that only those who have been initiated had the right to interpret the Bible. In the tradition of their North African predecessors, Donatists denied Catholics the right to interpret the Bible. Here they followed Tertullian in his writings against the Jews, and Macrobius' writings against those who opposed him on clerical celibacy.[106] What was unusual was Augustine's defense of the interpretation of the Bible by those outside his church.[107] But then he could not deny Donatists the Scripture while simultaneously affirming the validity of their baptism.

Elsewhere, Augustine's comments on the Donatist use of the Bible reinforced what we have seen. According to Augustine, Donatists proposed the text, "When the Son of Man comes, do you think he will find faith on the earth?" Augustine said that when Donatists referred to it, they had apostasy in mind, whereas he himself was thinking of perfection in the moral life.[108] This is a plausible explanation. For the Donatists in their identity as *collecta*, the prime sin would have been apostasy, whether manifested in actually offering worship to Roman deities or in delivering the Scriptures to be burned. This would explain how the bishops at the Council of Cirta could all but ignore the murders committed by Purpurius of Limata and quibble about what kinds of books, heretical or orthodox, Bishop Silvanus delivered to the flames.[109]

Donatists identified themselves not simply as the *collecta* of Israel but as the holy people of God who were holy because the Lord their God was holy (*inter alia*, Deut. 16:8; Lev. 11:44–45; 19:2, 20, 26, incidentally the same books that contain the peculiar use of the *collecta*). In the letter of Parmenian, the Law taught

Donatists to claim holiness as a challenge and as their heritage. Holiness, that is, lack of blemish, was a prerequisite for those who offered acceptable sacrifices, especially for Donatist clergy.[110] If the Donatists were to be holy as the Lord their God was holy, they would glorify God and God would glorify them. In addition, those whom they spurned the Lord would also spurn.[111]

The Donatists had quite a physicalist notion of holiness. Like its counterpart, evil, it was communicated by touch, even by proximity. The corollary to their self-perception as holy was the necessity of physical separation from sinners, lest that holiness be soiled. Petilian, Parmenian, Cresconius, and Gaudentius were all concerned with separation as a sign of the true Church. The Law, the prophets, the writings, and the teachings of Paul all commanded immediate and radical separation. Many biblical texts used in the martyr stories and the *Gesta* reappeared during this period to reinforce this teaching.[112] Among the descriptive passages of the Old Testament are those that set up typological relationships. Donatists portrayed themselves as the prophets and priests who kept the Law, and their opponents as those who offered unworthy and unclean sacrifices. Additional texts were taken from the New Testament. Verses that warned against associating with those who committed sexual sins were used to justify separation from the Catholics. The author of Eph. 5:11–12 ("Do not participate in works of darkness") urged separation. In 1 Cor. 5:6 ("A little leaven raises the whole lump"), Paul had warned his correspondents against associating with those who committed sexual transgressions.[113]

This was the sort of exegesis Optatus had reported when the Donatists interpreted Wis. 3:16 as a description of idolatry in terms of sexual sins: "the children of adulterers do not grow up." Donatists employed all these texts to warn against association with the Catholics. The Donatists of the fifth century continued and intensified this characterization. Since the Catholic crime was loyalty to the mistakes of their forebears in faith, Mensurius and Caecelian, and since ordained bishops were considered as fathers in faith to their ordinand sons, the texts the Donatists chose reflected the theme of Catholic lineage. The Bible-based rhetoric of the Donatists branded Catholics children of a harlot and those who would suffer for the sins of their ancestors.[114] Donatists used the words of the Bible to denounce the Catholics as false prophets and unfaithful priests. They did so by using the very words of the true prophets and faithful priests of the Bible.

Donatists at the Conference of Carthage protested that the Catholics refused to take seriously their obligation to purge evil from their midst and were waiting for God to do it at the Final Judgment. Donatists found this not simply a manifestation of Catholic laziness but also a danger to the salvation of the whole community. They drew on the command to Aaron and his sons, the priests of Israel, in Lev. 10:9–10 to show how God had commanded separation in the present: "[The Lord] says, 'It shall be an eternal law among your descendants to divide the sacred from the profane, the clean from the unclean.'"[115] They applied this responsibility given to the priests of Israel to the Catholic priests. Since the Donatists viewed the Catholics as insufficiently attentive to the dangers of sin within their community, they condemned the Catholic priests for their laxity. They appropriated Ezekiel's denunciation of the priests of Israel who failed their charge by not separating good and evil. They drove home their point by quoting several texts against the mixture of good and evil, including 2 Cor. 6:14–15, again a text used in the *Acts of the Abitinian Martyrs*: "What fellowship is there between the faithful and the faithless, what communion between light and darkness?"[116]

Besides condemning the Catholic priests for dereliction of duty, the Donatists used the Bible to attempt to impress on their counterparts the seriousness of communicating with sinners. They gathered positive models of biblical figures who abstained from unclean sacrifices and were holy, and negative examples of those who communicated and suffered devastation. Scripture provided Elisha, Elijah, and Amos as exemplary figures who refrained from communing in the mysteries of the schismatic Samaritans.[117] The unnamed prophet of 1 Kgs. 13:11–28 and the priests of Jerusalem who offered polluted sacrifices were the negative illustrations.[118] Direct condemnation came from two more texts emphasizing the danger to all members of the community of physical contact with unclean sacrifices: "Their sacrifices are like the bread of mourning: all who touch them are defiled by them" (Hos. 9:4) and "That is the way it is with this people, this nation: anyone who approaches them in this place is defiled" (Hag. 2:14). The texts share the same verb, "defiled," which by anaphora increases its rhetorical force. In casting their opponents in the roles of the people denounced in the Scriptures, the Donatists appointed themselves as the true priests and prophets for their own era. As their predecessors had done with the stories of the martyrs, so the Donatists at the Conference of Carthage envisioned their religious fidelity primarily in Old Testament terms. They were the faithful prophets and priests; the Donatist church was the assembly of Israel. Donatists at the Conference continued the hermeneutical method of the *Acts of the Abitinian Martyrs* without likening themselves to the martyrs. They followed people such as Purpurius of Limata, who saw the bishop of Cirta as the local antitype of Moses and the *seniores laici* as the elders of Israel. Donatists were the *collecta*, the faithful remnant opposing those who capitulated to the larger society without themselves paying the ultimate price for refusal to capitulate. The Catholics were the idolaters; the Donatists were those who kept the Law. The link between sexual immorality and idolatry was just as carefully used among Donatists as it had been by the prophets.

Holiness, for the Donatists of the fifth century, was similar to the martyrs' closeness to God in the martyr stories. However, the martyrs' proximity to the divine was a function of impending death, and Donatists in Augustine's time were not facing an imminent separation from the world by martyrdom. So for these Donatists holiness required a different sort of separation, one that demanded a daily attempt at segregation from Catholics. Under these circumstances, the model of the faithful of Israel in the midst of an apostate people inspired them. If the Donatists were the *collecta* of Israel, the Catholics could only be the unfaithful idolaters. Naturally then, the Donatists condemned the Catholics.

The way the Donatists used the Bible to describe themselves and the Catholics helps to understand their exegetical practices. The Donatists had conceived of themselves as the faithful *collecta*, continuing to worship the true God, to observe the commands of their Lord in the midst of an unfaithful people. Their image of the Catholics as that unfaithful people brings their own self-identity into sharper focus. But since both Donatists and Catholics professed the same creed, Donatists had to differentiate themselves from Catholics in noncredal ways. This they did with scriptural verses that helped them to distance themselves from the Catholics on matters of practice.[119] They used verses on true fidelity, ritual purity, and violence.

In earlier years, Donatists had availed themselves of verses that provided derogatory Old Testament types for Catholics, especially for their clergy. Many of those verses were used again during Augustine's lifetime. To Donatists, Catholics were like the schismatics who opposed Moses. The earth should break open and swallow the Catholics, as it had their prototypes.[120] They were like dead and rotting flies that ruin a cask of oil, or the dead body that pollutes the person who touches it.[121] Their sacrifices were polluted, and since that pollution was contagious it had to be avoided.[122]

Because Donatists had already defined their own fidelity in terms of the observance of the Law, they described Catholics in terms of apostasy through schism, the unforgivable sin against the Holy Spirit.[123] The Catholic Church was no church at all but the whore sitting on many waters.[124] This contained a reference to the water of Baptism, but, more importantly, one sees again the language of sexual infidelity associated with idolatry applied to the Catholics. The claims that the prophets of old made were revived by those who identified with the faithful of Israel. Like their predecessors in iniquity, the Catholics left the Lord and his community to wander in the desert.[125] Not only were they sinners, they were imprudent fools, false prophets, and wolves in the guise of sheep.[126]

Donatists excoriated Catholics for their resort to violence. Their use of arms was condemned in biblical terms. They were swift to shed blood and did not know the way of peace, just like Paul's opponents or those of Isaiah.[127] Cresconius used Ezek. 20:18 to identify his contemporary Donatist opponents not only with Mensurius and Caecelian but also with the idolaters of the Bible as he warned them: "Do not walk according to the laws of your ancestors."[128] The Law of God was invoked against their seizure of Donatist property: "Thou shalt not covet."[129]

Donatists found scriptural texts to condemn Catholics for resorting to imperial authority to enforce claims against them. Donatists themselves had upon occasion appealed to the power of the emperors, but the issue on which they appealed was the right to church funds, land, or buildings. The Donatists resented the Catholic appeal for the enforcement of belief. Gaudentius taught that God had given human beings free will and expected them to use it.[130] God's way was one of instruction and persuasion, not intimidation and force:

> The all-powerful God gave the proclamation to the people of Israel through prophets; he did not order it through kings. The savior of souls, the Lord Christ, sent fishermen to establish the faith, not soldiers.[131]

Fulgentius would add that if one were to follow the Gospel mandate "Compel them to come in that my house may be filled," at least one should compel entrance into the small company, that true Church without wrinkle or spot, not into that "assembly of vanity," the Catholic church.[132]

Donatists saw themselves as the holy and pure Church, faithful to God's law. Their bishop and orator Petilian envisioned his Catholic opponents by contrast as the descendants of the *traditores* who committed the words of God to the flames. If their ancestors had committed the archetypical traitorous act, handing over the Word of God to crucifixion, present-day Catholics were no better than their father Judas. As true Christians were clothed in Christ at Baptism, Catholics were clothed in Judas. Judas, not Christ, died for them.[133]

In sum, the Donatists of Augustine's time found in the Bible language to characterize their Catholic opponents. The evidence of their writings shows the continuity of this practice with that of their predecessors. Catholics were described in the same terms that the prophets had used against those of their community who had participated in the worship of alien gods or in the oppression of their neighbors. Their cultic acts were polluted in either case. Their offenses were described in terms of sexual infidelity. Once again, as in the past, drawing lines, not between Donatists and the rest of the world but specifically between Donatists and Catholics, had become necessary. This time the danger was not so much easy assimilation, as it had been in the third quarter of the fourth century, but buckling under the pressure of financial and legal disabilities.

In sum, the Donatists established a world on the same temporal plane as the Bible and then they populated it with a people characterized by biblical verses. That self-identification marked them as a persecuted people (although not as martyrs), as the *collecta*, a new Israel that has the exclusive right to interpret the Law and the challenge to be holy. In contrast to imagining themselves as the betrayed Christ or the patient Paul, Donatists pictured their Catholic opponents as the traitorous Judas. In contrast to Donatist fidelity, Catholics were the apostates against whom the prophets preached.

THE MESSAGES OF THE DONATISTS

As we have seen, the Donatists considered the Bible the eternal law of God. Its commands had to be taken seriously, for fidelity to the commands of God was the very basis of Donatist identity as the *collecta*. In addition, the biblical texts functioned as prophecy. Perhaps one of the most revealing comments on the Donatist view of the Bible in this light comes from Petilian's treatment of Judas as a type for Catholics. Remarking on the death of Judas, he discussed the various biblical verses that spoke of the situation. Jesus had prayed, "Father, I have saved all whom you have given to me; and none of them have perished except the son of perdition, so that the Scripture might be fulfilled" (John 17:12). David, as author of the Psalms, predicted, "Let another take his office [*episcopatum*], let his wife be a widow and his children orphans" (Ps. 109:8–9).[134] Petilian's analysis of the verses is very clear: "How great is the Spirit of the prophets, so that it has seen the whole future as if present, so that so many ages earlier the traitor [*traditor*] yet to be born might be condemned."[135] If the Spirit of the prophets predicted the death of Judas centuries before it would happen *as if the event were happening in the present*, and if there was only one Holy Spirit, Donatist reasoning would assert that the same Spirit spoke in the past to condemn Judas' sons, Mensurius and Caecelian, and was still speaking in the words of the Bible. However, in the Donatists' situation, the Spirit was providing analyses of current events and guidance for present action. The words of the texts that condemned Judas, *episcopatum* and *traditor*, were ready-made for the North African situation. Thus, as the Bible predicted events that came to pass in the first century, so it provided direct commands to be obeyed in the fifth.

Whether the Bible is seen as law or typological prophecy, the Donatist appropriation of the biblical message was not doctrinal (What ought I to believe?) but practical (What ought I to do?). This portion of the chapter will examine the legal and prophetic messages the Donatists read in the Bible. The subjects of the commands given to Donatists are first, of course, about separation from the Catholics, and second and derivatively about their respective sacraments, primarily Baptism. Donatists, following their Cyprianic heritage, claimed to have the only true Baptism.[136] They found messages on both subjects in the Bible.

On the subject of the relations between the two groups, the first and greatest of the commandments Scripture provided was that of the duty and necessity of separation. The prime text in this case was directed toward the Donatist bishops and priests, for in the biblical story God spoke these words to their typological model, the priests of Israel: "It shall be an eternal law for your descendants to make a division between the holy and the irreligious, and between the clean and the unclean."[137]

Many direct commands about the necessity of separation were woven into Donatist tracts. Some were couched in terms of the avoidance of demeaning social relationships: "Do not participate [*communicare*] in unfruitful works"; "You shall not participate [*communicaueris*] in the sins of another; keep yourself pure"; and "Don't take food with this sort of person."[138] Others utilized baptismal imagery: "Keep yourself from the water of strangers"; "Do not bear the yoke with nonbelievers."[139] Biblical texts that praised actions of separation became commands for the Donatists. The most frequently repeated was "I do not sit in the assembly of vanity."[140]

There are many indications of the sense of the urgency of separation in the Donatist presentations at the Conference of Carthage and in the letters and pamphlets of Donatist leaders.

At a conference, Donatist debaters were not entirely free to chose the biblical texts they used in debate. However, their response to the verses chosen by the Catholics shows them in continuity with their ancestors in choosing typology over allegory. Their responses also show their continuing evolution from a church of the martyrs to a church of the separated and sanctified. An examination of Catholic citations and argumentation sets the stage for a consideration of the distinctive exegesis of the Donatists on the issue of the urgency of separation, an important message for independent survival. This tactic would help the Donatist faithful resist pressures to assimilate.

At the Conference of Carthage, the Catholic *mandatum*, or official position paper had, using quotations from the Bible, raised the issue of the necessity and timing of the separation of the just from sinners, a favorite Donatist theme. In the opening statement of the Catholic party, their bishops linked the delay in separation that they found in the parables of the wheat and the tares (Matt. 13:37–39) and the dragnet (13:47–49) to the mixed state of the wheat and chaff in John the Baptist's parable of the threshing floor (Matt. 3:12). Interpreting the first two by the third, they advanced the contention that not only were good and bad mixed *within the Church* but that the separation of the two would not occur until the end of the world.[141] Using Rom. 1:18b, "They conceal the truth of God by their injustice," they accused the Donatists of suppressing the facts of the controversy and the evidence of the Bible.[142]

The Catholics had raised issues dear to Donatist ecclesiology. Donatists in their turn used some of the identical verses to answer

the Catholics, interpreting them in their own way and adding con-
firmatory verses from other parts of the Bible.

First, they contended that parables of separation, like those of
the wheat and the tares or the dragnet, dealt with division of sinners from the holy *just as soon as their identity was known*, not in the
distant future. They rejected the Catholic assertion that the Baptist's parable of the threshing floor dealt with sinners *within the
Church* by noting that in it the floor was specifically likened not to
the Church, but to the world. If the Lord God put into the Bible
the specific verbal equation of the world and the threshing floor,
who were they or the Catholics to contradict the words of the creator of that world?[143]

In their turn, the Donatists used Rom. 1:18b to counter the
Catholic charge against them. They accused the Catholics of
silencing the truth, for their Catholic opponents had truncated the
quotation. Here again, literalism is important. The Donatists then
continued the quotation from Romans, using vv. 18a–24 to call
down the wrath of God upon their opponents:

> The anger of God will be revealed from heaven against all the
> impiety and injustice of their people, for what is known about
> God is manifest to them who conceal the truth of God by their
> injustice, for what can be known about God is plain to them:
> God himself made it plain to them . . . they may not be excused,
> for although they knew God, they did not honor God or offer
> him thanks. . . .[144]

The Catholics, like the unbelievers of Paul's day, should have
known the truth and reverenced God, for God's invisible power
and divinity had been revealed to them through the visible world.
Ignoring what they should have known, their minds were dark-
ened. They preferred worship of earthly things to that of the
divine. The Donatists, then, called God's wrath down on the
Catholics because they, like the Gentiles Paul referred to in
Romans, should have known better, yet they were idolaters.

The basic reason behind the need for separation was to avoid
ritual pollution resulting from associating with those who had
committed the sin of apostasy. This sin inhered in the Catholics as

descendants and supporters of the *traditores*. Thus God commanded the Donatists to avoid contagion. "Go back, go back, leave and do not touch the unclean"; and "Do not touch me for I am clean."[145]

According to the Donatist interpretation of Rom. 1:18, the Catholics were the idolaters Paul (and God) condemned. The Donatists did not consider the charge of idolatry mere hyperbole. It was literal idolatry that the Donatists remembered. They could recall an incident from the Macarian persecution when the Catholics celebrated their Eucharist at an altar on which a bust of Constantine had been enthroned.[146]

Catholics considered the advice given in 1 Tim. 5:22b, "You shall not defile yourselves with the sins of another," to command moral but not physical separation.[147] Donatists again countered the Catholic interpretation by appealing to the text of the entire verse: "You shall not lay hands on anyone rashly nor shall you defile yourselves with the sins of another." Their interpretation was quite materialist.[148] They emphasized the first part of the verse, with an accent on the prohibition of touching a person, which the Catholics had omitted, for the Donatists believed that the Bible was prohibiting not only moral association but also physical contact. They found support in Num. 16:26, which prohibited touching not only the persons of the rebellious Korah, Dathan, and Abiram, but even any object belonging to them. They quoted the "nolite tangere" of Isa. 52:11, God's warning against touching anything unclean. Their final word comes from 2 Cor. 6:16–18, a key passage used in the *Acts of the Abitinian Martyrs*. It commanded radical separation between the faithful and the unfaithful on the grounds that God dwells only with the former.[149]

This horror of contagion was enormous, but the social costs of segregation were also tremendous. The price was high for the community. Some may have perceived it as ruthless. Once the Church found sin in its midst, it was swift to deal with it because the Bible commanded the separation of the clean and the unclean. Donatists lived up to their responsibilities. They degraded clerics, excommunicated anyone who deserved it, and kept alive the ancient forms of canonical penance.[150]

The price of faith was also high for the individual. According to Augustine, Gaudentius used the story of Razias (2 Macc. 14:37–46) as a lively example of heroism on this point to inspire Donatists to resist association with apostates and to impress on Catholics the deadly seriousness with which they took the duty to separate from the impure.[151] Razias was one of the elders of Jerusalem during the revolt of the Maccabees. He regarded capture at the hands of sinners, that is, the troops of the Syrian commander Nicanor, as pollution, a calamity worse than death, so he decided to kill himself. When the soldiers were rushing the tower in which he had secluded himself and were burning down its door, Razias tried to stab himself. In the struggle with the soldiers, he was unable to effect his own death. Wounded, he threw himself from the tower. Still not dead, he drew himself up on a rocky crag and disemboweled himself before a crowd of bystanders.

Considering all the Catholic propaganda about Donatists committing suicide when no one would martyr them,[152] one might question whether this passage could perhaps be something Augustine added to his report of Gaudentius' letter in order to discredit the Donatists. Augustine's own report centered on Razias as an example of cowardice in the face of tribulation. He could find no reason to praise Razias and he was, in fact, embarrassed by the inclusion of this story in Scripture. He finally fastened on Razias' love of his city as the reason why he was mentioned in the Bible. He was first and foremost, for Augustine, an example of a bad reason for suicide. Suicide is a topic Augustine found quite fascinating.[153]

However, a closer look at the context of the story within Gaudentius' letter militates against Razias being an example for Donatist suicide. Gaudentius presented Razias not so much as a martyr as someone who avoided contact with evil at all costs. Speaking of evil as a physically palpable substance capable of being touched or avoided was characteristically Donatist. Thus, one may see Razias as a biblical example offered by the Donatists not to encourage suicide, but rather to discourage contact with Catholics.

Commands also dealt with conduct during persecution, when

Donatists were harassed by Catholics. First of all, Donatists ought not be afraid of the words of sinners. Second, they were to beware of false prophets, recognizing them by their evil fruits.[154]

In a more positive vein, Donatists were to be imitators of the steadfastness of Christ and the patience of Paul, and, despite the beastly activities (*feralia*) of the Catholics, the Donatists were to love them.[155]

In Donatist eyes, the Law provided commands for Catholics too. The Bible called on them to be wise and to recognize themselves as the objects of biblical admonition.[156] They were not to walk according to the prescriptions of their ancestors nor were they to be mere hearers of the word. They were to be doers who would purge evil from their midst.[157] In Gaudentius' appeal against the enforcement of anti-Donatist legislation, he used the words of Scripture as a reminder to Catholics to observe the commandments of the Law not to kill Donatists or to covet their churches and lands.[158] More comprehensively, the command went out to Catholics to return to the life to which they had been called, fidelity to the Law.[159]

Besides commands relating to Donatist-Catholic relationships, the Bible provided guidance regarding the sacrament of Baptism. Behind all of these commands stand the two images of Donatist-Catholic relationships: Christ betrayed by Judas, and the prophets of God preaching against an apostate nation.

Judas had been gone from the upper room when Jesus washed the feet of the apostles. He alone of the inner circle was not clean.[160] His spiritual descendants were tainted, too, as was their baptism.

Donatists also distanced themselves from the Catholics by the use of biblical verses that dealt with approved cult. Catholics may have professed the same creed as the Donatists, but that would do them no good. For those who did not gather with the Lord scattered, and not all who said "Lord, Lord" entered the kingdom of heaven.[161] Catholic sacraments may have been similar to the Donatists', but that was not sufficient. The prophet Jeremiah taught the Donatists to be wary of liturgical claims of wicked priests. Donatists' biblical formation had taught them that God accepted worship only in the approved sanctuary.[162] Catholics and Donatists may have acknowledged the same God, but that was not enough, for even the demons confessed Christ.[163]

In the Donatist works embedded in Augustine's, one finds reference to many of the biblical verses about Baptism that had been used by the Donatists in earlier documents. Prime among these sacramental texts was "Let not the oil of the sinner anoint my head."[164] It was especially useful because it could be used to refer to either baptismal or clerical anointing. Some biblical images that had figured prominently in Optatus' answer to Parmenian on the *dotes*, for example, the enclosed garden and the dove, did not recur with any frequency, not even in Augustine's answer to Parmenian.[165] The argument had shifted away from texts on the unity of Baptism to the healing offered by Donatist baptism and the pollution found in the Catholic sacrament. Although Donatists could not deny that Catholics baptized, or at least performed a ceremony very, very similar to their own, they still could impugn the effects of the Catholic rite.

Texts not found or not important before Augustine's time expanded what had previously been only a minor theme, the purity of the water of Baptism. If the Catholics were stained by the sins of their spiritual ancestors, and if sin was a contagious pollution, it would be obvious that their baptismal water was diseased. The Bible offered the Donatists confirmation of their logic. On this subject, there was one foundational text, the one Parmenian had chosen years before, Jer. 2:13:

> Heaven trembled because the people of God have done two malevolent deeds: they have abandoned the fountain of living water and they have dug for themselves leaky cisterns which cannot hold water.[166]

Optatus had felt forced to reply to it, and it appeared in Augustine's answer to Parmenian.[167] No other document employed it, but its original application spawned the use of several other texts about impure, deceitful water. Catholic baptism was "lying water which did not contain faith."[168] Using biblical passages, Donatists exhorted their audience not to go to others or to drink the water of outsiders.[169]

Anyone baptized by a Catholic was as unclean as one who had touched a dead body, so the Bible said, "What good does a person's washing do when he is baptized by a dead man?"[170] Petilian interpreted this death spiritually and applied it, as was customary in North Africa, to those who had been *traditores*.[171] Their baptism could not save but placed the soul of the baptized person in spiritual jeopardy.

Most of these new texts, like their progenitor Jer. 2:13 ("[T]hey have abandoned the fountain of living water . . .") came from the prophets who were hurling invective against those in Israel who worshiped alien gods. Even the verses from Proverbs bear enmity toward the women and the wisdom of those outside the community of the faithful.

This division between inside and outside was echoed in two other biblical verses to which Augustine alluded. The first was the Donatist use of Gen. 6:14. In this verse, God commanded Noah to cover the ark inside and out with pitch. Augustine claimed that one of the Donatist bishops who preached in the city of Hippo had interpreted this verse as a mandate to keep true Baptism inside their church and keep the baptism of outsiders out.[172] This report should be taken as accurately reflecting Donatist exegetical practice. It conforms perfectly to their interpretation of the enclosed garden of Cant. 4:12, in which the wall of the garden kept the outside out as well as the inside in.[173]

The second new verse dealing with the division between the inside and the outside was John 19:34. Here water flowed from the side of Christ, indicating for the Donatists that only on the inside, the Body of Christ that is the Church, was Baptism to be found.[174]

Both of these verses became part of the rationale for Donatist separation.

The Donatist attack on Baptism done outside their Church utilized one well-known verse, Eph. 4:5, and at least two previously unused passages, Acts 2:38 and 19:1–5. The first, "one Lord, one faith, one Baptism," needs no comment.[175] The latter two are more oblique. In the first of these, Jews who listened to Peter on Pentecost were baptized. Cresconius maintained that even though they had been baptized in the Red Sea at the Exodus, they still submitted to a greater Baptism, the only real one.[176] Thus the Bible vindicated Donatist rebaptism of Catholic converts. In Acts 19:1–5, Paul met Ephesians who had been baptized by John the Baptist. Upon hearing that they had not received the Holy Spirit, he did not simply lay hands on them but rebaptized them. According to Cresconius, this passage too showed that there was no true Baptism outside the true Church.[177]

Donatist baptismal theology relied for its argumentation on a battery of biblical texts. Augustine cited verses used by earlier Donatists, primarily those mentioning oil and water, the elements of the sacrament. The texts appearing first in this period emphasized purity of the Donatist sacrament and the impurity of the Catholic rite. These verses were reinforced by and reinforced texts of separation.

DONATIST INTERPRETIVE STRATEGIES

The important tasks for the Donatists of this period were self-definition in the face of Catholic and imperial harassment and the maintenance of boundaries, especially with respect to the administration of sacraments. Donatist use of Scripture during the period from the 390s to the Vandal invasion exhibited continuity with the basic hermeneutical methods of previous Donatists on three counts. First, Donatists relied on Scriptures for an understanding of their own situation. The Bible itself interpreted their world. In so doing, the Bible became their world. As the pages of Scripture told of oppression and promised glory, so their world was one of persecution in which they waited for the age in which there would be no more weeping. But, unlike the pre-Donatist martyr stories, they did not anticipate an end to oppression any time soon. Their tactics promoted survival for the duration.

Second, the Donatists took to heart the world they adopted from the Bible, and they modeled themselves on the persecuted

172 The Bible in Christian North Africa

people of that world. Conversely, they saw the Catholics as the characters in the Scriptures who harassed their models. Third, this utilization of the characters from the pages of Scripture licensed the application of the messages embodied in their stories of their world and its characters. When the world of the Bible became their own world and the characters of that world populated North Africa, the commands God gave the biblical characters became divinely authorized mandates for Donatists and Catholics. Donatists appropriated God's injunctions in a literal manner because they believed that when God inspired the writers of Scripture to compose their verses, God provided not only for the situation of the authors but for the fifth century too.

There are two significant differences in the application of these principles during this late pre-Vandal period. The first involved models for imitation, and the second came in the area of the content of the biblical messages the Donatists appropriated from Scripture. The differences occurred because the socioreligious situation of the Donatists of Augustine's age diverged from that of their predecessors.

In Augustine's day, Donatist authors employed new biblical models for their behavior: Razias, Paul, and Jesus. Razias' chief function was to be the moral model for the lengths to which one ought to go to avoid mingling with Catholics. Interest in Paul was common to both Donatists and Catholics, although Donatists had more opportunity to exploit his mistreatment as a model for their lives than did Catholics, who looked to Paul for guidance in questions of theology. Finally, Christ as model was a function of Petilian's spirituality and, through Petilian, the model influenced the larger Donatist community. The chief attribute Donatist theologians wrote about was his patience in suffering, again, an appropriate model for the legal situation of the Donatists.

The word "model" rather than "type" is used advisedly in this context. A type is a figure that provides a world and a role into which an admirer can step. A model provides habits, or virtues, that a person admires and imitates. Razias and Paul did not function as types for the Donatists, as did the Maccabee brothers and the companions of Daniel for an earlier generation. Petilian and

Gaudentius did not invite Donatists to imitate the person, the life, and the death of Paul or of Razias, but the specific virtues they manifested. Even Jesus in his passion became a type for Donatists only when paired with the traitor Judas. Otherwise, it was his virtues, not his death, that Donatists highlighted.

As noted above, the martyrs did not function as models in this period. The deaths of Razias, Paul, and Jesus were not focal points. This should occasion no surprise when one considers the socioreligious environment of the Donatist authors. Especially in the years after 405, after the reimposition of anti-Donatist legislation in these years, Donatists faced penalties ranging from fines and flogging to the confiscation of property. However, even though the death penalty was legislated several times, they were not really facing death for their beliefs.[178]

The predicament was not so much the execution of the sentence as living under pressure to conform to Catholicism, in fear of being reported. In these straits, they needed encouragement to live a life of fidelity in the face of their foes. Consequently, Jesus, in his final discourse, fully aware of the danger facing him from Judas, was a good model.

However, better than any model was the prime prototype for Donatist self-understanding: the faithful of Israel, who had to bear with temptation to defect year after year. This steadfast assembly provided not simply a model whose virtues were to be imitated, but a type whose whole world could be adopted as the world of the Donatists. The way of life of the *collecta*, as imagined by the Donatists on the basis of their Bible, became the Donatist way of life. The enemies of the true Israel became the enemies of the Donatists, and the enemies of the Donatists became, in typological process, the enemies of the leaders of Israel, the prophets.

The second difference in the application of Donatist hermeneutics revolves around the content of biblical commands the Donatists of the fifth century gleaned from Scriptures. The perdurance of the *collecta* as type allowed Donatists to appropriate what they interpreted as Israel's attitude toward Law. Typology allowed them to apply the verses of command from the Bible to their own situation, justifying separation from the Catholics, the denunciation of Catholic clergy, and the rejection of Catholic rites. In effect, the direct application of these commands supported the continued existence of the Donatists as a separate group. This was one of the most important functions the Bible played in the history of Donatism.

Thus, even in the Augustinian period, as in previous times, by their typological and literal reading of the Bible, Donatists participated in the events of biblical history. They were not betrayed simply by the *traditores*, Mensurius and Caecelian of Carthage, or even by their descendants. They were handed over to the Roman authorities by Judas himself. They did not battle merely Catholics but the polluted apostates who opposed prophets. As with their predecessors, Donatists of Augustine's time interpreted the Scriptures and found strength for survival by playing out the stories of the Bible in their own lives.

CHAPTER 6

A New Image of Donatism

In the kingdom of heaven every wise scribe is like the head of a family who draws out from the storeroom both the new and the old (Matt. 13:52).

THIS SURVEY OF DONATIST USE of the Bible has produced some not unexpected conclusions. Most generally, one can say that Donatism was a living, developing religion during the years between its inception during the persecutions under Diocletian and the advent of the Vandals about a century and a quarter later. The portrait painted in this work is not the traditional one of a static, martyr-bound, millennialist movement, but one that shows the movement responding to the larger world in a variety of ways over the course of its history. The legalization of Christianity, the renewal of persecution, the attainment of majority status, and once again being outlawed all evoked responses designed to maintain and advance the movement in new circumstances. Donatist responses have been examined through the twists and turns in the biblical interpretation presented by the surviving literature of the movement and glimpsed in the works of its opponents.

The recovery of the lost image of Donatism was made possible by a suspicious retrieval of the history of Donatism from biased sources on both sides. The tools were a combination of the use of world-building and world-maintenance theories of anthropologists of religion, as well as the tools of historically based scriptural interpretation. Derived from the first is the idea that every community uses language to construct a world in which one can more or less comfortably live from a chaotic collection of sensations of the world. Once there is a world in which to live, it is populated by heroes and villains. Finally, the commands of Scripture are appropriated or ignored depending on the world, its inhabitants, and their circumstances. From the second discipline comes the idea that one can recover the social situation of the Donatist communities that produced the surviving literature and the hints of community life gathered from the writings of opponents by working backward from the product to the community.

This quest for historic Donatism in its various incarnations began with the roots of the movement in North African Christianity. The first chapter of this book surveyed the material Donatists gleaned from Tertullian, Cyprian, and the martyrs under Decius, Valerian, and Diocletian. From the ancestral storeroom trove, Donatists drew what they needed, when they needed it, and promptly. From Tertullian, Donatism inherited a propensity for literalism and an aversion to allegory. He bequeathed them an urgency about the commands of Scripture. From Cyprian, they received an ecclesiology of a pure Church in a world soiled by idolatry. He left to them a collection of biblical texts that treated questions such as the advisability of martyrdom, the status of the Church, and the validity of sacraments performed by those outside the Church. Cyprian filled in the commands on issues germane to the daily life of a persecuted Church. From both of these ancestors, Donatists inherited a sense of the unity of the Old and New Testaments and a propensity for typology. This method of biblical interpretation allowed the Donatists to give primacy to the literal words of the Bible while bringing the biblical world, its personal types, and its divine commands to each succeeding generation. Donatists would take the method and unleash it from the moorings Tertullian gave it by tying it only to the events of history. Donatists were able to apply it to a much broader range of texts than the authors of the second century. Not only events of the past but even events of the eschaton could be grist for the typological mill.

The contribution of the martyrs' stories was a method of building a world with words, populating it with heroes and villains, and giving the reader the literary vision to read in the stories commands for community life, all in narrative form. The prime story of the Severan period, when Christians faced the first systematic persecutions, the *Passio Perpetuae*, taught the earliest Donatists to build an apocalyptic world of their own. Martyr stories from the mid-third century taught them to populate the world of martyrdom with biblical champions such as Jesus and the Maccabees, and villains such as Judas and the idolatrous, assimilating Jews of Antiochus' era. From the martyr stories of the late third and early fourth centuries, Donatists learned to appropriate commands for daily living, for life among idolaters, whether that life required martyrdom or asceticism. From all these ancestors, Donatism drew on a devotion to the Holy Spirit as the Comforter who provided them with the ability not only to interpret Scripture but also to act out those Scriptures in their daily lives.

In our survey of Donatist martyr stories of the early fourth century, we saw that the earliest Donatists painted an apocalyptic world in which the old and the young, the senator mindful of his age, like Dativus of Abitina, and the girls almost too young to be prosecuted, like Maxima and her sisters in faith, all testified to their Christianity. Martyrs were more authoritative than bishops, and the prime command of the Bible was separation from the church of the *traditores* and their complicity in persecuting true Christians.

So far, so good; this is the traditional picture of Donatism, the one readers meet in Optatus, Augustine, and manuals of church history. But what happened after Constantine's grant of religious liberty to Christians? What happened, especially, when there were no more persecutions?

The movement did not die out. It sustained itself on the basis of the prime image bequeathed to it by the *Acts of the Abitinian Martyrs* in the early fourth century. According to that story, the most important thing Christians could do was to gather in community, literally, *collectam facere*, to make the assembly, the gathering of Christians who held the Law of the Lord, the Scriptures, in their hearts, like the Abitinian confessors of 304. This image of the *collecta* came from the self-identity of Israel on pilgrimage from the slavery of Egypt to the freedom of the Promised Land. On the road, its greatest gift from God was the Law—for Donatists, the Bible, whether inscribed on the pages of a physical book or, more importantly, in the hearts and lives of true believers. The Old Testament texts that supported the image of the Law-loving *collecta* provided the community the strength to sojourn in a land of idolaters, keeping itself pure and separating from those who did evil in the sight of the Lord. This self-image sustained them through the state persecution of Donatism from 317 to 321 and again from 346 to 348.

But what of periods of peace? As we saw in the third chapter, Donatism did not wane but gathered strength. It the period between the Constantinian and Macarian persecutions, it used the Bible to buttress its self-image as gathered community in the midst of evil. Using the portrait of the *collecta*, one never stated but implicit in Cyprian, it maintained community boundaries by accenting not martyrdom but purity, purity of ecclesiastical lineage, ritual practice, and daily life. During this period Donatists reinforced themselves as *collecta* by adding to the repertoire of images Moses for their leaders and the rebels against him for their internal enemies. When people within the movement faced division, the Bible told them how to deal with the situations. Words about persecution became words about community division. The literalist and typological tendencies inherited especially from Tertullian allowed them to reinforce group boundaries, characterize themselves and their opponents, and issue directives to maintain the community.

Here we begin to see that the sustaining image of Donatism was never simply the Church of the Martyrs, but that of the *collecta*.

Later in the fourth century, especially after the reign of Julian, the Donatist majority church learned to cope with the realities of life as a broad-based popular movement that grew to the point of having its own schisms. The ecclesiologies studied in the fourth chapter show how the Donatist church, usually seen as the Church of the Pure, came to terms with evil *within* the Church.

Again, the Donatist use of the Bible showed the ways in which they could deal with the evil while still maintaining group boundaries. From Parmenian's use of the Bible, Donatists learned that corrupt members would not vitiate the strength of the Church itself. The church of the pure could and did contain the not-so-pure. The personal and the ecclesial were no longer conjoined as they had been at the beginning of the movement. God gave the Church the requisite gifts, those necessary to maintain it in holiness, even when individual members failed. Thanks to Parmenian, the Church in Donatist eyes became an entity independent of the moral status of its members, long before Augustine wrote *The City of God*.

Tyconius went even farther than his bishop Parmenian, and, using the Bible, he envisioned the Church as simultaneously being both Body of Christ and, in some mysterious way, containing evil as a constitutive element in the body of the *collecta* still on pilgrimage in this world.

Here we see that the textbook portrayal of Donatism as the Church of the Pure and of no others has also been inaccurate.

In the fifth chapter, we saw how persecution returned to the Donatist world. But it was a persecution without martyrs. Under those circumstances, Donatism did not collapse and vanish from the scene, as so many historians would lead their readers to believe. It did not and could not rely on an image of the Church of the Martyrs or the Church of the Pure. Instead, it continued as the *collecta* with good and evil members. It drew lines in the North African sand between itself and the church of the children of the *traditores* of old. Drawing those lines was an urgent task, one commanded by the Donatist self-image as *collecta* and by the words of command found in the Bible. Separatism, not martyrdom; separatism, not purity, was the watchword of the age. Separatism demanded swift discipline within its ranks and at its edges. It was the separatist community, those faithful to God *as a group*. The Bible provided the warrants and the urgency because, as Tyconius had said and as all Donatists believed, what was happening in the Bible was really and truly happening in the present and especially in Africa.

In the end, the exercise of the typological model of the *collecta* of Israel provided for Donatist stability and cohesion in changing times, when neither the Church of the Martyrs nor the Church of the Pure could have fit the image they saw daily in the mirror of their own history. Optatus, Augustine, and textbooks of church history have for centuries fastened on one partial image of the Donatist church. Because they saw it only as the Church of the Martyrs or the Church of the Pure, they could not explain how it attracted the rich and powerful, why it survived when there was no persecution, and how it continued when it was obvious that it contained both saints and sinners. It maintained itself because it was not simply composed of the good and the pure but of those God had chosen, the *collecta* that the power of God maintained through the Law engraved on their hearts, the Bible they enacted in their lives.

Notes

PREFACE

1. Optatus of Milevis, *S. Optati Milevitani Libri VII*, ed. Carolus Ziwza, CSEL 26 (Prague and Vienna: Tempsky; Leipzig: Freytag, 1893); and Augustine's various anti-Donatist tracts, which are most conveniently assembled as *Sancti Aurelii Augustini Scripta contra Donatistas,* ed. M. Petschenig, CSEL 51–53 (Vienna: Tempsky; Leipzig: Freytag, 1908–10).

2. See, for example, his *The Legends of the Saints*, trans. Donald Attwater (New York: Fordham University Press, 1962), 12–48.

3. *Actes de la Conférence de Carthage en 411*, SC 194, 195, 224, 373, ed. Serge Lancel (Paris: Cerf, 1972–91).

4. W. H. C. Frend, *The Donatist Church: A Movement of Protest in Roman North Africa* (Oxford: Clarendon Press, 1952; repr. 1970).

5. It was not until the late nineteenth century, under the influence of the rising Marxist movement, that the Donatist controversy was construed as anything but a religious dispute. For the history of scholarship of Donatism, see André Mandouze, "Le donatisme représente-t-il la résistance à Rome de l'Afrique tardive?" in *Assimilation et résistance à la culture Greco-romaine dans le monde ancien: Travaux de VI*ᵉ *Congrès International d'Études Classiques (Madrid, Septembre 1974)*, ed. D. M. Pippidi (Bucharest: Editura Academiei; Paris: Société d'Édition "Les Belles Lettres," 1976), 357–66, esp. 359–60.

6. For a full discussion of the criteria and their use, see Maureen A. Tilley, "A Treasure Hidden in a Field: Unearthing Heretical Hermeneutics," *Explorations* 9:1 (Fall 1990): 55–69.

7. Optatus 2.8 (CSEL 26.44).

8. Optatus 2.8 (CSEL 26.44).

9. Cf. *Actes de la Conférence de Carthage* 3.258 (SC 224.1202).

10. Optatus 3.7 (CSEL 26.89).

11. Cf. Optatus 3.4 (CSEL 26.81–82).

12. Cornelius Petrus Mayer, "Taufe und Erwählung. Zur Dialektik des sacramentum Begriffe in der antidonatistischen Schrift Augustins: De baptisma," in *Scientia augustiniana: Festschrift Adolar Zumkeller,* ed. Cornelius Petrus Mayer and Williges Eckermann (Würzburg: Augustinus, 1975), 24.

13. Optatus 2.8 (CSEL 26.44).

14. *Ep. ad Cath.* 16.40–41, 19.51, 24.69 (CSEL 52.283–84, 298, 315–16); and *Ep.* 93.28.24 in *Sancti Aurelii Augustini Hipponiensis Epistulae,* CSEL 34, ed. Al. Goldbacher (Prague and Vienna: Tempsky; Leipzig: Freytag, 1898), 469.

15. E.g., Optatus' construal of 2 Tim. 3:2, 8; see Optatus 7.5 (CSEL 26.176–78).

16. Classic formulations are Peter L. Berger, *The Sacred Canopy: Elements of a Sociological Theory of Religion* (Garden City, N.Y.: Doubleday, 1967; repr. Anchor 1969), 3–52; Berger and Thomas Luckmann, *The Social Construction of Reality* (Garden City, N.Y.: Doubleday, 1966; repr. Anchor 1967); and "Religion as a Cultural System," chapter 4 of Clifford Geertz, *The Interpretation of Cultures* (New York: Basic Books, 1973), esp. 89–102.

17. Berger, 47.

18. On the history of biblical critics' attempts to see the Bible as reflective of first-century problems and to move behind it to the person of Jesus, see Albert Schweitzer, *The Quest for the Historical Jesus: A Critical Study of Its Progress from Reimarus to Wrede,* trans. W. Montgomery from the first German edition, *Von Reimarus zu Wrede* (1906) (New York: Macmillan, 1961); Edgar V. McKnight, *What Is Form Criticism?* (Philadelphia: Fortress Press, 1969); Norman Perrin, *What Is Redaction Criticism?* (Philadelphia: Fortress Press , 1969); and James W. Robinson, *The New Quest for the Historical Jesus,* Studies in Biblical Theology 25 (London: SCM, 1959).

19. E.g., John G. Gager, "The Quest for Legitimacy and Consolidation," chapter 3 of *Kingdom and Community: The Social World of Early Christianity* (Englewood Cliffs, N.J.: Prentice-Hall, 1975); Wayne A. Meeks, *The First Urban Christians: The Social World of the Apostle Paul* (New Haven and London: Yale University Press, 1983); Howard Clark Kee, *Miracle in the Early Christian World: A Study in Sociohistorical Method* (New Haven and London: Yale University Press, 1983); and Kee, *Knowing the Truth: A Sociological Approach to New Testament Interpretation* (Minneapolis: Augsburg Fortress Press, 1989).

20. For two test cases of this method, see Maureen A. Tilley, "Scripture as an Element of Social Control: Two Martyr Stories of Christian North Africa," *Harvard Theological Review* 84:4 (1990): 383–97.

21. For a sketch of the ways in which the ancients interpreted the

power of language, see Jane P. Tompkins, "The Reader in History: The Changing Shape of Literary Response," chapter 12 of *Reader-Response Criticism: From Formalism to Post-Structuralism*, ed. Jane P. Tompkins (Baltimore and London: Johns Hopkins University Press, 1980), 201–32, esp. 202–6. For a detailed study of the power of Christian rhetoric to reshape the Roman world, see Averil Cameron, *Christianity and the Rhetoric of Empire: The Development of Christian Discourse*, Sather Classical Lectures 53 (Berkeley, Los Angeles, and Oxford: University of California Press, 1991).

INTRODUCTION

1. *Acta Martyrum Saturnini, Felicis, Dativi, Ampelii et aliorum*, also known as the *Acts of the Abitinian Martyrs* 9 (MPL 8.695D; cf. DMS 25–49).

2. See the survey of opinions on the beginning of the Donatist movement in W. H. C. Frend and K. Clancy, "When Did the Donatist Schism Begin?" *Journal of Theological Studies*, n.s., 28 (1977): 104–9; and Peter Brown, "Religious Coercion in the Later Roman Empire: The Case of North Africa," *History* 48 (1963): 284 (= *Religion and Society in the Age of Augustine* [London: Faber & Faber, 1972], 302).

3. One of the better views of Donatism through an Augustinian prism is Rémi Crespin, *Ministère et sainteté: Pastorale de clergé et solution de la crise donatiste dans la vie et la doctrine de saint Augustin* (Paris: Études Augustiniennes, 1965). Despite the subtitle, it attempts to understand what made Donatism attractive to North Africans and how Catholicism countered that attraction.

4. Ernesto Buonaiuti, *Il Cristianesimo nell' Africa romana* (Bari: Laterza, 1928); Jean-Paul Brisson, *Autonomisme et Christianisme dans l'Afrique romaine de Septime Sévère à l'invasion vandal* (Paris: Boccard, 1958); and Frend, *The Donatist Church*.

5. His *Histoire littéraire de l'Afrique chrétienne depuis les origines jusqu'à l'invasion arabe*, 7 vols. (Paris 1901–23; repr. Brussels: Culture et civilisation, 1963), an exhaustive study, is still taken as canonical in the most recent contribution to Donatist history, Jean-Louis Maier, *Le Dossier du Donatisme*, T&U 134, 135 (Berlin: Akademie-Verlag, 1987, 1989).

6. Nowhere is this clearer than with the Marxist historians of Donatism. Even the best, Theodora Büttner and Ernest Werner, *Circumcellionen und Adamiten; zwei Formen mittelalterlichen Haeresie* (Berlin: Akademie-Verlag, 1975), provide no role for theological concerns.

7. E.g., J. S. Alexander, "Aspects of Donatist Scriptural Interpretation at the Conference of Carthage," T&U 128, *Studia Patristica* 15 (1984): 125–30; Robert B. Eno, "Some nuances in the ecclesiology of the Donatists,"

REA 18 (1972), 46–50; and Paula Fredriksen Landes, "Tyconius and the End of the World," REA 28 (1982), 59–75.

8. Robert B. Eno, "Doctrinal Authority in Saint Augustine," *Augustinian Studies* 12 (1981): 161.

9. Mayer, 25; and Yves M.-J. Congar in his general introduction to *Oeuvres de saint Augustin*, BA, quatrième série: *Traités Anti-Donatistes*, edited with a French translation by G. Finaert, vols. 28–32 (Paris: Descleé de Brouwer, 1963–65), 28.52.

10. Frend, *The Donatist Church*, xv.

11. Cf. Monceaux 4.437–76, and the wholesale redating of epigraphy in Yvette Duval, *Loca Sanctorum Africae: Le culte des martyrs en Afrique du IVe au VIIe siècle*, 2 vols., Collection de l'École Française de Rome 58 and 59 (Rome: École Française, 1982).

12. *Retractationes* 1.21.3 in *Sancti Aurelii Augustini Retractationum Libri II*, ed. Almut Mutzenbecher, CCL 57 (Turnhout: Brepols, 1984), 69.

13. See, for example, Maureen A. Tilley, "Understanding Augustine Misunderstanding Tyconius," in *Studia Patristica* 27 (1993): 405–8.

CHAPTER 1

Donatist Predecessors

1. On the distinctive North African dress and its survival, as well as other distinguishing customs, see Susan Raven, *Rome in Africa*, 3d ed. (London and New York: Routledge, 1993), 146–47.

2. W. H. C. Frend, *The Donatist Church: A Movement of Protest in Roman North Africa* (Oxford: Clarendon Press, 1952; repr. 1970), 77–79, 86; Marcel Le Glay, *Saturne Africaine* (Paris: Boccard, 1966), 490–91.

3. For the Jewish origin, see W. H. C. Frend, "Jews and Christians in Third Century Carthage," in *Town and Country in the Early Christian Centuries* (London: Variorum, 1980). The speculation on an origin from Asia Minor depends largely on similarities in liturgy.

4. *Passio Sanctorum Scillitanorum* in *The Acts of the Christian Martyrs*, ed. and trans. Herbert Musurillo (Oxford: Clarendon Press, 1972). Unless otherwise noted, all of the martyr stories in this chapter are from Musurillo.

5. *Passio* 6, 8, 14, 16, and 17 (Musurillo, 86–88).

6. See the echoes of Greek expressions in *Passio Sanctarum Perpetuae et Felicitatis* 4.9 and 12.2 (Musurillo, 110, 120).

7. See the list of episcopal sees in *Sententiae episcoporum de haereticis baptizandis*, in *S. Thasci Caecili Cypriani. Opera Omnia*, ed. William Hartel, CSEL 3:1–3 (Vienna: Geroldi, 1871), 1.435–61.

8. See *De Spectaculis* and *De Aleatoribus* in *S. Thasci Caecilii Cypriani Opera Omnia* (CSEL 3:3.2–13, 92–104).

9. The most accessible English-language survey of early North African literature is *A History of Early Christian Doctrine before the Council of Nicaea*, Vol. 3: *The Origins of Latin Christianity*, by Jean Daniélou, trans. David Smith and John Austin Baker (London: Darton, Longman & Todd; Philadelphia: Westminster Press, 1977). Despite its general title, it is devoted almost exclusively to North Africa.

10. Cicero, *De Inventione. De optimo Genere oratorum. Topica*, with an English translation by H. M. Hubbell, LCL (Cambridge: Harvard University Press; and London: William Heinemann, 1949); [Cicero] *Rhetorica ad Herrenium Libri IV. De Ratione dicendi*, with an English translation by Harry Caplan, LCL (Cambridge: Harvard University Press; London: Heinemann, 1954); and Quintilian, *The Institutio Oratoria of Quintilian*, with an English translation by H. E. Butler, 4 vols., LCL (London: Heinemann; New York: Putnam's, 1921). For indisputable evidence of Tertullian's dependence on these sources, see Timothy D. Barnes, *Tertullian: A Historical and Literary Study* (Oxford: Clarendon Press, 1971), 22–29, 197–206, esp. 196; and Robert Dick Sider, *Ancient Rhetoric and the Art of Tertullian* (Oxford: Clarendon Press, 1971); and "Tertullian: *On the Shows*: An Analysis," *Journal of Theological Studies*, n.s., 29 (1978): 339–65.

11. On Tertullian's knowledge of Irenaeus, see J. H. Waszink, "Tertullian's Principles and Methods of Exegesis," in *Early Christian Literature and the Classical Intellectual Tradition. In honorem Robert M. Grant*, ed. William R. Schoedel and Robert L. Wilken (Paris: Beauchesne, 1971), 21; and W. H. C. Frend, *Martyrdom and Persecution in the Early Church: A Study of a Conflict from the Maccabees to Donatus* (New York: New York University Press, 1967), 268. On the influence of Irenaeus, Justin, and Melito of Sardis, see Gottfried Zimmermann, *Die hermeneutischen Prinzipien Tertullians*, inaugural diss., University of Leipzig (Würzburg: Konrad Triltsch, 1937), 36–37. Zimmermann sees Justin as the primary influence on Tertullian.

12. *Digest* 32.69: *"Non aliter a significatione uerborum recedi oportet, quam cum manifestum est aliud sensisse testatorem,"* in *The Digest of Justinian*, ed. Theodor Mommsen and Paul Krueger, with an English translation by Alan Watson, 4 vols. (Philadelphia: University of Pennsylvania Press, 1985), 3.92.

13. *St. Irenaeus' Proof of the Apostolic Preaching* 36, 43, trans. and annotated by Joseph P. Smith (Westminster, Md.: Newman; London: Longmans, Green, 1952), 70–71, 75.

14. Tertullian, *Adv. Marc.* 3.12.1–4, in *Quintii Septimi Florentis Tertulliani Opera*, ed. E. Dekkers, CCL 1, 2 (Turnhout: Brepols, 1953), 1.523–24. Cf. 4.7.1–2 (CCL 1.553), 4.8.1–2, 4 (CCL 1.556, 557), 4.10.2 (CCL 1.562).

15. *Adv. Marc.* 4.11.12, 4.19.6, 5.5.7 (CCL 1.586, 592, 676–77); *Bapt.* 11.2 (CCL 1.286); *Herm.* 19.1, 27.2 (CCL 1.412, 419–20). Tertullian does admit that Jesus also used allegory and parables; see *Res. mort.* 37.1–9 (CCL 2.969–70) and *Scorp.* 11.4 (CCL 2.1091).

16. See 1.9–13 of *Rhetorica ad Herennium* (LCL 24–42); and Quintillian, *Instit. Or.* 5.5, 5.7.1–2, 7.6.1–8, 8.1, 8.7 (LCL 2.164, 168–69; 3.134–40, 194, 198–200). One of Tertullian's more skillful applications is *Adv. Marc.* 3.12.1–4 (CCL 1.523–24).

17. *Adv. Marc.* 4.1–2 (CCL 1.547).

18. Tertullian repeatedly reconciled seemingly contradictory statements in his answers to Marcion's "Antitheses." See, e.g., *Adv. Marc.* 4.11.10–11 (CCL 1.568), as well as *Res. mort.* 6.3–5, 7.1–7 (CCL 2.928 and 930), and *De jej.* 2.2–4 (CCL 2.1258).

19. E.g., *Ep. Barn.* 6.1–19 in *The Apostolic Fathers,* with an English translation by Kirsopp Lake, 2 vols., LCL (London: Heinemann; and New York: Putnam's, 1930), 1.358–62. All citations of the Apostolic Fathers are from the LCL edition. Cf. L. W. Barnard, "The Use of Testimonies in the Early Church and in the Epistle of Barnabas," in *Studies in the Apostolic Fathers and Their Background* (New York: Schocken, 1966), esp. 112.

20. E.g., *Adv. Marc.* 3.4.1–5 (CCL 1.511–2), *Ux.* 41–6.4 (CCL 1.377–81) and *Mon.* 12.1–5 (CCL 2.1247–8).

21. *Praescr. Haer.* 37 (CCL 1.217); cf. *Digest* 22.5.1–25 (pp. 2.650–53).

22. Cf. *1 Clement* 8, and 42–4, and *Epistle to the Philippians of Saint Polycarp* 3.2, 9.1–3 (LCL 1.20, 78–80, 286, 294).

23. *Ad Herennium* 2.6.9 (LCL 72–74).

24. Irenaeus, *Adv. Haer.* 3.3.1–2, 4.26.4; 4.32.1, 4.33.8 in *Contre les Hérésies,* ed. Adelin Rousseau, 10 vols., SC, Book 1: vols. 263, 264; Book 2: vols. 293, 294; Book 3: vol. 100 in two parts; Book 4: vols. 210, 211; Book 5: vols. 152, 153 (Paris: Cerf, 1965–82), 100.30–3, 211.722/23, 796/97, and 820/21; *Proof* 3 (Smith 49). See the discussion of these sections in Robert M. Grant and David Tracy, *A Short History of the Interpretation of the Bible,* 2d ed., revised and enlarged (Philadelphia: Fortress Press, 1984), 48–51. Tertullian: on apostolic authority, *Praescr. Haer.* 32.1–3 (CCL 1.212–13); on the lives of believers, *Praescr. Haer.* 37.1, 43 *ad fin.* (CCL 1.217 and 223); on reason and natural law, *Apol.* 17.1–3 (CCL 1.117), *Cor. Mil.* 5.1 (CCL 2.1045); on custom, *Cor. Mil.* 4.1 (CCL 2.1043); on the *regula fidei, Praescr. Haer.* 9, 12.5–6, 13–14.5, 19.1–3 (CCL 1.195, 197–98, 201), *Virg. Vel.* 1.3 (CCL 2.1209), *Mon.* 2.4 (CCL 2.1230). For more comprehensive discussions of these aspects of Tertullian's interpretive practice, see Timothy F. Merrill, "Tertullian: The Hermeneutical Vision of *De Praescriptione Haereticorum* and Pentateuchal Exegesis," *The Patristic and Byzantine Review* 6 (1987): 153–67, esp. 152–54; Monceaux, 1.344–46; T. P. O'Malley, *Tertullian and the Bible: Language, Imagery, Exegesis*

(Nijmegen and Utrecht: Dekker and Ven de Vegt, 1967), 130; Waszink, 24–26; Otto Kuss, "Zur Hermeneutik Tertullians," in *Neuetestamentliche Aufsätze. Festschrift für Josef Schmid zum 70 Geburtstag*, ed. J. Blinzler, O. Kuss, and F. Musser (Regensburg: Pustet, 1963), 158; and Adhemar d'Ales, *La Théologie de Tertullien*, 3d. ed. (Paris: Beauchesne, 1905), 254–61.

25. *Adv. Marc.* 3.5.7 (CCL 1.513).

26. *Mon.* 4.1–2 (CCL 2.1233), *Virg. Vel.* 1.5 (CCL 2.1210). Cf. *Idol.* 4.5 (CCL 2.1104).

27. Demonstrated by his practice in *Orat.* 8.5 (CCL 1.262), *Adv. Marc.*, *passim*, *Praescr. Haer.* 17.1–5 (CCL 1.200), *Res. Mort.* 10.1–5 (CCL 2.932–33).

28. See O'Malley, 131, 149–50, for examples.

29. See his method displayed in *Proof* 42B–97 (Smith 75–108). Cf. *Adv. Haer.* 4.32.1 (SC 211.496/97).

30. *Adv. Marc.*, all of books 4 and 5.

31. Irenaeus, *Proof*, 40B, 44–46 (Smith 73, 76–77); Tertullian, *Adv. Marc.* 2.27.3 (CCL 1.506).

32. Justin, *Dialogue with Trypho* 7.3, in Justin, *Dialogue avec Tryphon*, Greek text with French translation, introduction, and notes, trans. and ed. Georges Archambault, 2 vols., Textes et Documents 8 and 11 (Paris: Picard, 1909), 8.38/39.

33. *Dialogue* 12.1–13.4 (Textes et Documents 8.96–108).

34. *Dialogue* 11.2 (Textes et Documents 8.52).

35. *Jud.* 2.1–10, 6.1 (CCL 2.1341–4, 1352). R. P. C. Hanson noted that although Tertullian evacuated the Mosaic law of any legal force, calling it an "immature gospel," he invested verses of the New Testament with a similar but more enduring legalism. See his "Notes on Tertullian's Interpretation of Scripture," *Journal of Theological Studies*, n.s., 12 (1961): 277; and examples in *Adv. Marc.* 4.17.2 (CCL 1.585) and *Mon.* 7.4, 8.1, 9.1, and 13.3 (CCL 2.1238, 1239, 1240, 1248–49).

36. *Praesc. Haer.* 15.4–16.2 (CCL 1.199–200). Cf. O'Malley, 119–20.

37. E.g., *Spect.* 3.1–8, 14.1 (CCL 1.230–31 and 239). Tertullian does not have a formal schema of rigid distinctions in the way the Bible may be interpreted. Such divisions enter Christian hermeneutics first with Augustine (in 391) who discussed interpretation *secundum historiam, secundum aetiologicam, secundum analogicam,* and *secundum allegoriam,* in *De utilitate credendi* 3.5–6 (CSEL 25:1.7–9, ed. Joseph Zycha [Prague and Vienna: Tempsky; Leipzig: Freytag, 1891]). Later, John Cassian (*ca.* 420) refined them in his *Conlationes XXIIII* 14.8.1 (ed. M. Petschenig, CSEL 13.404 [Vienna: Geroldi, 1886]). Cassian devoted his attention to the types of "spiritual" senses of Scripture: tropological, allegorical, and analogical. For the dating of these developments, see Johannes Quasten, *Patrology*, Vol. 4: *The Golden Age of Latin Patristic Literature from the Council of Nicea to the Council of Chalcedon*, ed. Angelo DiBerardino, trans. Placid Solari (Westminster, Md.:

Christian Classics, 1986), 4.362, and Karlfried Froehlich, *Biblical Interpretation in the Early Church* (Philadelphia: Fortress Press, 1984), 28.

38. *Orat.* 8.1–6 (CCL 1.262), *Res. Mort.* 43.5 (CCL 2.979).

39. *Pud.* 14.1–2 (CCL 2.1306).

40. *Exhort. Cast.* 3.6, 4.5 (CCL 2.1019, 1021).

41. *Mon.* 14.2 (CCL 2.1249).

42. *Mon.* 14.4–5 (CCL 2.1249–50).

43. *Pud.* 8, 9, esp. 9.1 (CCL 2.1294–96); *Res. Mort.* 30.1 (CCL 2.959).

44. Irenaeus, *Adv. Haer.* 2.27.1; 4.26.1; 1.9.4 (SC 294.264, 211.712, 264.150). Cf. 4.26.1 (SC 211.714).

45. See *Res. Mort.* 28.1 (CCL 2.945).

46. *Res. mort.* 20.2 (CCL 2.945); *Apol.* 20.5 (CCL 1.122).

47. *Adv. Marc.* 3.5.2–4 (CCL 1.512–14), *Idol.* 9.1 (CCL 2.1107). This story also figures in 1 Enoch 8–10, a book Tertullian considered part of the canon. Astrologers were regularly expelled from Rome. By their claim to prescience they created opportunities for assassins to make their predictions come true.

48. *Praescr. Haer.* 6.6 (CCL 1.191).

49. For a set of Christological types, see *Adv. Marc.* 3.18.3–7 (CCL 1.531–33); for moral types, see *Praescr. Haer.* 3–4 (CCL 1.188–90).

50. Pontius, *Vita Cypriani* 2 in *S. Thasci Caecili Cypriani. Opera Omnia*, ed. William Hartel, CSEL 3/3 (Vienna: Geroldi, 1871), xci; Jerome, *Hieronymus. Liber De Viris inlustribus* 67, ed. Ernest Cushing Richardson, T&U 14/1 (Leipzig: J. C. Hinrichs'sche, 1896), 38.

51. Michael M. Sage, *Cyprian*, Patristic Monographic Series 1 (Cambridge, Mass.: Philadelphia Patristic Foundation, 1975), 103; Quasten, 2.341–43; *Acta Proconsularia* 3 in *S. Thasci Caecili Cypriani. Opera Omnia*, CXII.

52. Monceaux 2.238–40; *Ep.* 59.20, 63.1, 68.3 (CSEL 3/2.690, 701, 745–46), each with its supporting scriptures.

53. *Ep.* 67.3 (CSEL 3/2.737).

54. *Epp.* 76.3, 5 (CSEL 3/2.728–30).

55. *Ad Fort.* 1–2 (CSEL 3/1.321–23), and *Epp.* 6, 80 (CSEL 3/2.480–85, 839–40).

56. Michael A. Fahey, *Cyprian and the Bible: A Study in Third-Century Exegesis*, Beiträge zur Geschichte der biblischen Hermeneutik 9 (Tübingen: J.C.B. Mohr, 1971), 47.

57. Jerome 53 (Richardson, 31).

58. *Ep.* 55.27 (CSEL 3/2.646).

59. *Un.* 2 (CSEL 3/1.210), *Lap.* 10 (CSEL 3/1.244), *Dom.* 15 (CSEL 3/1.277), *Ep.* 58.1 (CSEL 3/2.657), *Ep.* 63.17 (CSEL 3/2.715). See Fahey, 35.

60. *Ep.* 66.10 (CSEL 3/2.734), *Mort.* 19 (CSEL 3/1.308–9), *Vita* 12–13 (CSEL 3/3.CII–CIV). See Sage, 203. Cyprian made allusions to Matt. 3:12, which has the wise men warned by a dream, more often than to all but two other verses in the Bible. See the citations of quotations and allusions in the Appendix to Fahey, 675–95.

61. Monceaux 2.317.

62. One exception is a discussion of the Trinity in *Ep.* 73.5 (CSEL 3/2.782).

63. *Ep.* 69 (CSEL 3/2.749–66). The quotations are taken from section 2, pp. 750–52.

64. *Ep.* 69.2 (CSEL 3/2.750–52).

65. E.g., *Epp.* 70.1, 72.1, 73.2, 74.2–3, 6, 11 (CSEL 3/2.767, 775, 779, 800, 802, 804, 808–9). Cf. *Sententiae episcoporum* 1 (CSEL 3/1.436).

66. *Ep.* 69.3–6, 11 (CSEL 3/2.752–54, 759–60).

67. The branches: John 15:6 in *Ep.* 73.10 (CSEL 3/2.785); gangrene: 2 Tim. 2:17 in *Ep.* 73.15 (CSEL 3/2.789); blemished priests: Lev. 21:21 in *Ep.* 72.2 (CSEL 3/2.777); the cistern: Jer. 2:13 in *Ep.* 70.1 (CSEL 3/2.767); the polluting dead: Eccl. 34:25 in *Ep.* 71.1 (CSEL 3/2.772); cf. Num. 19:2, Ps. 140:5 in *Ep.* 70.1–2 (CSEL 3/2.768).

68. Cf. the similar analyses in Monceaux 2.350 and Fahey, 52–55.

69. *Lap.* 20 (CSEL 3/1.252), *Un.* 12 (CSEL 3/1.220).

70. *Ep.* 73.9, 14, 17 (CSEL 3/2.784, 788, 791).

71. Num. 16:26 and Hos. 9:4 in *Ep.* 69.9 (CSEL 3/2.758).

72. Fahey, 48, citing G. Jouassard, "Les Pères devant le Bible, leur perspectives particulières," in *Etudes de critique et d'histoire religieuses* (Lyon: Bibliothèque de la faculté catholique de théologie de Lyon, 1948), 30.

73. *Un.* 10, 11, 17, 24 (CSEL 3/1.218, 219, 225, 231); *Lap.* 6, 7, 21 (CSEL 3/1.241–42, 253); *Pat.* 2, 4 (CSEL 3/1.397–98, 399–400); *Zel.* 8, 10, 12, 14 (CSEL 3/1.424, 425–26, 427, 428–29).

74. *Un.* 4, 6, 8, 16, 18 (CSEL 3/1.212–13, 214–15, 217, 224–25, 226–27).

75. *Un.* 23 (CSEL 3/1.230–31; cf. *Un.* 27 (CSEL 3/1.233).

76. For the prayer of the pentitents and the answer of God, see *Lap.* 31, 26 (CSEL 3/1.260, 263). Cf. *Lap.* 13, 18 (3/1.246, 250) for more "scriptwriting."

77. *Fort.* 1–2 (CSEL 3/1.317–18). *Ep.* 6 (CSEL 3/2.480–84) performs a similar function using similar verses. *Ep.* 58 (CSEL 3/2.656–66) uses very different passages.

78. Fahey, 48, 624–25.

79. Christ: *Test.* 1.8, 2.1 (*bis*) (CSEL 3/1.51, 62), *Ep.* 63.6 (CSEL 3/2.705). Baptism: "Quotiescumque autem aqua sola in scripturis nominatur, baptisma praedicatur," *Ep.* 69.2 (CSEL 3/2.751), *Ep.* 79.11 (3/2.808–9), *Ep.* 70.1 (CSEL 3/2.767). Eucharist: *Ep.* 63.3, 4–6, 11 (CSEL

3/2.702–5, 710). Priesthood: *Ep.* 59.4 (*bis*), 59.5 (*ter*) (CSEL 3/2. 670 and 672–73), and *Ep.* 77.4 (CSEL 3/2.738). Church: *Test.* 1.19 (*bis*), 20 (*ter*) (3/1.51–52), *Unit.* 4 (CSEL 3/1.213), *Dom.* 5 (CSEL 1.269), *Epp.* 74.11, 75.15 (*bis*) (CSEL 3/2.808, 820).

80. *Pat.* 10 (CSEL 3/1.404), the prophets as models for the martyrs; *Fort.* 4 (CSEL 3/1.324–25), Old Testament figures as models for the prayer life of Cyprian's community; *Ep.* 59.5–6 (CSEL 3/2.660–62) for Old Testament martyrs as models of suffering at the hands of members of the community. See Fahey, 556.

81. *Test.* 1.8 (CSEL 3/1.45), *Unit.* 18 (CSEL 3/1.226), *Epp.* 3.1, 63.4, 67.3, 69.8, 73.8 (CSEL 3/2.470, 703, 737, 756, 784).

82. *Fort.* 11 (CSEL 3/1.337–38): Saul vs. David, Ahab vs. Elijah, and Antiochus vs. Eleazar; *Test.* 2.16, *Zel.* 6 (CSEL 3/1.83, 442): Saul vs. David; *Un.* 18 (CSEL 3/1.226): Uzziah vs. Azariah; *Dom.* 21 (3/1.283): Elijah as a type of Christ; and *Op.* 11 (CSEL 3/1.382): Daniel as a type of Christ.

83. E.g., Abel and Cain in *Test.* 1.18 (CSEL 3/1.45), *Zel.* 5 (CSEL 3/1.421–22), *Fort.* 11 (CSEL 3/1.337), *Epp.* 6.2, 79.2 (CSEL 3/2.482, 668); Jacob and Esau in *Fort.* 11 (CSEL 3/1. 337), *Pat.* 10 (CSEL 3/1.404), *Zel.* 5 (CSEL 3/1.422), and *Ep.* 59.2 (CSEL 3/2.668); Joseph and his brothers in *Test.* 1.20 (CSEL 3/1.53), *Fort.* 11 (CSEL 3/1.337), *Zel.* 5 (CSEL 3/1.422), and *Ep.* 59.2 (CSEL 3/2.668). The first in each pair becomes a type of Christ and, by extension, the persecuted Christian.

84. Hannah vs. Peninnah, Rachel vs. Leah, Sarah vs. Hagar: *Test.* 1.20 (CSEL 3/1.52–53), *Dom.* 4 (CSEL 3/1.269).

85. *Un.* 18 (CSEL 3/1.226), *Epp.* 3.1, 67.3, 69.8–9, 73.8, 75.16 (CSEL 3/2.470, 737, 756–58, 784, 821).

86. *Un.* 17, 18 (CSEL 3/1.226) and *Epp.* 3.1, 59.4–5, 65.2–3, 66.3, 67.1–9, 72.2 (CSEL 3/2.470, 670–72, 723–25, 728, 736–43, 777). Cf. *The Letters of St. Cyprian of Carthage*, trans. and annotated by G. W. Clarke, 4 vols., Ancient Christian Writers (New York and Ramsey, N.J.: Newman, 1984–89), 1.156, n. 16, and 1.167, n. 15; and Maurice Wiles, "The Theological Legacy of St. Cyprian," *Journal of Ecclesiastical History* 14 (1963): 145–46.

87. On contagion: *Un.* 18 (CSEL 3/1.226–27), *Ep.* 59.5 *ad fin*, 65.2–3, 67.3, 72.2 (CSEL 3/2.673, 723–24, 737, 777). On the application of Old Testament purity sayings to laity: *Virg.* 1–2, *passim* (CSEL 3/1.187–88), and *Ep.* 64.4 (CSEL 3/1.719–20).

88. *Lap.* 5 (CSEL 3/1.240) and *Ep.* 58.2 (CSEL 3/2.657–58).

89. *Ep.* 10.3–4 (CSEL 3/2.492–93). Cf. *Epp.* 57.5, 76.5 (CSEL 3/2.653, 832).

90. Clarke, 1.233. This belief was at least as old as the end of the second century; cf. Tertullian, *Pud.* 22 (CCL 2.1228–30), and the *Passio Sanctarum Perpetuae et Felicitatis* 7 in *The Acts of the Christian Martyrs*, ed. Herbert Musurillo (Oxford: Clarendon Press, 1972), 114.

91. *Fort.* 11–12 (CSEL 3/1.342–43); cf. *Mort.* 2 *ad fin* (CSEL 3/1.298).

92. *Lap.* 17 (CSEL 3/1.249).

93. *Lap.* 18 (CSEL 3/1.250).

94. Cf. the treatment of this passage by Maurice Bévenot who calls it a "rhetorical interpretation" in his commentary on *St. Cyprian. The Lapsed. The Unity of the Catholic Church*, Ancient Christian Writers 25 (Westminster, Md.: Newman; London: Longmans, Green, 1957), 86, n. 83.

95. *Ep.* 10.4 (CSEL 3/2.492–93).

96. *Ep.* 58.5 (CSEL 3/2.660).

97. *Ep.* 27.3 (CSEL 3/2.543): "non martyres euangelium faciant, sed per euangelium martyres fiant."

98. Matt. 28:19 in *Ep.* 27.3 (CSEL 3/2.543).

99. Jer. 23:16–17 in *Ep.* 43.5 (CSEL 3/2.593–94); cf. *Ep.* 7.3, 15.1 *ad fin*, 16.2 *ad fin* (CSEL 3/2.506, 514, 519).

100. *Ep.* 43.4 (CSEL 3/2.593). Cyprian was able to apply this verse easily to *isti presbyteri* of Carthage because his Bible did not name the elders as *senes* as in the Vulgate but as *duorum presbyterorum veterum.* The play on the word *presbyteri* is also found in Irenaeus, *Adv. Haer.* 4.26.2 (SC 100.718/19), in a section that is also devoted, like *Ep.* 43, to rebellious presbyters.

101. *Gesta* 3.22, 25–27, 30 (SC 224.934–40).

102. Musurillo 106–31. See my commentary in "The Passion of Perpetua and Felicity," in *Searching the Scriptures.* Vol. 2: *A Feminist Commentary*, ed. Elisabeth Schüssler Fiorenza (New York: Crossroad, 1994), 829–58.

103. W. H. C. Frend, *Martyrdom and Persecution*, 240.

104. Tertullian, *Mart.* 1 (CCL 1.3) and *Fuga, passim* (CCL 2.1133ff.).

105. *Passio Perpetuae* 1.2 (Musurillo 106).

106. *Passio Perpetuae* 4.4 and 12.1–7 (Musurillo 110, 120).

107. *Passio Perpetuae* 4.3 (Musurillo 110).

108. *Passio Perpetuae* 20.10 (Musurillo 128).

109. The *Vita Caecilii Cypriani* and the *Acta Proconsularia* are found in *S. Thasci Caecili Cypriani Opera Omnia*, CSEL 3/3.xc–cxiv. The *Acta* are also in Musurillo, 168–75. Citations of the *Vita* and the *Acta* in this chapter are from CSEL 3/3.

110. *Acta Proconsularia* 2 (CSEL 3/3.cxi); *Vita Cypriani* 11 (CSEL 3/3.ciii).

111. *Vita Cypriani* 11 (CSEL 3/3.cii).

112. *Vita Cypriani* 3, 10, 11, 13 (CSEL 3/3.xciii, c–ci, cii, civ).

113. *Vita Cypriani* 14–18 (CSEL 3/3.cv–cx).

114. Deut. 4:35, Exod. 20:11 in *Acta Proconsularia* 1.1 (CSEL 3/3.cx).

115. *Passio Mariani et Iacobi* 12.5–7 (Musurillo 210–12).

116. *Passio Mariani et Iacobi* 8.8, 12.7 (Musurillo 206, 210).

117. *Passio Mariani et Iacobi* 6.10, 14 (Musurillo 202).

118. *Passio Mariani et Iacobi* 13.1, 13.3 (Musurillo 212).

119. *Passio Sanctorum Mariani et Iacobi* 1.3 (Musurillo 196).

120. *Passio Mariani et Iacobi* 8.1–11, 11.2 (Musurillo 204–6, 208).

121. *Passio Montani et Lucii* 10.2, 11.1–7, 14.5 (Musurillo 222–24, 226).

122. See Tertullian, *Mart.* 1 (CCL 1.3) and *Fuga, passim* (CCL 2.1133ff.).

123. On the history of the attribution of the *Passio* to Pontius, see Musurillo xxxv.

124. The *Passio Perpetuae* and the *Passio Montani et Lucii* are so strikingly similar in structure (letter followed by narrative), ethos, visions, and exclamatory perorations that a deliberate patterning of the latter on the former has been suggested. See the discussion in Musurillo xxxv.

125. *Passio Montani et Lucii* 21.3–4 (Musurillo 234).

126. *Passio Montani et Lucii* 3.4 (Musurillo 216).

127. *Passio Montani et Lucii* 11.3 (Musurillo 222).

128. *Passio Montani et Lucii* 13.5–6 (Musurillo 226).

129. *Passio Montani et Lucii* 16.3–5 (Musurillo 230).

130. Heavenly reward: Eccl. 12:7 in the *Passio Montani et Lucii* 7.4 (Musurillo 218), Matt. 21:11 and 18:19 in 15:4 (226); perseverance: Prov. 21:1 in 12.4–5 (224), John 14:2 in 17.1 (230), and 2 Cor. 6:9 in 19.5–6 (232); unity: Luke 12:33 in 9.2 (220) (cf. Matt. 25:35), 1 John 4:7, Col. 3:14, Matt. 7:7, Matt. 18:19 (cf. 1 John 5:13, 15), 2 Tim. 2:12 (cf. Rev. 20:4), Matt. 5:9, Rom. 8:17 in 10.1–8 (222), John 15:12 in 23.3 (236).

131. *Acta Maximiliani* 1.3 (Musurillo 244).

132. Rev. 7:2 in the *Acta Maximiliani* 2.4 (Musurillo 246).

133. John 9:23 in *Acta Maximiliani* 2.3, Matt. 16:16, Rom. 4:25, Acts 2:22, Heb. 2:10 in 2.5 (Musurillo 246), and Matt. 19:29 in 3.3 (248).

134. Prov. 25:22: "Deus tibi bene faciat," in the *Acta Marcelli* (Musurillo 254).

135. See the *Passio Montani et Lucii* 14.1 (Musurillo 226). Cf. 2 Macc. 7:13, 4 Macc. 9:9 for the curses hurled by martyrs at their judge.

136. 2 Pet. 1:11, Bar. 6:38, Exod. 4:11 in the *Acta Marcelli* 1.1 (Musurillo 250), Mark 14:61 in 2.1 (250), and Sir. 1:27 in 4.2 (252).

137. Deut. 4:35 in *Acta Crispinae* 1.4 (Musurillo 302), 1 Thess. 1:9 in 1.6 (302–4), Exod. 20:11 in 1.7 (304), Jer. 10:11, Neh. 7:2, Gen. 1:10 in 2.3 (304), Phil. 3:8–9 in 2.2 (304), Ezek. 20:7, Wis. 14:16, Wis. 13:10 in 2.4 (304–6).

138. *Passio Sanctae Crispinae* 3.1 (Musurillo 306).

139. The *Passio* is from the AB 9 (1890), 116–23.

140. Phil. 1:21 in *Passio Typasii* 7.33 (AB 9.122) and Rev. 5:13 in 8.38 (123).

141. *Passio Typasii* 5.27 (AB 6.120).

142. Matt. 4:24 in *Passio Typasii* 7.35–36 (122).

143. See Peter Brown, "The Rise and Function of the Holy Man in Late Antiquity," *Journal of Roman Studies* 6 (1971): 80–101.

144. For the proceedings of the Council, see Augustine, *Contr. Cresc.* 3.27.30 (CSEL 52.435–37). On the various dates, 303–5, see Adrian Fortescue, *Donatism* (London: Burns and Oates, 1917), 2; and Serge Lancel, "Les débuts du Donatisme: la Date du 'Protocole de Cirta' et de l'élection épiscopale de Silvanus, REA 25 (1979), 217–19. Based on Lancel's arguments, I accept a date of 305.

CHAPTER 2
Stories of the Martyrs

1. Cf. Galerius' edict of toleration and Constantine's edict of Milan, sections 2, 6, and 10 (313) quoted in Lactantius, *De morte persecutorum* 34 and 48 (MPL 7.219–20, 267–70).

2. Frend, *Martyrdom*, 409.

3. Constantine to Anulinus, proconsul of Africa, in Eusebius 10.5.13–17 and 10.6.1–2 (LCL 2.452–54, 260–62); and Constantine to Caecilian, bishop of Carthage, in Eusebius 10.7.1–2 (2.462–64).

4. On Constantinian interventions in the affairs of the North African Church, see Eusebius, 10.5.1–10.7.2 (LCL 2.445–64), various letters of Constantine in the Appendix to *S. Optati Milevitani Libri VII* (CSEL 26.208–16); Augustine, *Ep.* 88.4 (CSEL 34.410–11); and *Contra Cresconium* 3.70.81 in *Sancti Aurelii Augustini Scripta contra Donatistas* (CSEL 52.486–87).

5. It is difficult to determine exactly when Catholic and imperial authorities began to treat Donatists not merely as schismatics but as heretics. Frend, *The Donatist Church*, 3, n. 1, pinpoints the time at 405 when they are drawn into the net of antiheretical legislation. This fails to give full weight to anti-Donatist legislation that began as early as 314, when Constantine fulminated against the Donatists who appealed to him from the judgment of other Christian bishops (CSEL 26.208). On a practical level, the distinction is not significant, for legislation in 326 specifically combined the categories of schismatic and heretic to refuse them legal privileges. See *Cod. Theod.* 16.4.5 in *The Theodosian Code and Novels and the Sirmondian Constitutions*, trans. with commentary by Clyde Pharr (Princeton: Princeton University Press, 1952), [450]. All citations to the Code are by section number followed by Pharr's pages in brackets.

6. See below, pp. 60, 68.

7. On events of this first period, see Frend, *The Donatist Church*, 159–61.

8. *Acta Martyrum Saturnini Presbyteri, Felicis, Dativi, Ampelii et aliorum*, hereafter *Acts of the Abitinian Martyrs* (MPL 8.688–713).

9. Eusebius, 10.8.11 (LCL 2.471); for the repeal by Constantine in 324, see *Cod. Theod.* 15.14.1 [437].

10. *Acts of the Abitinian Martyrs*, introduction (MPL 8.689).

11. This judgment presumes that the treatment of Caecilian as still a deacon is not an archaizing subterfuge of the editor. Considering the remainder of the story, especially the prologue, reference to Caecilian as bishop would have generated much better polemical effect. If the account were an entirely Donatist piece of propaganda with no basis in reality, one would expect some challenge upon the introduction of the act as official evidence at the Conference of Carthage in 411. It is also difficult to believe the acts would have continued to circulate and to be employed liturgically by the Catholics as they were at least until the time of Augustine if they were wholly a creation of the Donatists. For the introduction of the *Acts* into the proceedings of the Conference, see Augustine, *Breviculus Collationis cum Donatistis* 3.17.32 (CSEL 53.81); for their liturgical usage, see Victor Saxer, *Morts, martyrs, reliques en Afrique chrétienne aux premières siècles: Les témoignages de Tertullian, Cyprien et Augustin à la lumière de l'archéologie africaine,* Théologie historique 55 (Paris: Beauchesne, 1980), 226–27, 321.

12. See p. 51.

13. The Donatist version is MPL 8.689B–703B; the Catholic version is MPL 8.703C–15B.

14. *Acts of the Abitinian Martyrs* 18 (MPL 8.701B). For the use of the *Acts* by the Donatists at the Conference of Carthage, see chapter 5, p. 155.

15. Their story is recorded in AB 9 (1890), 110–16.

16. CIL 8.14902 and the Communication of Heron de Villefosse in *Comptes rendus de l'Académie des Inscriptions,* April 11, 1906, 141.

17. MPL 8.751D–58A.

18. Brisson, *Autonomisme et Christianisme,* 310, considers it a sermon of Donatus preached in March 318 or 319. Frend, *The Donatist Church,* 321 (cf. 159–60), makes no claims about the identity of the author but ascribes it to the year 320.

19. François Dolbeau, "La Passion des saints Lucius et Montanus: Histoire et édition du texte," REA 29 (1983): 64–65.

20. 2 Chr. 13:11, Gen. 26:5, Mark 10:19 in *Acts of the Abitinian Martyrs* 4 (MPL 8.692C); 2 Cor. 3:3 in *Acts* 9, 11, and 12 (MPL 8.695D, 696C–D). 1 Pet. 1:25 quoting Isa. 40:7–8 in *Passio Maximae* 3 (AB 9.113).

21. Unity: Deut. 4:35 in *Acts of the Abitinian Martyrs* 4 (MPL 8.693A) and 2 Kgs. (4 Kgs. Vulgate) 17:53 in *Passio Maximae* 2 (AB 9.113); Christology: Acts 4:12 in *Acts of the Abitinian Martyrs* 12 (MPL 8.697B).

22. See especially the claim of the Abitinians to embody the Scripture in *Acts of the Abitinian Martyrs* 4.7, 12.8, 12.10, 14.4 (MPL 8.693A, 697C, 698D, 698D) and the concentration on the defense of scripture as a physical book in 18.1–3 (MPL 8.701A–C).

23. See the proto-Donatist attitude toward Catholic cooperation with the Roman authorities in the *Acts of the Abitinian Martyrs* 2 and 18 (MPL 8.690B–C, 701A–C).

24. Various details from Revelation in *Acts of the Abitinian Martyrs* 2 (MPL 8.690B), Eph. 6:14–17 and 5:19 in 3 (MPL 8.691B and C). Acts 5:38–39 is used repeatedly in 2, 4, 9 and 15 (MPL 8.690B, 692C, 695C, 699B).

25. 2 Tim. 2:12 in *Acts of the Abitinian Martyrs* 1 (MPL 8.689C); Rev. 6:2 in *Sermo de passione* 14 (MPL 8.758A).

26. *Acts of the Abitinian Martyrs* 14 (MPL 698D); cf. 2 Macc. 7:37 and Matt. 12:50 and Mark 3:35.

27. Ps. 31:23 (32:23 Vulgate) in *Passio Maximae* 4 (AB 9.114).

28. See especially sections 2 and 5 (MPL 8.754B–D, 755A–B).

29. Matt. 23:15, Hos. 9:4, Hag. 2:12–13 in *Acts of the Abitinian Martyrs* 19 (MPL 8.702C).

30. 2 Cor. 6:13–15 in *Acts of the Abitinian Martyrs* 19 (MPL 8.701D), Rev. 22:18–19 and 2 Macc. 7:9 in *Acts* 18 (MPL 8.701B–C).

31. Dan. 3:7 in *Passio Maximae* 1 (AB 9.111; DMS 17–24).

32. Matt. 26:63 in *Passio Maximae* 2 (AB 9.112; DMS 52–60).

33. Luke 6:16, Matt. 24:24, Matt. 7:15, 16 in *Sermo de passione* 1 (MPL 753A).

34. Isa. 55:8 in *Sermo de passione* 14 (MPL 8.757D–758A), Matt. 10:26 and Isa. 28:15 in 5 (MPL 8.755B).

35. The prime pre-Donatist legal texts are found in Matt. 5:44–48 (the Sermon on the Mount) and Rom. 12:21 (overcome evil by good) in *Vita Cypriani* 9 (CSEL 3/3.xcix–c). Even those which deal with the Christian way of life are taken exclusively from the New Testament: Matt. 9:13, 12:17, 12:7, 19:17 in *Vita Cypriani* 2 (CSEL 3/3.xcii); and 2 Cor. 6:9 in *Passio sanctorum Montani et Lucii* 19 (Musurillo 232). Donatist texts on the law of God are from the Old Testament: 2 Chr. 13:11 (cf. Deut. 6:17), Gen. 26:5, Mark 10:19 (but set in the context of a recitation of Exod. 20:12–16) in *Acts of the Abitinian Martyrs* 4 (MPL 8.692C). *The Acts of the Abitinian Martyrs* 9 (*bis*), 11, and 12 (MPL 8.695D, 697C) may use the words of 2 Cor. 3:3, but the concept of the law of God written in the heart was a concept widespread throughout the Old Testament precisely in sections so dear to the Donatists; see Josh. 22:5, 2 Kgs. (4 Kgs. Vulgate) 10:31, Ps. 36:31, Ps. 118:34, and especially Isa. 51:7 and Jer. 31:33. In the *Passio Maximae* 3 (AB 9.113), the one reference to the law of God is based on 1 Pet. 1:25 quoting Isa. 40:7–8.

36. In the *Acts of the Abitinian Martyrs*, *collecta*, *collectam facere*, or *collectam celebrare* describe the community and the reason for their arrest at least seventeen times. For the biblical use of *collecta*, see Deut. 16:8, Lev. 23:36, 2 Chr.7:9 and Neh. (2 Esdr. Vulgate) 8:18. These latter two are the closest in spirit to the Abitinian use. In the New Testament, the sole referent of this word is Paul's collection for the church at Jerusalem in 1 Cor. 16:1–2.

37. The Donatists did not make extensive use of "holy war" texts from Joshua and Judges. Their identity was not shaped by that part of the Bible and its war of conquest, but by the prophetic texts of separation, a different sort of battle.

38. Prayers: Acts 7:59, various verses from the Psalms, and Jer. 17:17 in *Acts of the Abitinian Martyrs* 4 (MPL 8.692C, 693A), Ps. 30:18 in 6 (*bis*) and 9 (MPL 8.693D, 695D); holiness: 2 Cor. 6:16–17, "nolite conjungi cum infidelibis."

39. 2 Macc. 6 and 7 in *Acts of the Abitinian Martyrs* 6, 14, and 16 (MPL 8.693D, 698A, 700B).

40. *Dignitatis suae memor:* 2 Macc. 6:23 (cf. 4 Macc. 5:36) and *Acts* 6 (MPL 8.693D); *tyrannus:* 2 Macc. 7:27, 4 Macc. 5:1, 14, 6:1, 9:32, etc., and *Acts of the Abitinian Martyrs* 10, 15 (MPL 8.696A and 699B); *carnifex, carnifices:* 2 Macc. 7:29 and *Acts* 6, 7, and 8 *inter alia* (MPL 8.693C, 694B, 695B); various phrases regarding lack of eternal life for the persecutors: 2 Macc. 7:14, 4 Macc. 9:32, 10:11 and *Acts* 18 (MPL 8.701C).

41. Judg. 15:11 and Ps. 65:12, "Transivimus per ignem et aquam, et pervenimus in refrigerium," in *Passio Maximae* 2, 5 (AB 9.113, 115). *Refrigerium* appears in North African vocabulary not only as a place of coolness and refreshment in this life but also on tombstones as a euphemism for the afterlife.

42. Matt. 26:63 and a conflation of Matt. 27:48 and 27:34 with Jer. 23:15 in *Passio Maximae* 2 and 3 (AB 9.112 and 113).

43. See *Passio Maximae* 6 (AB 9.116).

44. Cf. *Passio Perpetuae* 3, 5, 6, 9 (Musurillo 108–110, 112, 114, 116) and *Passio Maximae* 4 (AB 9.113–14).

45. John 15:16, 18–20 in *Sermo de passione* 7 (MPL 8.756A).

46. *Sermo de passione* 11 (MPL 8.757A). Cf. Matt. 23:35 (Vulgate): "ut veniat super vos omnis sanguis iustus qui effusus est super terram a sanguine Abel iusti usque ad sanguinem Zacchariae filii Barachiae quem occidistis inter templum et altare."

47. *Sermo de passione* 13 (MPL 8.757C). Cf. Matt. 26:31 and Zech. 13:7.

48. Luke 23:46 in *Sermo de passione* 6 (MPL 8.755C).

49. Repeatedly the interrogators of the Donatists were described as *carnifex;* the same epithet was applied to Antiochus in 2 Macc. 7:29. It was used nine times in the *Acts of the Abitinian Martyrs.* See, e.g., the *Acts of the Abitinian Martyrs* 21.3 (MPL 8.701C) and *Passio Maximae* 2.13 (AB 9.112).

50. Frend, *The Donatist Church,* 161–77.

51. Optatus 3.3 (CSEL 26.81).

52. On the events during the second periods of persecution, see Frend, *The Donatist Church,* 177–80.

53. Monceaux, 5.88–89; and Sebastiaen Lenain de Tillemont,

Memoires pour servir à l'histoire ecclésiastique des six premieres siècles, 16 vols., (Venice: Pitteri, 1732), 6.305.

54. *Passio Maximiani et Isaac* (MPL 8.770D–71D; cf. DMS 63–75).

55. For examples and a discussion of the reverence of animals for the bodies of the saints, see Maureen A. Tilley, "Martyrs, Monks, Insects, and Animals," in *The MedievalWorld of Nature*, ed. Joyce E. Salisbury (NewYork: Garland Press, 1993), 93–108.

56. *Passio Benedicti Martyris Marculi*, hereafter the *Passio Marculi* (MPL 8.760C–66D; cf. DMS 78–87).

57. Optatus 3.6 (CSEL 26.86) claimed that Marculus was killed. They knew Secunda had jumped from her balcony to join Maxima and Donatilla in *Passio Maximae* 4 (AB 9.113) and some suspected this was a Donatist cover-up for death by self-defenestration. Augustine knew the Catholic story of Marculus as suicide as well as the Donatist report of martyrdom, but he made no certain judgment. See *Cont. Cresc.* 3.49.54 (CSEL 52.461), *Contra Litteras Petiliani* 2.20.46 (CSEL 52.46) and *In Ioh. Ev.* 9.15, in *Sancti Aurelii Augustini In Iohannis Evangelium Tractatus CXXIV*, ed. Radbodus Willems, CCL 36 (Turnhout: Brepols, 1954), 120.

58. *Passio Maximiani* (MPL 8.771).

59. "*Vae tibi saeculum quia peristi*," in *Passio Maximiani* (MPL 8.771B). Cf. Rev. 18:10, 16, 19, 1 Cor. 7:31.

60. Rom. 8:29 in *Passio Marculi* (MPL 760D).

61. Phil. 1:23, "dissolvi et cum Christo esse multo melior est," and Luke 2:29–30 in *Passio Marculi* (MPL 8.764B).

62. Vineyard: Matt. 20:8 in *Passio Maximiani* (MPL 8.771C–D); thirst satisfied: Matt. 5:6; treasure: Luke 12:33; and tranquillity: 1 Pet. 3:14 in *Passio Marculi* (MPL 8.762D, 763B, 763D).

63. Gen. 22 and Cant. 5:2, "Ego, inquit, dormio, et cor meum vigilat," in *Passio Maximiani* (MPL 8.770B).

64. See the history of mutual destruction of church properties from the ruin of the cathedral in the *Sermo de passione* 4 (MPL 8.754) to the desecration of the Eucharist and holy oils in Optatus 2.19 (CSEL 26.53–54).

65. 2 Macc. 7:29 and Matt. 26:57 in the *Passio Marculi* (MPL 8.761A and B, 762B, 763D, 764A, 765A), and in the *Passio Maximiani* (MPL 8.769A).

CHAPTER 3
Donatists in Controversy

1. The *Gesta apud Zenophilum* is printed with several other documents relative to Donatism in the Appendix to *S. Optati Milevitani Libri VII*, ed.

Carolus Ziwza, CSEL 26 (Vienna and Prague: Tempsky; Leipzig: Freytag, 1893), 185–97. An English translation is appended to *The Work of St. Optatus Bishop of Milevis against the Donatists*, trans. O. R. Vassall-Phillips (London and New York: Longmans, Green, 1917), 349–81.

2. Eusebius, 10.5.1–17, 10.7.2 (LCL 2.444–65).

3. *Gesta apud Zenophilum* (CSEL 26.191).

4. *Gesta apud Zenophilum* (CSEL 26.191).

5. *Gesta apud Zenophilum* (CSEL 26.189). Panels of *seniores* managed the affairs of Christian communities in some of the cities of North Africa. The origin and exact extent of their authority are unknown. See Frend, *The Donatist Church*, 16, n. 2; and his "The Seniores Laici and the Origins of the Church in North Africa," *Journal of Theological Studies*, n.s., 12 (1961): 280–84. In the fourth century, *seniores* were the trustees of Church property and managers of episcopal elections.

6. *Gesta apud Zenophilum* (CSEL 26.190).

7. *Gesta apud Zenophilum* (CSEL 26.191).

8. Fortis to Silvanus (CSEL 26.190) and Sabinus to Fortis in *Gesta apud Zenophilum* (CSEL 26.192).

9. The text is found among the *opera spuria* in *S. Thasci Caecili Cypriani Opera Omnia* (CSEL 3/3.173–220). On the attribution to Macrobius, see Johannes Quasten, *The Ante-Nicene Literature after Irenaeus*, vol. 2 of *Patrology* (Westminster, Md.: Christian Classics, 1984), 369.

10. See chapter 2, pp. 69–70.

11. On spiritual marriage, see Elizabeth A. Clark, "John Chrysostom and the Subintroductae," in *Ascetic Piety and Women's Faith: Essays on Late Ancient Christianity*, Studies in Women and Religion 20 (Lewiston, N.Y., and Queenston, Ontario: Edwin Mellen, 1986), 265–91, esp. 266–70.

12. *De singularitate clericorum* 1 (CSEL 3/3.173).

13. *De singularitate clericorum* 2 (CSEL 3/3.175).

14. *De singularitate clericorum* 42 (CSEL 3/3.217).

15. *De singularitate clericorum* 3, 8 (CSEL 3/3.176, 181).

16. *De singularitate clericorum* 20 (CSEL 3/3.196).

17. *De singularitate clericorum* 15–26 (CSEL 3/3.201–3).

18. Wis. 2:21–22 in *De singularitate clericorum* 26 (CSEL 3/3.202).

19. Matt. 19:11 in *De singularitate clericorum* 10 (CSEL 3/3.184).

20. Both of these sermons are found in translation in Elizabeth A. Clark, *Jerome, Chrysostom, and Friends: Essays and Translations*, Studies in Women and Religion 2 (New York and Toronto: Edwin Mellen, 1979).

21. 1 Cor. 7:34 in Macrobius 6 (CSEL 3/3.179) and Chrysostom 6 and 7 (Clark, pp. 182 and 183); 1 Cor. 8:13 in Macrobius 11 (186) and Chrysostom 3 and 4 (171 and 173); 1 Cor. 10:24 in Macrobius 11 (187) and Chrysostom 4 (175); and 1 Cor. 10:32 in Macrobius 7 (181) and Chrysostom 7 (174).

22. Matt. 5:16 in Macrobius 7 (CSEL 3/3.181) and Chrysostom 7 (Clark, 186).

23. *Praescr.* 7.9 (CCL 1.193).

24. The text is in MPLS 1.288–94.

25. Alberto Pincherle in "Un sermone donatista attribuito a s. Ottato di Milevi," *Bilychnis* 22 (1923): 134–48; and "Due postille sul donatismo," *Ricerche Religiose* 18 (1947): 160–64, makes his case for Optatus of Thamugadi as author. Francesco Scorza Barcellona affirms Pincherle's rejection of Optatus of Milevis as author but underlines the weaknesses in Pincherle's arguments for the Bishop of Thamugadi in "L'interpretazione dei doni dei magi nel sermone natalizio de [Pseudo] Ottato di Milevi," *Studi Storico Religiosi* 2 (1978): 129–40. Only Eugenio Romero Pose, in "Ticonio y el sermone 'In natali sanctorum innocentium' (Exeg. de Matt. 2)," *Gregorianum* 60 (1979): 513–44, makes a case for Tyconian authorship. For a history of the scholarship on the identity of the author of the sermon, see Francesco Scorza Barcellona, "L'interpretazione dei doni dei magi nel sermone natalizio de [Pseudo] Ottato di Milevi," 129–30, 147–49. His confirmation of the text as Donatist in style and theology is persuasive; so also his hesitancy to attribute it to any of the specific candidates thus far offered.

26. See, e.g., *Sermo in natali sanctorum innocentium* 7 (MPLS 1.291) and Julian's rescript in Augustine, *Cont. litt. Pet.* 2.97.224 (CSEL 52.142).

27. *Sermo* 1 (MPLS 1.289).

28. *Sermo* 2 (MPLS 1.289).

29. *Sermo* 7 (MPLS 1.291).

30. *Sermo* 5 (MPLS 1.290).

31. "Inrisit te virgo filia Sion, super te caput movebit virgo filia Hierusalem" (Isa. 37:22) in *Sermo* 5–6 (MPLS 1.290). This use of scripture totally ignored the context of the quotation in Isaiah, effectively transferring derision from Zion to Zion's enemies. This error, although difficult to make in the Hebrew text, is easy both in the Greek and Latin when the poetry is read independently of its prose context and case endings in the nominative and the vocative are mistaken for each other.

32. *Sermo* 7 (MPLS 1.291).

33. *Sermo* 10 (MPLS 1.292–93); Scorza Barcellona, 131–32.

34. *Sermo* 8 (MPLS 1.292).

35. *Sermo* 10 (MPLS 1.293).

36. *Sermo* 12 (MPLS 1.194).

37. Both sides appealed to and accepted the authority of Constantine at the beginning of the schism, and both sides would continue to make such appeals throughout the fourth century. Both used imperial legislation that provided for the confiscation of the property of heretical groups. Catholics used it against Donatists, and Primianus, Donatist bishop of Carthage, successfully invoked the laws in 395 and 396 against the Maximianists, sup-

porters of an excommunicated deacon. See Augustine, *Contr. Cresc.* 4.4.4–5 (CSEL 52.501–2); Frend, *The Donatist Church*, 213–24; and Monceaux, 4.354–64. The legislation involved was most probably that of Arcadius and Honorius (395), *Cod. Theod.* 16.2.29 [445] misprinted in Frend, 219, as 16.2.9. Cf. *Cod. Theod.* 16.5.8 (July 19, 381) on the confiscation of the churches of heretics, and 16.1.3 (July 30, 381) on the delivery of confiscated property to orthodox bishops [452 and 440]. Though originally directed against Arians, they could have served in the North African situation.

CHAPTER 4
New Times, New Ecclesiologies:
Parmenian and Tyconius

1. According to Optatus 3.3 (CSEL 26.73–74), Donatus would not allow Donatist churches to accept the subsidies of Paul and Macarius which Donatus, no doubt, interpreted as bribes. Translations of Optatus in this chapter are from Vassall-Phillips. For the interpretation of the funds as alms, see Giovanni Alberto Cecconi, "Elemosina e propaganda: Un' analisi della 'Macariana persecutio' nel III libri di Ottato di Milevi," REA 36 (1990), 42–66.

2. For the change in policy between Julian and his successors and the progress of the resulting Rogatist schism from Donatism, see Augustine, *Epp.* 87, 93 (CSEL 34.397–406, 444–96); Monceaux 4.128–29; W. H. C. Frend, *The Rise of Christianity* (Philadelphia: Fortress, 1984), 657; and *The Donatist Church*, 197–99.

3. See Optatus 2.18–19 (CSEL 26.51–55) for incidents of violence attributed to Donatists specifically.

4. Ammianus Marcellinus 27.9.1–2 in *Ammianus Marcellinus, with an English Translation*, ed. John C. Rolfe, LCL, 3 vols. (Cambridge: Harvard University Press; London: Heinemann, 1939), 3.56.

5. *Cod. Theod.* 16.6.1 (in 373), 16.6.2 (in 377), and 16.5.4 (in 380) [463–64 and 450]. See also Monceaux 4.47.

6. For Valentinian's attitude, see Socrates, *Church History* 4.29 in *A Select Library of Nicene and Post-Nicene Fathers*, second series, vol. 2, *Socrates, Sozomenus: Church Histories*, trans. A. C. Zenos (Grand Rapids: Eerdmans, 1979), 113; and A. H. M. Jones, *The Later Roman Empire 284–604*, 3 vols. (Oxford: Blackwell, 1964), 1.150.

7. Monceaux 4.45; and Frend, *The Donatist Church*, 171.

8. Augustine, *Contr. ep. Parm.* 1.11.17 (CSEL 51.39).

9. Jerome, *Liber de viris inlustribus* 110 (Richardson, 50).

10. Optatus 2.16 (CSEL 26.50–51); Frend, *The Donatist Church*,

187–88. On the edict of unity and the Macarian persecutions, see above, 69–70.

11. *Gesta* 1.65, 133 *ad fin.* (SC 195.679, 772). See the discussion in Lancel's introductory notes (SC 194.124).

12. Monceaux 5.244–45. Yves M.-J. Congar sketches the chronology of the interaction between the works of Parmenian and both Optatus and Augustine in his introduction to and notes on Augustine's *Contra Epistulam Parmeniani*, BA 28.201–4 and 718–19.

13. On the history of the debate on the authenticity and integrity of the seventh book, see Tillemont, 6.308, Ziwza in CSEL 26.ix–xi, and Monceaux 5.250–54. Vassall-Phillips isolates the three passages he thinks are not from Optatus. They are printed separately at the end of Book VII in his translation (298–310). Monceaux (2.254) thinks they were written by clerics from Optatus' diocese. Ziwza prints all parts of the seventh book together, marking the suspect passages in the apparatus. If the suspect passages did not come from the pen of Optatus, they still contain texts that their author attributed to the Donatists.

14. See Augustine, *Ep.* 93.13.51 (CSEL 34.494–96); and A. C. De Veer, "L'exploitation du schisme maximianiste par Saint Augustin dans la lutte contre le Donatisme," *Recherches Augustiniennes* 3 (1965): 219–37.

15. E.g., he characterized Donatists as being in control of the violence of the Circumcellions when he knew and wrote elsewhere that they were not. See Optatus 3.4 (CSEL 26.81; cf. 26.82).

16. The best biography to date is Peter Brown's *Augustine: A Biography* (Berkeley and Los Angeles: University of California Press, 1967).

17. Augustine acknowledges his debt to Optatus in *Contr. Ep. Parm.* 1.3.5 (CSEL 51.24).

18. On the difference Augustine's non-African education made, see "Afer Scribens Afris: The Church in Augustine and the African Tradition," in Robert Markus, *Saeculum: History and Society in the Theology of Saint Augustine* (Cambridge: Cambridge University Press, 1988), 105–32.

19. For the dating of *Contr. Ep. Parm.*, see Brown, *Augustine*, 184.

20. *Contr. Ep. Parm.* 1.3.9 (CSEL 51.28).

21. Cyprian, *Ep.* 73.1 (CSEL 3/2.778) and *Unit.* 5–8 (CSEL 3/1.213–17); the bishops of North Africa in council at Carthage in 256, *Sententiae episcoporum de haereticis baptizandis* (CSEL 3/1.435–61).

22. Augustine, *Contr. Ep. Parm.* 2.8.21, 2.11.23 (CSEL 51.69, 73).

23. Augustine, *Contr. Ep. Parm.* 2.14.32 (CSEL 51.83); cf. *Acts of the Abitinian Martyrs* 19 (MPL 8.702C).

24. *Contr. Ep. Parm.* 2.8.18 (CSEL 51.67).

25. Optatus did not dispute Parmenian's general theory here, only the inclusion of the *umbilicus* as one of them. See Optatus 2.8 (CSEL 26.44).

26. Thomislaus Šagi-Bunić provides a well-nuanced reconstruction of

Parmenian's sacramental theology in "Controversaria de baptismate inter Parmenianum et S. Optatum Milevitanum," *Laurentianum* 3 (1962): 167–209.

27. Augustine, *Contr. Ep. Parm.* 2.11.23–24 and 2.14.32–2.15.33 (CSEL 51.73–74 and 84–85).

28. *Inter alia* Augustine, *Contr. Ep. Parm.* 2.11.24 (CSEL 51.73–76) and *De bapt.* 4.17.24, 6.1.1 (CSEL 51.250–51, 297–98).

29. For Cyprian's use of the Canticle, see p. 33.

30. Cant. 4:7 and Eph. 5:27 in *Gesta* 3.58 (SC 224.1198).

31. E.g., *Acts of the Abitinian Martyrs* 1, 5, 6, 11 (MPL 8.692C, 693C, 694B, 696D); and p. 57.

32. Since this version is known both to Tertullian, *De bapt.* 5 (CCL 1.281), and was becoming a common reading even in Constantinople by 400, there is no reason to believe that this was a creation of Optatus and was not known to and used by Parmenian. On the history of the interpretation of John 5:4, see Raymond Brown, *The Gospel According to John I–XII*, Anchor Bible 29 (Garden City, N.Y.: Doubleday, 1966), 207; and Bruce Manning Metzger, *The Text of the New Testament: Its Transmission, Corruption, and Restoration*, 2d ed. (New York and Oxford: Oxford University Press, 1968), 80, 194.

33. Tertullian, *De bapt.* 5–6 (CCL 1.281–82). See E. Amann, "L'Ange du Baptême dans Tertullien," *Revue des sciences religieuses* 1 (1921): 221. He traces Parmenian's ideas on the role of the angel in Baptism to Tertullian.

34. *Contr. Ep. Parm.* 2.11.23 (CSEL 51.73).

35. Vassall-Phillips, 79, n. 1; and Congar, BA 28.67.

36. Optatus 1.12 (CSEL 26.14); Vassall-Phillips, 24–25. See Tertullian, *De pud.* 21.9 (CCL 2.1327); and Cyprian, *Unit.* 4 (CSEL 3/1.212–13).

37. Cf. Optatus 2.1, 14 (CSEL 26.32–33, 48–49).

38. Optatus 1.10 (CSEL 26.12); Vassall-Phillips, 10.

39. E.g., Augustine, *De bapt.* 5.17.23 (CSEL 51.282).

40. E.g., *Contr. Ep. Parm.* 3.3.17–19 (CSEL 51.121–22).

41. *Contr. Ep. Parm.* 3.5.27 commenting on Dan. 2:34–35.

42. On interpretation in context, see Macrobius, *De singularitate clericorum* 15–26 (CSEL 3/3.201–3) on p. 84; and *Gesta* 3.258 (SC 224.1202), p. 165.

43. John 14:27 ("I leave you peace") in *Gesta apud Zenophilum* (CSEL 26.190, 192). Various verses from John 15 in Cyprian, *Unit.* 14 (CSEL 3/1.222) and *Ep.* 73.10 (CSEL 3/2.785); *Sermo de passione Donati et Advocati* 7 (MPL 8.756A); and *Passio Montani et Lucii* 22.3, 23.3 (Musurillo 234, 236).

44. Optatus 2.9 (CSEL 26.45); Vassall-Phillips, 85–86.

45. On the intra-Donatist quarrel on rebaptism, see Frend, *The Donatist Church*, 167–68, 189, 224.

46. Optatus 5.10 (CSEL 26.140).

47. *Gesta* 3.258 (SC 224.1202).

48. Optatus 4.7 (CSEL 26.112)

49. *Contr. Ep. Parm.* 2.2.4 (CSEL 51.104).

50. *Gesta* 2.4 (SC 224.926).

51. Optatus 2.19, 2.23, 6.1 (CSEL 26.54, 60, 145). Miraculously, an angel caught the vial and saved its contents.

52. Optatus 4.8 (CSEL 26.114).

53. *Gesta* 3.258 (SC 224.1210).

54. Optatus 4.9 (CSEL 26.114).

55. *Contr. Ep. Parm.* 2.10.20 (CSEL 51.66), where Augustine insists that it applies to the Donatists themselves.

56. Optatus 3.12 (CSEL 26.100) says this was an unfounded though very powerful rumor.

57. Augustine and the biographer Gennadius of Marseilles (*fl.* 470) provide the only surviving details of his life. See Gennadius, *Liber de viris inlustribus* 18, ed. Ernest Cushing Richardson, T&U 14/2 (Leipzig: J. C. Hinrichs'sch, 1896), 68. Augustine makes his most illuminating remarks on Tyconius in *Contr. Ep. Parm.* 1.1.1 (CSEL 51.19–20), 2.13.31 (CSEL 51.83); *Ep.* 93.10.43–44 (CSEL 34.486–87). These are succinctly summarized in the notes on *Cont. Ep. Parm.* by Congar in BA 28.718–20. They are woven into lively narrative in Monceaux 6.166–71.

58. On Tyconius as apologist and the novelty of his tactics, see Alberto Pincherle, "Alla Ricerca di Ticonio," *Studi Storico-Religiosi* 2 (1978): 360. Cf. Monceaux 5.175.

59. Augustine, *Ep.* 93.10.44 (CSEL 34.487).

60. Robert B. Eno, "Some nuances," 48.

61. See Jean-Paul Brisson, *Glorie et misère de l'Afrique chrétienne* (Paris: Laffont, 1948), 191–92; G. Morin, "Une lettre apocryphe inédite de st Jérôme au pape Damase," *Revue Bénédictine* 35 (1923): 121–25; Alberto Pincherle, "L'arianesimo e la Chiesa africana nel IV secolo," *Bilychnis* 25/3 (1925), 97–106; Donatien DeBruyne, "Une lettre apocryphe de Jérôme fabriquée par un Donatiste," *Zeitschrift für die neuetestamentliche Wissenschaft* 30 (1931): 70–76; and Frend, *The Donatist Church*, 170.

62. *Contr. Ep. Parm.* 2.2.4 (CSEL 51.47).

63. On the disciplinary rather than punitive aspect of the excommunication, see Augustine, *Contr. Ep. Parm.* 3.6.29 (CSEL 51.136–37).

64. For a detailed analysis of the incompatibility of Tyconius' ecclesiology and that of Augustinian Christianity, see L. J. van der Lof, "Warum wurde Tyconius nicht katholisch?" *Zeitschrift für die neuetestamentliche Wissenschaft und die Kunde der ältern Kirche* 57 (1966): 260–83.

65. *Saeculum*, 115–16.

66. The *Commentary* survives only in citations in, and in its influence

on, a multitude of other commentaries. Because there has been no reconstruction of the text, the comments that follow depend almost exclusively on the *Liber Regularum* for assertions about Tyconius' hermeneutics. The Turin fragments represent the most extended Tyconian material outside of the *Liber Regularum*. They do not contradict but rather sustain many of the following assertions. See *The Turin Fragments of Tyconius' Commentary on Revelation*, ed. Francesco Lo Bue (Cambridge: Cambridge University Press, 1963).

67. The critical edition is still *The Book of Rules of Tyconius*, ed. F. C. Burkitt (Cambridge: Cambridge University Press, 1894). Burkitt's edition and a translation are found in *Tyconius: The Book of Rules*, trans. with an introduction and notes by William S. Babcock (Atlanta: Scholars, 1989). In the present work, references are to section numbers and pages in Burkitt. All translations of Tyconius are my own.

68. See *De doctrina christiana* 3.30.42–3.37.56 in *De doctrina christiana; De vera religione*, ed. Joseph Martin, CCL 32 (Turnhout: Brepols, 1962), 102–16. On Augustine's misinterpretations of Tyconius, see Tilley, "Understanding Augustine," 405–8.

69. *Liber Regularum* (hereafter *LR*) 3 (18–19). See the premier study of Tyconius by Traugott Hahn, *Tyconius-Studien: Eine Beitrag zur Kirchen- und Dogmengeschichte des vierten Jahrhunderts* (Leipzig: Dietrich'sche, 1900), 37–38.

70. Gerald Bonner, "*Quid Imperatori cum Ecclesia*? St. Augustine on History and Society," *Augustinian Studies* 2 (1971): 235; Markus, *Saeculum*, 22–71.

71. *LR* 2 (11) and 4 (31); see Pamela Mary Bright, *Liber Regularum Tyconii: A Study of the Hermeneutical Theory of Tyconius—Theologian and Exegete of the North African Tradition* (Ph.D. diss., University of Notre Dame, 1987), 114. A slightly revised version of this work was issued under the title *"The Rules of Tyconius": Its Purpose and Inner Logic*, Christianity and Judaism in Antiquity 2 (Notre Dame: University of Notre Dame, 1988). All references to Bright's work are to her dissertation.

72. *LR* prologue and 1 (1 and 4).

73. This tactic was certainly within the larger North African tradition. Tertullian had tried to deprive the Valentinians of their biblically based arguments by asserting that the Bible was not theirs to interpret because it belonged not to heretics but only to the one, true Church. See *Praesc. Haer.* 15.4–16.2 (CCL 1.199–200).

74. *LR* 3 (16); cf. 4 (39–41).

75. *LR* 1, 2 (1, 3, 4, 8). Cf. the treatment of the faculty of reason in Bright, 89.

76. Cf. Bright, 54–55, 80.

77. This translation is made from a text constructed from the various quotations of the passage by Tyconius in the *Liber Regularum*. It is supplemented by connectives from the Vulgate.

78. *LR* 1 (5), 2 (8), 3 (30), 4 (31, 50, 52), 6 (67), 7 (74, 84).

79. Among the narratives he omitted 1 and 4 Kings, 2 Chronicles, Ruth, Tobit, Judith, and Esther. He worked in all of the prophetic books except Habakkuk and Malachi. In the New Testament he passed over 2 and 3 John and all of the Catholic epistles except 1 Peter.

80. Burkitt, 104–9, provides a list of scriptures cited; Bright, 52, discusses the numbers in more detail.

81. *LR* 1 (1).

82. *LR* 1 (2); cf. Isa. 53:4–5.

83. See chapter 3, 86–89.

84. E.g., the Church in Isa. 61:10, Rev. 22:17, and Matt. 25:1; Christ in Isa. 45:1. See *LR* 1 (3–4).

85. *LR* 3 (28).

86. *LR* 1 (2).

87. *LR* 2 (8).

88. Isa. 45:3–4, 29:13; and Cant. 1:5 in *LR* 2 (8, 10).

89. *LR* 2, 3 (8–10).

90. *LR* 3 (28).

91. Isa. 43:5–8, 43:27—44:1, 63:9–40, 33:20, 23 in *LR* 2 (9–10); Isa. 10:16–19 and Zech. 14:11–16 in *LR* 4 (48); and Jer. 17:19–27 in *LR* 5 (63–64).

92. Nineveh: Jonah 3:3, Nahum 3:3, 16, and Zeph. 2:13—3:5; Egypt: Isa. 19:1–3 and 19:19–20 in *LR* 4 (41–44).

93. Ezek. 26:15–18 in *LR* 4 (45–46).

94. Hahn, 33, n. 1, and pp. 42–43, was alarmed at the lack of Pauline (perhaps Protestant) theology in Tyconius' treatment of the Law. Joseph Ratzinger interpreted it to make Tyconius a proto-Lutheran in his "Beobachtungen zum Kirchenbegriff des Tyconius im *Liber Regularum*," REA 2 (1956), 173–85, esp. 181. William S. Babcock perceptively compares Tyconius and Augustine on grace and free will in "Augustine and Tyconius: A Study in the Latin Appropriation of Paul," in *Studia Patristica* 17/3 (Oxford and New York: Pergamon, 1982), 1209–15.

95. *LR* 3 (24–25).

96. *LR* 4 (31–32).

97. *LR* 4 (31). Cf. Cicero, *De inventione* 1.22.32 and 1.28.42 (LCL, pp. 64, 80); *De oratore* 9.39–40 (LCL, pp. 410–12); and Quintilian, *De Institutio oratorica* 7.1.23–24 (LCL, pp. 18–20). Despite Tyconius' warning, Augustine and other commentators have explained the rule according to the standard rhetorical definition. See *De doctrina christiana* 3.34.47 (CCL 32.106–7). Cf. Burkitt, xv, for his explanation of genus statements as universally true and species statements as affirmations of the particular.

98. *LR* 4 (32–34).

99. *LR* 4 (37).

100. *LR* 5 (33); cf. Paula Fredriksen Landes, "Tyconius and the End of the World," REA 28 (1982), 59–72, esp. 42.

101. Fredriksen Landes, 62.

102. Ezek. 37:11–14, the dry bones, is interpreted in light of John 5:24–29, eternal life as a gift to the baptized. See *LR* 4 (36–37).

103. See chapter 1, pp. 26–27.

104. *LR* 5 (55); cf. *LR* 2 (11), where synecdoche explained seemingly contradictory passages regarding Israel.

105. *Vita Cypriani* 13 (CSEL 3/3.civ); cf. 2 Pet. 3:8, where one day equals a thousand years; and Ps. 84:10, where one day is better than a thousand.

106. *LR* 5 (56). Obviously Tyconius was not familiar with the common calculation of pregnancy by lunar months. Under this system a ten-month pregnancy was normal and posed no significant exegetical problem.

107. *LR* 5 (56).

108. In *LR* 5 (60), seven: Rev. 1:4 and Ps. 119:164; ten: Rev. 2:10; one hundred: Luke 18:30 and Mark 10:30; ten thousand: Dan. 7:10 and Ps. 68:17; one dozen: Matt. 19:28; a dozen dozens: Rev. 7:4.

109. Matt. 25:14–30 and Luke 19:12–27 in *LR* 5 (61).

110. 1 John 2:18, 2 Cor. 6:2, Luke 4:19 in *LR* 5 (60).

111. Fredriksen Landes, 67–69.

112. Luke 17:26–36 in *LR* 6 (66).

113. *LR* 6 (67).

114. Paul: Rom. 5:12–21; 1 Cor. 15:22, 45–49; cf. Eph. 1:10. Irenaeus: *inter alia, Adversus Haereses* 3.16.6; 3.18.1, 7; 3.21.10; 3.22.3–4 (SC 211.312–14, 342, 366–70). See the discussion in J. N. D. Kelly, *Early Christian Doctrines* (San Francisco: Harper & Row, 1978), 170–74.

115. *LR* 6 (67).

116. *LR* 6 (66–67).

117. *LR* 3 (29). See the debate between Catholics and Donatists on the meaning of the parable in *Gesta* 3.266 (SC 224.1226); Augustine, *Contr. Ep. Parm.* 1.14, 2.5 (CSEL 51.25–27, 48); *Contra litt. Petil.* 3.2.3 (CSEL 52.162); *Enn. in Ps.* 149.3 (CCL 40.2179–80); *Sermones in Vetere Testamento* 4.3, 47.18 (CCL 41.43, 590). Cf. *Cont. Cresc.* 2.22.27, 3.65.75 (CSEL 52.386, 481).

118. *LR* 6 (67–68).

119. 1 John 2:3–4, 9; 4:20; 3:14–15 in *LR* 6 (68–69).

120. *LR* 6 (70). This must have been a popular anti-Donatist text if one is to judge from the frequency of its use within the subsequent thirty years. See the debate at the Conference of Carthage in *Gesta* 1.55, 3.174 (SC 195.660, 224.1120); and Augustine: *Contr. Ep. Parm.* 2.11.24, 2.18.37, 3.5.25 (CSEL 51.75, 92, 131); *De bapt.* 4.7.10, 4.11.17, 7.50.98 (CSEL 51.233, 241, 270); *Contr. Cresc.* 1.7.9, 4.26.33 (CSEL 52.331–32, 531); *Brev. Coll.* 3.8.11 (CSEL 53.61).

121. 1 John 5:21 in *LR* 6 (70).

122. Donatists of the Augustinian period were especially determined to use anti-idolatry texts against their opponents; however, they rarely used the same verses Tyconius did.

123. *LR* 7 (70).

124. E.g., Wis. 6:1–4, Isa. 14:12–14, 25 in *LR* 7 (72).

125. *LR* 7 (72–73).

126. *LR* 7 (73–74).

127. *LR* 7 (75).

128. Ezek. 28:2–19 in *LR* 7 (77–80).

129. Cf. Bright, 32.

CHAPTER 5
Harassment and Persecution Again

1. The long history of two bishops in many towns is reflected in the roll call of the bishops at the Conference of Carthage in 411 when they recognize their opposing bishops by sight. See *Actes* 1.120–129 (SC 195.708–40).

2. For an extended treatment of imperial policy against traditional religions and Arians in the 380s, including relevant legislation, see Pierre Chuvin, *A Chronicle of the Last Pagans*, trans. B. A. Archer (Cambridge and London: Harvard University Press, 1990), 49–72; A. H. M. Jones, *The Decline of the Ancient World* (London and New York: Longman, 1966), 67–71; and Frank R. Trombley, *Hellenic Religion and Christianization, c. 370–529*, Études préliminaires aux religions orientales dans l'empire romain 115/1 (Leiden, New York, and Cologne: Brill, 1993), 1–72.

3. W. H. C. Frend, "The Donatist Church and St. Paul," in *Le epistole paoline nei manichei, i donatisti e il primo Agostino*, Sussidi Patristici 5 (Rome: Instituto Patristico Augustinianum, 1989), 117–18.

4. Frend, *The Donatist Church*, 200.

5. *Cod. Th.* 16.1.2, revocation of the right to make wills and to inherit (February 28, 380) [440]; *Cod. Th.* 16.4.1, making troubling the church a crime of treason (January 23, 382) [449]; *Cod. Th.* 16.4.2, legislation proscribing public religious debates (June 16, 388) [449].

6. Jordanes, *Iordanes Romana et Getica*, 320, in *Monumenta Germaniae Historica* 5/1, ed. Theodor Mommsen (Berlin: Weidmann, 1882), 41.

7. For the identity and biographies of the appointees, see A. Pallu de Lessert, *Fastes des provinces africaines (Proconsulaire, Numidie, Maurétanies) sous la domination romaine*, 2 vols. (Paris, 1896–1901; repr. Rome: "L'Erma" di Bretschneider, 1969).

8. For a full treatment of each of the following Donatist leaders, see Monceaux, volume 5, and, for those who participated in the Conference of Carthage, Serge Lancel's *Actes* (SC 194), 198–238.

9. The charges against Primian are listed in the account of the Council of Cabarsussa found in Augustine's *Enn. in Ps. XXVI* #2.20 in *Sancti Aurelii Augustini Ennarationes in Psalmos I–L*, CCL 38, ed. Eligius Dekkers and Johannes Fraipont (Turnhout: Brepols, 1956), 361–66. They included the alienation of both lower clergy and the lay officials of the diocese, the placement of bishops in dioceses not already vacated, the humiliation of one of his presbyters. This priest was forced to crawl through a sewer as punishment for having ministered to the sick without the bishop's permission.

10. Augustine, *Ep.* 43.9.26 (CSEL 34.108).

11. On the disputed dating of Maximian's ordination (between June 24, 393, and April 24, 394), see Jean-Louis Maier, *Le Dossier du Donatisme* (Berlin: Akademie-Verlag, 1987, 1989), 2.84.

12. See Augustine, *Enn. in Ps. 21* #2.31 (CCL 38.133–34) and *Contr. Cresc.* 3.56.62 (CSEL 52.467–68). Frend, *The Donatist Church*, 219, construes their ability to go to law in this way and to be successful as implicit imperial admission that the Donatist church is recognized as *the* Christian church in North Africa. While this interpretation is indeed possible, an alternative would be that the Primianists had a longer claim to the property and record of such.

13. See Augustine, *Contra litt. Petil.* 2.23.53 (CSEL 52.51); and *Ep.* 108.2.5 (CSEL 34/2.615–16). For a full discussion of the relationship between the two bishops and the political implications of their alliance with Gildo, see Monceaux 6.117–20.

14. *Ep.* 87.1 (CSEL 34.397), and *Gesta cum Emerito* (CSEL 53.181–96).

15. On the dating of Optatus' death, see Frend, *The Donatist Church*, 226.

16. See Frend, *The Donatist Church*, 221–22.

17. On Gaudentius as moderate in character though an extremist in rhetoric, see L. J. van der Lof, "Gaudentius of Thamugadi," *Augustiniana* 67/1–2 (1967): 5–13.

18. *Cod. Th.* 15.5.20 prohibits heretics from assembling (May 19, 391) [454], confirming an imperial order, *Cod. Th.* 16.1.4, supporting the right of assembly only for orthodox churches (January 23, 386) [440].

19. See De Veer, 219–37.

20. See the comments of Frend, *The Donatist Church*, 240, on Augustine, *Ep.* 29.11 (CSEL 34/1.121–22).

21. See Augustine, *Contr. Cresc.* 3.46.50 (CSEL 52.457–58); *Ep.* 185.4.15 (CSEL 57.14); and Frend, *The Donatist Church*, 260.

22. *Cod. Th.* 16.5.21 (June 15, 392) [454].

23. *Cod. Th.* 16.4.3 (July 18, 392) [449].

24. *Cod. Th.* 16.5.22 (April 15, 394) [454].

25. *Cod. Th.* 16.5.24 (July 9, 394) [454].

26. *Cod. Th.* 16.5.26 (March 30, 395) [455].

27. *Cod. Th.* 16.5.25 (March 13, 395) [454] and 9.39.3 (March/May 13, 398) [255].

28. Augustine, *Contr. Cresc.* 3.49.54 (CSEL 52.461–62).

29. On the perception of Donatists as threats to civil order (but not as revolutionaries per se), see Mandouze, 357–66.

30. *Cod. Th.* 7.8.7 (June 8, 400) [166] and *Regula Ecclesiae Carthaginensis Excepta* §67 of June 16, 401, in *Concilia Africae a. 325 – a. 525*, ed. Charles Munier, CCL 149 (Turnhout: Brepols, 1974), 199–200.

31. Frend, *The Donatist Church*, 224, 228.

32. *Cod. Th.* 16.5.37–38 (February 12 and 25, 405) [456] and 16.11.2 (March 5, 405) [476].

33. *Cod. Th.* 16.5.41, 16.6.3–5 (November 15, 407) [457]; and Frend, *The Donatist Church*, 264–65.

34. E.g., *Cod. Th.* 16.5.42 (November 15, 408) [457], Donatists not allowed to serve in the imperial household; *Cod. Th.* 16.5.45 (November 27, 408) [458], their assemblies are forbidden, their property confiscated, their adherents exiled; *Cod. Th.* 15.5.46 and 47 (January 15 and 26, 409) [458], penalties for government officials who fail to enforce the laws.

35. Sirmondian Constitution 14 (January 15, 409) [484–485], and *Cod. Th.* 16.5.51 (August 25, 410) [459].

36. E.g. *Cod. Th.* 16.5.52 (January 30, 412) [459], greater fines than before and the exile of priests as well as bishops; *Cod. Th.* 16.6.6 (March 21, 413) [465], prohibiting the Donatist practice of baptism of Catholic converts; *Cod. Th.* 16.5.54 (June 17, 414) [460], deprivation of civil rights, exile, and fines.

37. *Cod. Th.* 16.5.56 (August 25, 415) [461].

38. See pp. 97–99.

39. After 413 he wrote against the Donatists only occasionally. By that time he was much more preoccupied by the Pelagian controversy, and there is no perceptible shift in his stance toward the Donatists.

40. See especially *Ep.* 93.2.5 (CSEL 34.449–450) with his exegesis of Luke 14:23, "Compel them to come in." For an analysis of the development of Augustine's thought on the use of force, see *inter alia*, Peter Brown, "St. Augustine's Attitude to Religious Coercion," *Journal of Roman Studies* 54 (1964): 107–16; and Robert Markus, "Coge intrare: Die Kirche und die politische Macht," in *Die Kirche angesichts der konstantinischen Wende*, ed. George Schwaiger (Munich: Schöningh, 1975).

41. Augustine's anti-Donatist works that make no significant reference to Donatist exegesis are *Psalmus contra partem Donati*, an abecedarian song (393); *Sermo ad Caesareensis ecclesiae plebem*, an address delivered in the presence of their Donatist bishop Emeritus (418); and *De gestis cum Emerito*, the record of a very one-sided debate (418). The works that merely repeat

information from Optatus or the *Gesta* of the Conference of Carthage are *De baptismo contra Donatistas*, an attempt to deny the Donatists their Cyprianic heritage supporting the invalidity of heretical baptism (400); *Breviculus collationis cum Donatistas*, a summary of the *Gesta* of the Conference of Carthage (411); and *Ad Donatistas post collationem*, a refutation of the arguments in the Donatist mandate at the Conference (411/412).

42. CSEL 57.1–44. None of the letters more recently attributed to Augustine in *Lettres 1*–29**, ed. and with a French translation and commentary by Johannes Divjak, BA 46B (Paris: Études augustiniennes, 1987), contributes significantly to a history of Donatist exegesis.

43. An example of Augustine's preoccupation with his own concerns in reporting on Donatist materials is his treatment of Tyconius' *Liber Regularum* in *De doct. chr.* 3.30.43–3.37.55 (CCL 32.103–15). For an analysis of his distortions, see Tilley, "Understanding Augustine," 405–8.

44. These are printed in Monceaux 5.307–39. Section and page number references will be to Monceaux's reconstruction (under the name of the Donatist author).

45. The *Liber Genealogicus* is found in *Monumenta Germaniae Historica Auctores Antiquissimi*, vol. 9: *Chronica Minora Saec. IV. V. VI. VII*, ed. Theodore Mommsen (Berlin: Weidmann, 1892; reprint ed., Munich: Strauss and Cramer, 1981), 154–96. All references to the *Liber Genealogicus* will be by the initials *LG*, the section numbers, and, in parentheses, the pages in Mommsen.

46. On the authorship and sources of the *Liber*, see Monceaux 6.249.

47. The Augustinian works and the *Contra Fulgentium* are found in *Sancti Aurelii Augustini Scripta contra Donatistas*, 3 vols., CSEL 51–53, ed. M. Petschenig (Vienna: Tempsky; and Leipzig: Freytag, 1908–10). They are also in *Oeuvres de Saint Augustin, Traités Antidonatistes*, with French translation by G. Finaert, BA 28–32 (Bruges: Desclée de Brouwer, 1963–68). The introductions and notes by various authors are very helpful. On the dating of the *Contra Fulgentium*, see Monceaux 6.22.

48. *Gesta* 3.249 (SC 224.1186).

49. *Brev. coll.* 3.10.20 (CSEL 53.70).

50. See chapter 1, pp. 43–45.

51. See chapter 2, p. 65.

52. *Ep.* 93.3.9 (CSEL 34.453). Nebuchadnezzar was a figure for both periods, for he persecuted Shadrach, Mishach, and Abednego (Dan. 3:1–21) and later punished those who defamed their God (Dan. 3:91–96).

53. The stories of faithful people include Enoch (Gen. 5:24), Noah (Gen. 7:1), Lot (Gen. 9:12), and two of the twelve tribes of Israel (3 Kgs. 11–12) in *Ep. ad Cath.* 13.33 (CSEL 52.274).

54. *LG* 626 (196).

55. Victorinus of Pettau, *Scholia in Apocalypsim* 2.4, in *Victorini Epi-*

scopi Petavionensis Opera, ed. Johannes Hausleiter, CSEL 49 (Vienna: F. Tempsky; Leipzig: G. Freytag, 1916), 39.

56. *Acts of the Abitinian Martyrs* 18, 19 (MPL 8.701B and D). See especially *Gesta* 3.28 (SC 224.1201).

57. *Gesta* 3.265 (SC 224.1224–26).

58. The Church: Eph. 5:27 in *Gesta* 3.75, 3.249, 3.258 (SC 224.1038, 1186, 1198); Isa. 62:11–12, Cant. 4:7, and 2 Cor. 11:2 in 3.258 (SC 224.1196, 1198). The unclean: Isa. 52:1, 35:3–7, 8–10 in *Gesta* 3.258 (SC 224.1196–98). The world: John 17:25, Rom. 3:19, John 15:19, 1 John 4–5, and 1 John 2:15 in *Gesta* 3.266 (SC 224.1226).

59. Matt. 13:47–48 in *Gesta* 3.258, 3.263 (SC 224.1202, 1222).

60. *Ps. ABC* 9–13 (CSEL 51.1), *Enn. in Ps.* 64.9 (CCL 39.832–33), *Ep.* 105.5.15 (CSEL 34.609).

61. *Gesta* 3.258 (SC 224.1202).

62. Augustine, *Ad Don. post coll.* 27 (CSEL 53.126).

63. *Gesta* 3.266 (SC 224.1226).

64. *Gesta* 3.99 (SC 224.1060) and Augustine's debate in 397/398 with Fortunatus, the Donatist bishop of Cirta, in *Ep.* 44.2.3–3.5 (CSEL 34.111–14). See the argument of Eno, "Some nuances," 46–50.

65. *Aeneid* 1.12–13 paraphrased in *LG* 196 (169).

66. Cyprian, *Epp.* 69.2, 74.11 (CSEL 3/2.751, 808–9).

67. "[A]nnuntia mihi, quem dilexit anima mea, ubi pascis, ubi cubas in meridie . . . ?" Note the final word, which can be translated either "in the south" (a Donatist interpretation) or "at midday" (favored by the Catholics).

68. Cf. Mayer, 24.

69. In *Ep. ad Cath.* 16.40 (CSEL 52.286–87), he maintained that if the Donatists wanted to use *meridie* for the south, they had commended Egypt, true south, and not Africa, which was situated at the compass-point marked "*auster*" or southwest. In *Ep. ad Cath.* 16.41 (CSEL 52.283–84), he objected that the Church could not ask the Lord where the Church reposed, as if the one were two. In *Ep.* 93.8.24 (CSEL 34.469) and *Ep. ad Cath.* 19.51 (CSEL 52.298), he maintained that if the Church were in the south, then the Maximianists who separated from the Donatists ought to be more holy because their area, Byzacena, was farther south than Numidia, the stronghold of the Donatists. Finally, in *Ep. ad Cath.* 24.69 (CSEL 52.315–16), Augustine countered that Mt. Sion was in the north (Ps. 47:3), so the Church could not be in the south.

70. *Inter alia, Un.* 1.4–6 (CSEL 3/1.212–14) and *Ep.* 69.2 (CSEL 3/2.750–52).

71. *Contr. Cresc.* 3.66.75 (CSEL 52.480).

72. In his article on Augustine's *De baptismo*, Mayer, 26, asserts that the certainty with which the Donatists maintained the salubrious effects of

their baptism gave rise to a predestinarianism in the Donatist church. Mayer grounds his opinion solely on his reading of one of Augustine's polemics against the Donatists. There is no evidence of this sort of predestinarianism in Donatist works themselves, especially with respect to individuals. In fact, the second letter of Gaudentius (especially sections 7 and 13) so defended the vital role in God's plan for the exercise of free will as to undermine Mayer's argument.

73. *Ep. ad Cath.* 9.23 (CSEL 52.257).

74. For the Bible as God's last will and testament, see P. de Luis Vizcaíno, "La Sagrada Escritura como 'Testamento' de Dios en la obra antidonatista de S. Agustin," *Estudio Agustiniano* 15 (1980): 3–37.

75. *Ad Donat. post coll.* 8.11–12 (CSEL 53.109).

76. For the differences between Augustine and Tyconius on the role of free will, see William S. Babcock, "Augustine's Interpretation of Romans (A.D. 394–396)," *Augustinian Studies* 10 (1979): 55–74, esp. 69–72; and "Augustine and Tyconius," 1209–15.

77. Gen. 5:24, 7:1, 9:12; 3 Kgs. 11:11 in *Ep. ad Cath.* 13.33 (CSEL 52.274).

78. *Ep. ad Cath.* 14.36 (CSEL 5.178).

79. *Liber Regularum* 6 (Burkitt, p. 67).

80. *LG* 20–23 (161).

81. *LG* 43–44 (163).

82. *LG* 546 (192).

83. *LG* 614 (194).

84. See his commentary on the Antichrist of Rev. 13:8 in *Scholia in Apocalypsim* 13.3 (CSEL 49.123–24). This is not Victorinus pure and simple, but Jerome's recension. However, the extract in the *Liber* indicates that it is Jerome's version that the Donatist editors know.

85. Victorinus' own reading of the verse showed the number of the beast as 666, but some variants of the text, including a reading in Tyconius, had the number as 616, which would, indeed, match the numerical value of Nero's name. See Bruce M. Metzger, *A Textual Commentary on the New Testament* (New York: United Bible Societies, 1971), 751–52.

86. *LG* 615–19 (194–95).

87. *LG* 441 (182).

88. Wis. 3:6 in Petilian 28 (318).

89. Matt. 5:10–12, Matt. 5:39, and John 16:2–3 in Petilian 40, 50, 52 (322, 324, 325); and in Gaudentius 2.8 (332).

90. John 12:24 and 2 Tim. 3:12 in Petilian 49 (324) and Gaudentius 2.8 (332).

91. *Sermo in natali sanctorum innocentium* 7 (CSEL 3/3.290–91).

92. Petilian 51 (324).

93. Petilian's fascination with the suffering Jesus came from his read-

ing of the martyr *acta*. The bulk of Petilian's references are identical to those in the martyr stories. The biblical verses as well as references to Jesus as model do not appear in any Donatist works reflected in Augustine except Petilian's work or in works based on the proceedings of the Conference of Carthage, where Petilian was the prime Donatist orator.

94. Fulgentius 5 (337).

95. Gaudentius 2.10 (332).

96. Petilian 51 (324)

97. Petilian 17 (315).

98. 1 Cor. 4:16, 2 Cor. 11:20, 23, 26 in Petilian 43, 50 (322, 324).

99. On the rediscovery of Paul, see P. Brown, *Augustine*, 151–53, 272, and the bibliography given in Babcock, "Augustine's Interpretation of Romans," 7–8 and n.8.

100. For an analysis of the verses in Donatist writings, see Frend, "The Donatist Church and St. Paul," 85–123. The article also includes catalogs of Pauline verses used by the bishops at the Council of Carthage in 256 and those used by Donatists during the period 390 to the Vandal invasion.

101. Examples of Donatist use: *legalibus testimoniis, legalibus documentis, lex diuina, caelestibus testimoniis* in *Gesta* 3.249 (SC 24.1186); and of Catholic use: *euangelio, epistulis apostolicis, actibus apostolorum* and *testimoniis legis et prophetarum* and *lege et prophetis et psalmis* in 1.55 (SC 195.648, 652).

102. Exod. 23:7, Rom. 2:13, 3:13 in Gaudentius 2.3–4 (331).

103. 1 Tim. 1:8, Exod. 20:13–17, Matt. 5:19, 1 Cor. 6:18, Matt. 12:32, and Matt. 5:39, in Petilian, 36–38 (321).

104. On the Abitinian use of *collecta*, see pp. 65, 159–60, 177–78; on the *Acts* at the Conference, see Augustine, *Brev. Coll.* 3.17.32 (CSEL 53.81).

105. *Contr. Cresc.* 1.10.13 (CSEL 52.336).

106. Tertullian, *Iud.* 2.1–10, 6.1 (CCL 2.1341–44, 1352), discussed in chapter 1, and Macrobius, *De singularitate clericorum* 10, 26, discussed in chapter 3.

107. *Contr. Cresc.* 1.11.14 (CSEL 52.336).

108. Luke 18:8 in *Ep. ad Cath.* 15.38 (CSEL 52.280) and *Ep.* 93.11.49 (CSEL 34.492).

109. Proceedings of the Council of Cirta in Augustine, *Contr. Cresc.* 3.27.30 (CSEL 52.436–37).

110. Exod. 19:22, 30:20–21, Lev. 22:21 in *Contr. ep. Parm.* 2.7.12 (CSEL 51.57). Cf. 1 Macc. 4:42.

111. 1 Kgs. 2:30 in *Contr. ep. Parm.* 2.19.38 (CSEL 51.97).

112. Lev. 10:9–10 (the command to divide the holy from the profane) in *Contr. ep. Parm.* 2.21.40 (CSEL 51.95); Ps. 140:5 (avoidance of the oil of the sinner) in *Contr. ep. Parm.* 2.10.20, 2.10.22, 3.2.4 (CSEL 51.66, 71, 104) and *Contr. Cresc.* 2.23.28, 4.16.18 (CSEL 52.387, 518) and Fulgentius

6 (337); Isa. 52:11 (a call for separation) in *Contr. ep. Parm.* 3.4.20 (CSEL 51.125); 2 Cor. 6:14–15 (another call for separation) in Petilian 29 (318); 1 Tim. 5:22 (avoiding the contamination of the sins of other people) in *Contr. ep. Parm.* 2.21.40 (CSEL 51.95), Petilian 63 (328), *Contr. Cresc.* 3.36.40 (CSEL 52.447), and Gaudentius 2.10 (332).

113. *Contr. ep. Parm.* 2.20.39, 2.22.42 (CSEL 51.94–95, 97).

114. Citations of Hos. 2:4–5 and Isa. 4:20–21 in *Gesta* 3.258 (SC 224.1210). See also *Gesta* 3.221–247 (SC 224.1162–86), Bishop Petilian's exchange with Augustine over who ordained Augustine.

115. *Gesta* 3.258 (SC 224.1200).

116. Also Jer. 23:28 and Sir. 13:21, all in *Gesta* 3.258 (SC 224.1200–1202); *Acts of the Abitinian Martyrs* 19 (MPL 8.701D).

117. No specific incidents are mentioned for Elijah and Elisha; Amos 7:10. All in *Gesta* 3.258 (SC 224.1204–6).

118. Isa. 1:11–15 and Mal. 1:6–7 in *Gesta* 3.258 (SC 224.1206–8).

119. Tadeuz Kotula, "Point de vue sur le Christianisme Nord-Africain à l'Époque du Bas-Empire," in *Miscellanea Historiae Ecclesiasticae* (Warsaw: Polska Akademia Nauk; Louvain-la-Neuve: Bureau de la Revue d'Histoire Ecclésiastique; Brussels: Nauwelaerts, 1983), 117, calls the differentiation one of religious and nonreligious factors. It is anachronistic to distinguish the two with these terms because all of life was religious for Donatists. "Credal" and "practical" or "devotional" are more adequate oppositions because they preserve the overarching religious construction Donatists placed on all of life.

120. Numbers 16 in Petilian 34 (320), and Augustine, *Ep.* 53.3.6 (CSEL 34.157). Cf. Num. 16:26 in *Gesta* 3.258 (SC 224.1214–16).

121. Dead flies: Eccl. 10:1 in Optatus 7.4 (CSEL 26.173–74), *Contr. ep. Parm.* 2.10.20 (CSEL 51.66), *Contr. Cresc.* 2.24.29 and 27.33 (CSEL 52.388 and 393) and Fulgentius 9 (337); dead body: *Gesta* 1.55 (SC 195.666), *Contr. ep. Parm.* 2.10.20 (CSEL 51.66), *Petilian* 4 (311), *Contr. Cresc.* 4.16.18 (CSEL 52.518).

122. Isa. 66:3 in Optatus 4.1, 6 (CSEL 26.102, 112), *Gesta* 3.258 (SC 224.1206), Petilian 34 (320), Fulgentius 6 (337); Hag. 2:10–14 in *Acts of the Abitinian Martyrs* 19 (MPL 8.702C–D), Optatus 6.2, 3 (CSEL 26.146, 148), *Gesta* 3.258 (SC 224.1208), and Fulgentius 10.338; 1 Tim. 5:22 in *Gesta* 3.258 (SC 224.1214), *Contr. ep. Parm.* 2.21.40 (CSEL 51.95), Petilian 63 (328), *Contr. Cresc.* 3.36.40 (CSEL 53.447), and Gaudentius 2.10 (332).

123. Matt. 12:32 in Petilian 38 (320) and *Contr. Cresc.* 4.8.10 (CSEL 52.491). See also *Ep.* 185.11.48 (CSEL 57.41), where Augustine extrapolated from the Donatist interpretation of the sin against the Holy Spirit as schism to an imaginative dialogue between Donatists and Catholics. In the interchange he has Donatists ask why, if this sin is unforgivable, Catholics

would try to convert them. Augustine's answer is that the real sin against the Holy Spirit is hardness of heart until death, that is, the rejection of the possibility of the remission of sins.

124. Rev. 17:1–2, 15 in Fulgentius 7 (337).

125. Jer. 2:13 in Fulgentius 1 (336).

126. Prov. 23:9 and 1 Macc. 2:62 in *Contr. Cresc.* 3.46.50, 4.64.82 (CSEL 52.457, 580); and Matt. 7:15–16 in *Ep.* 44.3.4 (CSEL 34.112).

127. Rom. 3:15, 17, reflecting Ps. 13:3–4 and Isa. 59:7–8, in *Contr. Cresc.* 4.52.62 (CSEL 52.559), *Contr. ep. Parm.* 2.3.7 (CSEL 51.52), and Petilian 9 (313).

128. *Contr. Cresc.* 4.45.54 (CSEL 52.552).

129. Exod. 20:17 in Gaudentius 2.13 (332).

130. Sir. 15:14 in Gaudentius 2.7 (332).

131. Gaudentius 2.13 (333).

132. Luke 14:23, a favorite Augustinian text, with Eph. 5:27, in Fulgentius 15 (333). Cf. Augustine, *Contr. Cresc.* 1.25.28 (CSEL 53.227).

133. Gal. 3:27, Matt. 27:4–5 in Petilian 5, 30 (312, 319).

134. Petilian 5 (312).

135. Petilian 5 (312).

136. Augustine, representing Catholics, was willing to admit the validity of Baptism within either communion, but its effectiveness only among Catholics. See his *De bapt.* 1.3.4 (CSEL 53.148).

137. Lev. 10:9–10 in *Contr. ep. Parm.* 2.23.43 (CSEL 51.98).

138. Eph. 5:11–12, 1 Tim. 5:22, and 1 Cor. 5:11 in *Contr. ep. Parm.* 2.20.39, 2.21.40, 3.2.7 (CSEL 51.94–95, 108); *Contr. Cresc.* 3.36.40 (CSEL 52.447); and Petilian 63 (328). *Communicare* in the patristic period had left behind the simple concept of sharing and was used in situations of a superior mixing socially with an inferior, or of a good person associating with an evil one. It did not bear eucharistic overtones.

139. Prov. 5:15 and 2 Cor. 6:14 in *Ep. ad Cath.* 23.65 (CSEL 52.342) and Petilian 29 (318).

140. Ps. 25:4–5 in *Contr. ep. Parm.* 3.5.26 (CSEL 51.132), *Brev. coll.* 3.19.18 (CSEL 53.67), and *Ad Don. post coll.* 5.7 (CSEL 53.105).

141. *Gesta* 1.55 (SC 195.656); cf. *Gesta* 3.261 (SC 224.1222).

142. *Gesta* 1.55 (SC 195.664) and John 3:17 in 3.265 (SC 1224–26).

143. *Gesta* 3.258 (SC 224.1198, 1202) and 3.263 (SC 114.1222).

144. *Gesta* 3.258 (SC 224.1212).

145. Isa. 52:11, 65:5 in *Contr. ep. Parm.* 3.4.20 (CSEL 51.125), *Brev. coll.* 3.19.18 (CSEL 53.67), *Ad. Don. post coll.* 5.7 (CSEL 53.104).

146. Optatus 3.12 (CSEL 26.100).

147. *Gesta* 3.258 (SC 224.1198, 1202) and 3.263 (SC 224.1222).

148. *Gesta* 3.258 (SC 224.1214).

149. *Gesta* 3.258 (SC 224.1214–16); *Acts of the Abitinian Martyrs* 19 (MPL 8.701D–702A).

150. See chapter 5, p. 133.

151. Gaudentius 2.11 (333); cf. Augustine's comments in *Contra Gaud.* 1.28.32–32.41 (CSEL 53.231–41).

152. See Optatus 3.6 (CSEL 26.86); Augustine, *Contr. Cresc.* 3.49.54 (CSEL 52.461), *Contr. litt. Petil.* 2.20.46 (CSEL 52.46), *In Ioh. Ev.* 9.15 (CCL 36.120). For a Christian precedent on voluntary martyrdom, see Tertullian, *Scap.* 5.1 (CCL 2.1131). See also the discussion of the *Passio Marculi* (chapter 2, p. 71) and the story of Secunda jumping from her balcony to join her sisters in faith on their way to judgment in *Passio Ss. Maximae, Donatillae et Secundae* 4 (AB 9.113).

153. Augustine's comments on Razias: *Contr. Gaud.* 1.28.32, 1.31.36–37 (CSEL 53.230, 235–36). Other discussions of suicide: *Civ. Dei* 1.17–28 (CCL 47.17–30) and *Ep.* 204.6 (CSEL 57.320).

154. 1 Macc. 2:62 and Matt. 7:15–16 in *Contr. Cresc.* 3.46.50 (CSEL 52.457) and Petilian 10 (313).

155. 1 Cor. 4:16, 2 Cor. 11:26, and John 13:34–35 in Petilian 43 (322).

156. Ps. 2:10–13 in Petilian 55 (325).

157. Ezek. 20:18, Rom. 2:13, and 1 Cor. 5:13 in *Contr. Cresc.* 4.45.54 (CSEL 52.552); Gaudentius 2.5 (331); *Contr. ep. Parm.* 3.1.1 (CSEL 51.99).

158. Exod. 23:7 and 20:17 in Gaudentius 2.3, 24 (331, 332).

159. Eph. 4:1–3 in Petilian 40 (321).

160. John 13:10–11 and 15:3–4 in Petilian 16 (315).

161. Matt. 12:30 and Matt. 7:21–32 in *De unico bapt.* 7.10 (CSEL 53.11). Cf. Petilian 35 (320).

162. Jer. 7:14 and Deut. 12:13 in Fulgentius 12 (338).

163. Jas. 2:19 in *De unico bapt.* 10.17 (CSEL 53.18).

164. Ps. 140:5 in Optatus 4.7 (CSEL 26.112, 114); *Contr. ep. Parm.* 2.10.20, 2.10.22, 3.2.4 (CSEL 51.66, 71, 104); *Contr. Cresc.* 2.23.28, 4.16.18 (CSEL 52.387, 518); and Fulgentius 6 (337).

165. Cant. 4:12, the enclosed garden is found twice: *Contr. Cresc.* 4.66.77 (CSEL 52.576) and Fulgentius 5 (336–37); the dove appears only in *De bapt.* 1.11.15 (51.160).

166. Optatus 4.9 (CSEL 26.114).

167. Optatus 4:9 (*ter*) (CSEL 26.114–16) and Augustine, *Contr. ep. Parm.* 2.10.66 (CSEL 51.66).

168. Jer. 5:18 in *Contr. ep. Parm.* 2.10.20 (CSEL 51.66), *Contr. Cresc.* 2.23.28 (CSEL 52.387), and *Ep. ad Cath.* 23.64 (CSEL 52.311).

169. Prov. 15:15–17 in *Ep. ad Cath.* 23.65–66 (CSEL 52.312–13).

170. Sir. 34:30 (Vulgate): "Qui baptizatur a mortuo, non ei prodest

lavatio ejus" in Petilian 4 (311); *Contr. ep. Parm.* 2.10.20 (CSEL 51.66); *Contr. Cresc.* 2.24.29, 2.27.33, 4.16.18 (CSEL 52.388, 393, 518), and *Ep.* 108.2.6 (CSEL 34/2.617).

171. Petilian 4 (311). See the note by B. Quinot, "Eccli., XXXIV, 25 (Sept. XXXI, 30)," in BA 30.753–57. He maintains that Cresconius enlarged on the sense of the word "dead" to include not only non-Christians, heretics, and *traditores*, but also sinners. However, I take Quinot's text, *Contr. Cresc.* 3.24.29 (CSEL 52.388), not to be a quotation from Cresconius but rather a polemical overstatement by Augustine. Augustine derived his own Donatist construction of Sir. 34:30 by juxtaposing to it Ps. 140:5, "Let not the oil of the sinner anoint my head." See also *Ep.* 105.3.12 (CSEL 34.603) for a manifestation of the Catholic problem of differentiating *traditores* from other sinners. Augustine quoted imperial legislation which averred that not knowing the sinful soul of one's baptizer might make repeated rebaptisms necessary. Donatists, who as a matter of principle differentiated well-known *traditio* from all other sins, would not be subject to such a problem. The context of the imperial legislation is lacking. The legislation is not from the *Cod. Th.* 16.6, despite Wilfrid Parsons's comments in *Saint Augustine. Letters*, Fathers of the Church 18 (New York: Fathers of the Church, 1953), 205.

172. *Ep. ad Cath.* 5.9 (CSEL 51.241). Augustine preferred to interpret the pitch, a flammable substance, as the burning charity, for, according to 1 Cor. 13:7, charity covers all.

173. Chapter 4, pp. 106–7

174. *Ep. ad Cath.* 24.68 (CSEL 51.314); Augustine focused on the fact that the water flowed *out* of the body, making it possible for Baptism to be conferred validly outside the Church.

175. Petilian 19 (316), Fulgentius 5 (337), *Contr. Cresc.* 1.28.33 (352), and *De unico bapt.* 10.17 (CSEL 53.18).

176. Acts 2:38 in *Contr. Cresc.* 3.10.10 (CSEL 52.418). Augustine maintained that this generations-old passage through water hardly counted as baptism for the Jews of Peter's day.

177. *Contr. Cresc.* 3.10.10 (CSEL 52.418). See also *Ep.* 93.11.48 (CSEL 34.490) for a discussion of whether, on the basis of the precedent of baptism after John, one ought to rebaptize heretics and schismatics, or heretics only.

178. See chapter 5, pp. 132, 136–37.

Bibliography

PRIMARY SOURCES AND TRANSLATIONS

Acta Martyrum Saturnini, Felicis, Dativi, Ampelii et aliorum [*Acts of the Abitinian Martyrs*]. MPL 8.689–715.

Acta Proconsularia. In *S. Thasci Caecili Cypriani. Opera Omnia*. Ed. William Hartel. CSEL 3/3. Vienna: Geroldi, 1871.

Actes de la Conférence de Carthage en 411. Ed. Serge Lancel. SC 194, 195, 224, and 373. Paris: Cerf, 1972–91.

The Acts of the Christian Martyrs. Trans. and ed. Herbert Musurillo. Oxford: Clarendon, 1972.

Ammianus Marcellinus. *Ammianus Marcellinus*. Trans. and ed. John C. Rolfe. LCL. 3 vols. Cambridge: Harvard; and London: Heinemann, 1939.

The Apostolic Fathers. With an English translation by Kirsopp Lake. LCL. 2 vols. London: Heinemann; and New York: Putnam's, 1930.

Augustine. *Lettres 1*–29**. Ed. with a French translation and commentary by Johannes Divjak. BA 46B. Paris: Études augustiniennes, 1987.

———. *Oeuvres de saint Augustin*. BA 4th series: *Traités Anti-Donatistes*. Ed. with a French translation by G. Finaert. Vols. 28–32. Paris: Descleé de Brouwer, 1963–65.

———. *Sancti Aurelii Augustini De doctrina christiana; De vera religione*. Ed. Joseph Martin. CCL 32. Turnhout: Brepols, 1962.

———. *Sancti Aurelii Augustini De utilitate credendi*. Ed. Joseph Zycha. CSEL 25/1. Prague and Vienna: Tempsky; Leipzig: Freytag, 1891.

———. *Sancti Aurelii Augustini Ennarationes in Psalmos I–L*. Ed. Eligius Dekkers and Johannes Fraipont. CCL 38. Turnhout: Brepols, 1956.

————. *Sancti Aurelii Augustini In Iohannis Evangelium Tractatus CXXIV*. Ed. Radbodus Willems. CCL 36. Turnhout: Brepols, 1954.

————. *Sancti Aurelii Augustini Hipponiensis Epistulae*. CSEL 34:1–2, 44, 57, and 58. Ed. Al. Goldbacher. Prague and Vienna: Tempsky; Leipzig: Freytag, 1895, 1898, 1904, 1911, and 1923.

————. *Sancti Aurelii Augustini Retractationum Libri II*. Ed. Almut Mutzenbecher. CCL 57. Turnhout: Brepols, 1984.

————. *Sancti Aurelii Augustini Scripta contra Donatistas*. Ed. M. Petschenig. CSEL 51–53. Vienna: Tempsky; Leipzig: Freytag, 1908–10.

John Cassian. *Conlationes XXIIII*. Ed. M. Petschenig. CSEL 13. Vienna: Geroldi, 1886.

Cicero. *De Inventione. De optimo Genere oratorum. Topica*. With an English translation by H. M. Hubbell. LCL. Cambridge: Harvard University Press; London: Heinemann, 1949.

[Cicero]. *Rhetorica ad Herrenium Libri IV. De Ratione dicendi*. With an English translation by Harry Caplan. LCL. Cambridge: Harvard University Press; London: Heinemann, 1954.

Concilia Africae a. 325 – a. 525. Ed. Charles Munier. CCL 149. Turnhout: Brepols, 1974.

Cyprian. *The Letters of St. Cyprian of Carthage*. Trans. and annotated by G. W. Clarke. 4 vols. Ancient Christian Writers. New York and Ramsey, N.J.: Newman, 1984–89.

————. *S. Thasci Caecili Cypriani. Opera Omnia*. Ed. William Hartel. CSEL 3/1–3. Vienna: Geroldi, 1871.

————. *St. Cyprian. The Lapsed. The Unity of the Catholic Church*. Trans. Maurice Bèvenot. Ancient Christian Writers 25. Westminster, Md.: Newman; London: Longmans, Green, 1957.

The Digest of Justinian. Ed. Theodor Mommsen and Paul Krueger with an English translation by Alan Watson. 4 vols. Philadelphia: University of Pennsylvania Press, 1985.

Donatist Martyr Stories: The Church in Conflict in Roman North Africa. Trans. with notes and introduction by Maureen A. Tilley. Translated Texts for Historians 24. Liverpool: Liverpool University, 1996.

Gennadius. *Liber de viris inlustribus*. Ed. Ernest Cushing Richardson. T&U 14/2. Leipzig: J. C. Hinrichs'sche, 1896.

Gesta apud Zenophilum. In *S. Optati Milevitani Libri VII*. Ed. Carolus Ziwza. CSEL 26. Vienna and Prague: Tempsky; Leipzig: Freytag, 1893.

Irenaeus. *Contre les Hérésies*. Ed. Adelin Rousseau. 10 vols. SC, Book 1: vols. 263 and 264; Book 2: vols. 293 and 294; Book 3: vols. 100 in two parts; Book 4: vols. 210 and 211; Book 5: vols. 152 and 153. Paris: Cerf, 1965–82.

————. *St. Irenaeus Proof of the Apostolic Preaching*. Trans. and annotated by

Joseph P. Smith. Westminster, Md.: Newman; London: Longmans, Green, 1952.

Jerome. *Hieronymus. Liber de viris inlustribus.* Ed. Ernest Cushing Richardson. T&U 14/1. Leipzig: J. C. Hinrichs'sche, 1896.

Jordanes. *Iordanes Romana et Getica.* In *Monumenta Germaniae Historica* 5/1. Ed. Theodor Mommsen. Berlin: Weidmann, 1882.

Justin, *Dialogue avec Tryphon.* Trans. and ed. Georges Archambault. Textes et Documents 8 and 11. Paris: Picard, 1909.

Lactantius. *De morte persecutorum.* In MPL 7.

Liber Genealogicus. In *Monumenta Germaniae Historica Auctores Antiquissimi,* vol. 9: *Chronica Minora Saec. IV. V. VI. VII.* Ed. Theodor Mommsen. Berlin: Weidmann, 1892; reprinted, Munich: Strauss and Cramer, 1981.

Macrobius. *De singularitate clericorum.* In *S. Thasci Caecili Cypriani Opera Omnia.* CSEL 3/3. Vienna: Geroldi, 1971.

Optatus of Milevis. *S. Optati Milevitani Libri VII.* Ed. Carolus Ziwza. CSEL 26. Prague and Vienna: Tempsky; Leipzig: Freytag, 1893.

———. *The Work of St. Optatus Bishop of Milevis against the Donatists.* Trans. O. R. Vassall-Phillips. London and New York: Longmans, Green, 1917.

Passio Benedicti Martyris Marculi. MPL 8.760–66.

Passio S. Typasii Veterani. AB 9 (1890): 116–23.

Passio Ss. Mariani et Iacobi. In Musurillo 194–213.

Passio Ss. Martyrum Maximiani et Isaac. MPL 8.767–74.

Passio Ss. Maximae, Donatillae et Secundae. AB 9 (1890): 110–16.

Pontius. *Vita Cypriani.* In *S. Thasci Caecili Cypriani. Opera Omnia.* Ed. William Hartel, CSEL 3/3. Vienna: Geroldi, 1871.

Quintilian. *The Institutio Oratoria of Quintilian.* With an English translation by H. E. Butler. 4 vols. LCL. London: Heinemann; and New York: Putnam's, 1921.

Sententia episcoporum de haereticis baptizandis. In *S. Thasci Caecili Cypriani. Opera Omnia.* Ed. William Hartel. CSEL 3/1. Vienna: Geroldi, 1871.

Sermo de Passione Ss. Donati et Advocati. MPL 8.752–58.

Sermo in natali sanctorum innocentium. MPLS 1.288–94.

Socrates. *Church History.* In *A Select Library of Nicene and Post-Nicene Fathers,* second series. Vol. 2: *Socrates, Sozomenus: Church Histories.* Trans. A. C. Zenos. Grand Rapids: Eerdmans, 1979.

Tertullian. *Quintii Septimi Florentis Tertulliani Opera.* Ed. E. Dekkers. CCL 1, 2. Turnhout: Brepols, 1953.

The Theodosian Code and Novels and the Sirmondian Constitutions. Translated with commentary by Clyde Pharr. Princeton: Princeton University Press, 1952.

Tyconius. *The Book of Rules of Tyconius.* Ed. F. C. Burkitt. Cambridge: Cambridge University Press, 1894.

————. *The Turin Fragments of Tyconius' Commentary on Revelation*. Ed. Francesco Lo Bue. Cambridge: Cambridge University Press, 1963.

————. *Tyconius: The Book of Rules*. Translated with an introduction and notes by William S. Babcock. Atlanta: Scholars Press, 1989.

Victorinus of Pettau. *Scholia in Apocalypsim*. In *Victorini Episcopi Petavionensis Opera*. Ed. Johannes Hausleiter. CSEL 49. Vienna: F. Tempsky; Leipzig: G. Freytag, 1916.

SECONDARY SOURCES

Alexander, J. S. "Aspects of Donatist Scriptural Interpretation at the Conference of Carthage." T&U 128. *Studia Patristica* 15 (1984): 125–30.

Amann, E. "L'Ange du Baptême dans Tertullien." *Revue des sciences religieuses* 1 (1921): 208–21.

Babcock, William S. "Augustine and Tyconius: A Study in the Latin Appropriation of Paul." *Studia Patristica* 17/3 (1982): 1209–15.

————. "Augustine's Interpretation of Romans (A.D. 394–396)." *Augustinian Studies* 10 (1979): 55–74.

Barnard, L. W. *Studies in the Apostolic Fathers and Their Background*. New York: Schocken, 1966.

Barnes, Timothy D. *Tertullian: A Historical and Literary Study*. Oxford: Clarendon Press, 1971.

Berger, Peter L. *The Sacred Canopy: Elements of a Sociological Theory of Religion*. Garden City, N.Y.: Doubleday, 1967. Reprint, Anchor, 1969.

————, and Thomas Luckmann. *The Social Construction of Reality*. Garden City, N.Y.: Doubleday, 1966. Reprint, Anchor 1967.

Bonner, Gerald. "*Quid Imperatori cum Ecclesia?* St. Augustine on History and Society." *Augustinian Studies* 2 (1971): 231–51.

Bright, Pamela Mary. *Liber Regularum Tyconii: A Study of the Hermeneutical Theory of Tyconius—Theologian and Exegete of the North African Tradition*. Ph.D. Diss., University of Notre Dame, 1987.

————. *"The Rules of Tyconius": Its Purpose and Inner Logic*. Christianity and Judaism in Antiquity 2. Notre Dame: University of Notre Dame Press, 1988.

Brisson, Jean-Paul. *Autonomisme et Christianisme dans l'Afrique romaine de Septime Sévère à l'invasion vandal*. Paris: Boccard, 1958.

————. *Glorie et misère de l'Afrique chrétienne*. Paris: Laffont, 1948.

Brown, Peter. *Augustine: A Biography*. Berkeley and Los Angeles: University of California Press, 1967.

————. "Religious Coercion in the Later Roman Empire: The Case of North Africa." *History* 48 (1963): 83–101 = *Religion and Society in the Age of Augustine*. London: Faber & Faber, 1972: 237–59.

————. "The Rise and Function of the Holy Man in Late Antiquity." *Journal of Roman Studies* 61 (1971): 80–101.

————. "St. Augustine's Attitude to Religious Coercion." *Journal of Roman Studies* 54 (1964): 107–16.

Brown, Raymond E. *The Gospel According to John I–XII*. Anchor Bible 29. Garden City, N.Y.: Doubleday, 1966.

Buonaiuti, Ernesto. *Il Cristianesimo nell' Africa romana*. Bari: Laterza, 1928.

Büttner, Theodora, and Ernest Werner. *Circumcellionen und Adamiten; zwei Formen mittelalterlichen Haeresie*. Berlin: Akademie-Verlag, 1975.

Cameron, Averil. *Christianity and the Rhetoric of Empire: The Development of Christian Discourse*. Sather Classical Lectures 53. Berkeley, Los Angeles, and Oxford: University of California Press, 1991.

Cecconi, Giovanni Alberto. "Elemosina e propaganda: Un' analisi della 'Macariana persecutio' nel III libri di Ottato di Milevi." REA 36 (1990): 42–66.

Chuvin, Pierre. *A Chronicle of the Last Pagans*. Trans. B. A. Archer. Cambridge and London: Harvard University Press, 1990.

Clark, Elizabeth A. *Ascetic Piety and Women's Faith: Essays on Late Ancient Christianity*. Studies in Women and Religion 20. Lewiston, N.Y., and Queenston, Ont.: Edwin Mellen, 1986.

————. *Jerome, Chrysostom, and Friends: Essays and Translations*. Studies in Women and Religion 2. New York and Toronto: Edwin Mellen, 1979.

Crespin, Rémi. *Ministère et sainteté: Pastorale de clergé et solution de la crise donatiste dans la vie et la doctrine de saint Augustin*. Paris: Études Augustiniennes, 1965.

d'Ales, Adhemar. *La Théologie de Tertullien*. 3d ed. Paris: Beauchesne, 1905.

Daniélou, Jean. *A History of Early Christian Doctrine before the Council of Nicaea*, Vol. 3: *The Origins of Latin Christianity*. Trans. David Smith and John Austin Baker. London: Darton, Longman & Todd; Philadelphia: Westminster Press, 1977.

DeBruyne, Donatien. "Une lettre apocryphe de Jérôme fabriquée par un Donatiste." *Zeitschrift für die neuetestamentliche Wissenschaft* 30 (1931): 70–76.

Delehaye, Hippolyte. *The Legends of the Saints*. Trans. Donald Attwater. New York: Fordham, 1962.

De Veer, A. C. "L'exploitation du schisme maximianiste par Saint Augustin dans la lutte contre le Donatisme." *Recherches Augustiniennes* 3 (1965): 219–37.

de Villefosse, Heron. "Communication." *Comptes rendus de l'Académie des Inscriptions,* April 11, 1906: 141.

Dolbeau, François. "La Passion des saints Lucius et Montanus: Histoire et édition du texte." REA 29 (1983): 39–65.

Duval, Yvette. *Loca Sanctorum Africae: Le culte des martyrs en Afrique du IVe au VIIe siècle.* 2 vols. Collection de l'École Française de Rome 58, 59. Rome: École Française, 1982.

Eno, Robert B. "Doctrinal Authority in Saint Augustine." *Augustinian Studies* 12 (1981): 133–72.

———. "Some nuances in the ecclesiology of the Donatists." REA 18 (1972): 46–50.

Fahey, Michael A. *Cyprian and the Bible: A Study in Third-Century Exegesis.* Beiträge zur Geschichte der biblischen Hermeneutik 9. Tübingen: J.C.B. Mohr, 1971.

Fortescue, Adrian. *Donatism.* London: Burns and Oates, 1917.

Frend, W. H. C. *The Donatist Church: A Movement of Protest in Roman North Africa.* Oxford: Clarendon Press, 1952; repr. 1970.

———. "The Donatist Church and St. Paul." In *Le epistole paoline nei manichei, i donatisti e il primo Agostino.* Sussidi Patristici 5. Rome: Instituto Patristico Augustinianum, 1989.

———. "Jews and Christians in Third Century Carthage." In *Town and Country in the Early Christian Centuries.* London: Variorum, 1980.

———. *Martyrdom and Persecution in the Early Church: A Study of a Conflict from the Maccabees to Donatus.* New York: New York University Press, 1967.

———. *The Rise of Christianity.* Philadelphia: Fortress Press, 1984.

———. "The Seniores Laici and the Origins of the Church in North Africa." *Journal of Theological Studies,* n.s., 12 (1961): 280–84.

———, and K. Clancy. "When Did the Donatist Schism Begin?" *Journal of Theological Studies,* n.s., 28 (1977):104–9.

Froehlich, Karlfried. *Biblical Interpretation in the Early Church.* Philadelphia: Fortress Press, 1984.

Gager, John G. *Kingdom and Community: The Social World of Early Christianity.* Englewood Cliffs, N.J.: Prentice-Hall, 1975.

Geertz, Clifford. *The Interpretation of Cultures.* New York: Basic Books, 1973.

Grant, Robert M., and David Tracy. *A Short History of the Interpretation of the Bible.* 2d ed., revised and enlarged. Philadelphia: Fortress Press, 1984.

Hahn, Traugott. *Tyconius-Studien: Eine Beitrag zur Kirchen- und Dogmengeschichte des vierten Jahrhunderts.* Leipzig: Dietrich'she, 1900.

Hanson, R. P. C. "Notes on Tertullian's Interpretation of Scripture." *Journal of Theological Studies,* n.s., 12 (1961): 273–79.

Jones, A. H. M. *The Decline of the Ancient World.* London and New York: Longman, 1966.

———. *The Later Roman Empire, 284–604.* 3 vols. Oxford: Blackwell, 1964.

Jouassard, G. "Les Pères devant le Bible, leur perspectives particulières." In *Études de critique et d'histoire religieuses.* Lyon: Bibliothèque de la faculté catholique de théologie de Lyon, 1948.

Kee, Howard Clark. *Knowing the Truth: A Sociological Approach to New Testament Interpretation.* Minneapolis: Augsburg Fortress Press, 1989.

————. *Miracle in the Early Christian World: A Study in Sociohistorical Method.* New Haven and London: Yale University Press, 1983.

Kelly, J. N. D. *Early Christian Doctrines.* San Francisco: Harper & Row, 1978.

Kotula, Tadeuz. "Point de vue sur le Christianisme Nord-Africain à l'Époque du Bas-Empire." In *Miscellanea Historiae Ecclesiasticae.* Warsaw: Polska Akademia Nauk; Louvain-la-Neuve: Bureau de la Revue d'Histoire Ecclésiastique; Brussels: Nauwelaerts, 1983.

Kuss, Otto. "Zur Hermeneutik Tertullians." In *Neuetestamentliche Aufsätze. Festschrift für Josef Schmid zum 70 Geburtstag.* Ed. J. Blinzler, O. Kuss, and F. Musser. Regensburg: Pustet, 1963.

Lancel, Serge. "Les débuts du Donatisme: la date du 'Protocole de Cirta' et de l'élection épiscopale de Silvanus." REA 25 (1979): 217–19.

Landes, Paul Fredriksen. "Tyconius and the End of the World." REA 28 (1982): 59–75.

Le Glay, Marcel. *Saturne Africaine.* Paris: Boccard, 1966.

Luis Vizcaíno, P. de. "La Sagrada Escritura como 'Testamento' de Dios en la obra antidonatista de S. Agustin." *Estudio Agustiniano* 15 (1980): 3–37.

Maier, Jean-Louis. *Le Dossier du Donatisme.* T&U 134, 135. Berlin: Akademie-Verlag, 1987, 1989.

Mandouze, André. "Le donatisme représente-t-il la résistance à Rome de l'Afrique tardive?" In *Assimilation et résistance à la culture Greco-romaine dans le monde ancien: Travaux de VIᵉ Congrès International d'Etudes Classiques (Madrid, Septembre 1974).* Ed. D. M. Pippidi. Bucharest: Editura Academiei; Paris: Société d'Édition "Les Belles Lettres," 1976.

Markus, Robert. "Coge intrare: Die Kirche und die politische Macht." *Die Kirche angesichts der konstantinischen Wende.* Ed. George Schwaiger. Munich: Schöningh, 1975.

————. *Saeculum: History and Society in the Theology of Saint Augustine.* Cambridge: Cambridge University Press, 1988.

Mayer, Cornelius Petrus. "Taufe und Erwählung. Zur Dialektik des sacramentum Begriffe in der antidonatistischen Schrift Augustins: De baptisma." *Scientia augustiniana: Festschrift Adolar Zumkeller.* Ed. Cornelius Petrus Mayer and Williges Eckermann. Würzburg: Augustinus, 1975.

McKnight, Edgar V. *What Is Form Criticism?* Philadelphia: Fortress Press, 1969.

Meeks, Wayne A. *The First Urban Christians: The Social World of the Apostle Paul.* New Haven and London: Yale University Press, 1983.

Merrill, Timothy F. "Tertullian: The Hermeneutical Vision of *De Praescriptione Haereticorum* and Pentateuchal Exegesis." *The Patristic and Byzantine Review* 6 (1987): 153–67.

Metzger, Bruce Manning. *The Text of the New Testament: Its Transmission, Cor-*

ruption, and Restoration. 2d ed. New York and Oxford: Oxford University Press, 1968.

―――. *A Textual Commentary on the New Testament.* New York: United Bible Societies, 1971.

Monceaux, Paul. *Histoire littéraire de l'Afrique chrétienne depuis les origines jusqu'à l'invasion arabe.* 7 vols. Paris, 1901–23; reprinted, Brussels: Culture et civilisation, 1963.

Morin, G. "Une lettre apocryphe inédite de st Jérôme au pape Damase." *Revue Bénédictine* 35 (1923): 121–25.

O'Malley, T. P. *Tertullian and the Bible: Language, Imagery, Exegesis.* Nijmegen and Utrecht: Dekker and Van de Vegt, 1967.

Pallu de Lessert, A. *Fastes des provinces africaines (Proconsulaire, Numidie, Maurétanies) sous la domination romaine.* 2 vols. Paris, 1896–1901; repr. Rome: "L'Erma" di Bretschneider, 1969.

Perrin, Norman. *What Is Redaction Criticism?* Philadelphia: Fortress Press, 1969.

Pincherle, Alberto. "Alla Ricerca di Ticonio." *Studi Storico-Religiosi* 2 (1978): 355–65.

―――. "L'arianesimo e la Chiesa africana nel IV secolo." *Bilychnis* 25/3 (1925): 97–106.

―――. "Due postille sul donatismo." *Ricerche Religiose* 18 (1947): 160–64.

―――. "Un sermone donatista attribuito a s. Ottato di Milevi." *Bilychnis* 22 (1923): 134–48.

Quasten, Johannes. *Patrology.* 4 vols. Westminster, Md.: Christian Classics, 1984–86.

Ratzinger, Joseph. "Beobachtungen zum Kirchenbegriff des Tyconius im *Liber Regularum.*" REA 2 (1956): 173–85.

Raven, Susan. *Rome in Africa.* 3d ed. London and New York: Routledge, 1993.

Robinson, James W. *The New Quest for the Historical Jesus.* Studies in Biblical Theology 25. London: SCM, 1959.

Romero Pose, Eugenio. "Ticonio y el sermone 'In natali sanctorum innocentium' (Exeg. de Mt. 2)." *Gregorianum* 60 (1979): 513–44.

Sage, Michael M. *Cyprian.* Patristic Monographic Series 1. Cambridge, Mass.: Philadelphia Patristic Foundation, 1975.

Šagi-Bunić, Thomislaus. "Controversaria de baptismate inter Parmenianum et S. Optatum Milevitanum." *Laurentianum* 3 (1962): 167–209.

Saxer, Victor. *Morts, martyrs, reliques en Afrique chrétienne aux premières siècles: Les témoignages de Tertullian, Cyprien et Augustin à la lumière de l'archéologie africaine.* Théologie historique 55. Paris: Beauchesne, 1980.

Schweitzer, Albert. *The Quest for the Historical Jesus: A Critical Study of Its Progress from Reimarus to Wrede.* Trans. W. Montgomery from the first

German edition, *Von Reimarus zu Wrede* (1906). New York: Macmillan, 1961.

Scorza Barcellona, Francesco. "L'interpretazione dei doni dei magi nel sermone natalizio de [Pseudo] Ottato di Milevi." *Studi Storico Religiosi* 2 (1978): 129–40.

Sider, Robert Dick. *Ancient Rhetoric and the Art of Tertullian*. Oxford: Clarendon Press, 1971.

———. "Tertullian: *On the Shows*: An Analysis." *Journal of Theological Studies*, n.s., 29 (1978): 339–65.

Tillemont, Sebastiaen Lenain de. *Memoires pour servir à l'histoire ecclésiastique des six premières siècles*. 16 vols. Venice: Pitteri, 1732.

Tilley, Maureen A. "Martyrs, Monks, Insects, and Animals." In *The Medieval World of Nature*. Ed. Joyce E. Salisbury. New York: Garland Press, 1993.

———. "Passion of Perpetua and Felicity." In *Searching the Scriptures*. Vol. 2: *A Feminist Commentary*. New York: Crossroad, 1994.

———. "Scripture as an Element of Social Control: Two Martyr Stories of Christian North Africa." *Harvard Theological Review* 84:4 (1990): 383–97.

———. "A Treasure Hidden in a Field: Unearthing Heretical Hermeneutics." *Explorations* 9:1 (Fall 1990): 55–69.

———. "Understanding Augustine Misunderstanding Tyconius." *Studia Patristica* 27 (1993): 405–8.

Tompkins, Jane P., ed. *Reader-Response Criticism: From Formalism to Post-Structuralism*. Baltimore and London: Johns Hopkins University Press, 1980.

Trombley, Frank R. *Hellenic Religion and Christianization, c. 370–529*. Études préliminaires aux religions orientales dans l'empire romain 115/1. Leiden, New York, and Cologne: Brill, 1993.

van der Lof, L. J. "Gaudentius of Thamugadi." *Augustiniana* 67/1–2 (1967): 5–13.

———. "Warum wurde Tyconius nicht katholisch?" *Zeitschrift für neuetestamentliche Wissenschaft und die Kunde der ältern Kirche* 57 (1966): 260–83.

Waszink, J. H. "Tertullian's Principles and Methods of Exegesis." In *Early Christian Literature and the Classical Intellectual Tradition. In honorem Robert M. Grant*. Ed. William R. Schoedel and Robert L. Wilken. Paris: Beauchesne, 1971.

Wiles, Maurice. "The Theological Legacy of St. Cyprian." *Journal of Ecclesiastical History* 14 (1963): 145–46.

Zimmermann, Gottfried. *Die hermeneutischen Prinzipien Tertullians*. Inaugural diss., University of Leipzig. Würzburg: Konrad Triltsch, 1937.

Index

Subject Index

Apostolic Fathers, 23
Asceticism, 49-50, 82-86, 88, 92
Augustine, Catholic bishop of Hippo Regius, 17, 96, 100-101 103, 109-10, 135, 138, 140-41, 142, 149, 150-51, 155

Baptism, 102, 106-7; ministers of, 102, 105-6; Novatianist 29-30; re-baptism 100-103, 106, 217, nn.171, 177; validity of 29, 32, 33, 156, 169-71, 215, n.136, 217, n.174
Bible, as Law, 65, 78, 117, 120-21, 137, 151, 155-57, 161, 168, 177-80, 195, n.35; as Law in Tertullian 187, n.35; inspiration of, 23, 31; unity of 23-24, 30, 32, 33, 40, 115-16

Caecilian, Catholic bishop of Carthage, 9-10, 142, 144, 157, 161, 194, n.11
Christology, 24, 27
Circumcellions, 94, 135, 200, n.15
Collecta, 55, 65, 76, 78, 80, 143, 155-56, 159-60, 161, 177-79
Conference of Carthage (411), 22, 134, 137, 140, 145-46, 155, 157-59, 164
Constantine and Constantinian religious policies, 56
Context, as an interpretive tool, 24
Council of Cirta (305), 49-52, 79, 101
Council of Bagaï (394), 133, 134
Cresconius, Donatist partisan, 156, 160, 171
Cyprian, 45, 51, 88, 109; predecessor to the Donatists, 28-41, typology in, 106; *Vita Cypriani*, 42, 44, 46, 122. *See also Acta Proconsularia*

De singularitate clericorum, 77, 82-86
Donatus, Donatist bishop of Carthage, 61, 69-70, 96, 131, 194, n.18, 200, n.1
Dotes (gifts of the Church) 102-6, 111

Eleazar, 66. *See also* Maccabees 6 in *Scripture Index*

Eschatology, 43, 54, 74, 107, 111-12, 114-15, 143, 146-47, 158, 175; language of, 63, 65; Tyconius and, 116-17, 122-23
Eucharist, 105, 166, 197, n.64

Firmus, revolutionary leader 94, 95, 132

Gaudentius, Donatist bishop of Thamugadi, 135, 154-55, 161, 167-68
Gesta of the Conference of Carthage, *See* Conference of Carthage (411)
Gesta apud Zenophilum, 77, 79-82, 92
Gildo, *comes Africae*, 95, 130, 132-36

Herod, *See Sermo in natali sanctorum innocentium*

Irenaeus, 22, 23, 24, 31
Irony as interpretative device, 81
Isaac as type, 75
Israel as type of the Church, 36, 37, 119, 158-59, 171. *See also Collecta*

Jesus as type or model, 30, 39, 44, 49, 67, 78, 86-89, 91, 118, 143, 154-55, 168, 190, nn.82, 83; 212, n.93
Judas as type, 161, 163, 168

lapsi 28-29, 46
Liber Regularum, 115-28, 154. *See also* Tyconius
Liber Genealogicus, 139, 143-44, 148, 152
Literal interpretation, in Cyprian 35-40; in Tertullian 25, 26

Maccabees, 39, 45, 47, 66, 78, 91, 167. *See also* entries in the *Scripture Index*.
Macrobius, Donatist bishop, 70, 82, 91-92
Marius Victorinus, 154
Maximian, Donatist bishop, and Maximianists, 101, 133-34, 135, 199, n.37, 208, n.11